MYSTAGOGY

Enrico Mazza

Translated by: Matthew J. O'Connell

MYSTAGOGY

A Theology of Liturgy in the Patristic Age

PUEBLO PUBLISHING COMPANY

New York

Design: Frank Kacmarcik

ISBN: 0-916134-93-8

Printed in the United States of America

Contents

Introduction ix
   I. *The Problem* ix
   II. *Mystagogy* ix
   III. *Scopes and Limits of the Present Study* xi

CHAPTER ONE
General Questions 1
   I. *Meaning of the Term "Mystagogy"* 1
   II. *Mystagogical Catechesis or Mystagogical Theology?* 2
A. The Problem 2
B. Some Examples 3
C. Conclusion 6
   III. *Mystagogy and Biblical Exegesis* 7
A. The Use of Scripture 7
B. Typology and Mystagogy 9
C. Typology and Allegory 10

CHAPTER TWO
Ambrose of Milan 14
   I. *The History of Salvation and Its Vocabulary* 14
A. Mystery (*Mysterium*) 16
B. Figure (*Figura*) 16
C. Shadow (*Umbra*) 18
D. Appearance (*Species*) 18
E. Image (*Image*) 19
F. Likeness (*Similitudo*) 20
G. Type (*Typus*) 21
H. Sacrament (*Sacramentum*) 21
   II. *The Mystagogy of St. Ambrose* 23
A. Celebrating the Mystery of the Opening (*Aperitionis celebrantes mysterium*) 25
B. How Ancient This Mystery Is (*Quam vetus mysterium est*) 26

C. It Is a Mystery and a Sanctifying Action (*Mysterium est et sanctificatio*) 27

D. Consecrated by the Mystery of the Cross (*Crucis mysterio consecrata*) 29

E. This Is That Great Mystery (*Hoc est illud magnum mysterium*) 30

F. Sacrament of Baptism—Mystery of Rebirth (*Baptismatis sacramentum—Regenerationis mysterium*) 31

G. They Handed Down This Mystery to Us (*Hoc nobis mysterium tradiderunt*) 32

H. Let Us Establish the Truth of the Mystery (*Adstruamus mysterii veritatem*) 32

I. Conclusion 33

  III. *The Typological Application, or Sacramentality* 34

A. Correspondence, Superimposition, Identity 34

B. Jewish Sacraments and Christian Sacraments 39

C. Conclusion 43

CHAPTER THREE

Theodore of Mopsuestia 45

  I. *The Catechetical Homilies of Theodore* 45

  II. *Questions of Vocabulary* 46

A. Figure, Sign, Mystery 46

B. The Use of *Typos* and the Problem of the Words Signifying Sacramentaility 47

  III. *The Purpose of the* Catechetical Homilies 49

A. Homily on the Lord's Prayer 50

B. Homilies on the Mysteries 51

C. Conclusion 54

  IV. *Mystagogy and Allegory* 55

A. The Vision of Isaiah 56

B. Eucharistic Communion 56

C. The Vestments 57

D. Baptismal Actions 58

  V. *The Relation Between the Sacraments and Natural Realities* 59

  VI. *The Eucharist as Type of the Passion* 61

A. The Passion in Relation to the Angelic Liturgy 61

B. The Passion in Relation to the Bread and Wine 65

  VII. *The Eucharist as Type of the Resurrection* 66

A. The Communion Rites as Types of the Resurrection 67

B. Epiclesis, Holy Spirit, Resurrection 70

C. The Eucharist as Remission of Sins 71

VIII. *The Heavenly Liturgy* 72
A. The Concept of Redemption 73
B. Sacrament and Salvation 74
C. The Angelic Liturgy and the *Sanctus* 78
D. Life in the Image of Heaven 81
E. The Actions of Jesus as Types 82
  IX. *Sacramental Realism* 85
   X. *The Gap Between Sacrament and Content* 93
A. Sacrament and Eschatology 93
B. Content or Fruit? 97
  XI. *Conclusion* 101

CHAPTER FOUR
John Chrysostom 105
  I. *The Catechetical Homilies of Chrysostom* 106
A. The Choice of Texts 106
B. The Date of the Texts 108
  II. *The Distinguishing Traits of Chrysostom's Mystagogy* 109
A. The Problem of the Moral Thematic 109
B. The Problem of the Eucharistic Thematic 114
  III. *"Morality" as a Theology of Initiation* 120
  IV. *The Angels* 124
  V. *The Symbolism of the Rites* 126
  VI. *The Mystery* 131
  VII. *Chrysostom's Typology* 134
VIII. *The Eyes of Faith and Sacramentality* 141
A. The Eyes of Faith in the Moral Life of the Faithful 143
B. The Eyes of Faith in the Liturgical Rites 143
C. Traces of Regression 147

CHAPTER FIVE
Cyril of Jerusalem 150
  I. *The Eucharist* 151
A. The Structure of the Anaphora 151
B. Cyril's Mystagogy 152
  II. *Baptism and Imitation* 154
A. Symbol 155
B. Imitation 156
C. Likeness 158
D. *Antitypos* 160
  III. *Cyril's Typology* 161
  IV. *Conclusion* 164

CHAPTER SIX
Final Reflections 165
    I. *Mystagogy as Theology* 165
    II. *Imitation and Typology* 167
    III. *A Cultural and Philosophical Problem?* 168
    IV. *A Final Question* 171
    V. *Conclusion* 174

Abbreviations 175

Select Bibliography 176

Notes 181

Index 219

Introduction

The sacraments have not always been interpreted in the same way throughout the history of the Church; rather there has been a series of sacramental theologies. Each successive theology, however, has as it were been grafted on to its predecessor without any break in continuity; as a result, it is quite difficult to pinpoint the line of demarcation between them.

This becomes especially clear when we look at the vocabulary for the sacraments. The terms proper to a given sacramental theology are taken over by its successor, even though the underlying ideas and type of thinking are in process of change. The persistence of sacramental vocabulary creates the impression that there is not only a strict continuity between these various theologies, but a practical identity, although there has, in fact, been a shift in thinking.

Another point that must be kept in mind is that the way of posing the problems to which an answer is sought has also changed. It is precisely these changes, in my opinion, that chiefly determine the lines along which the shift from one theology to another takes place. A change in vocabulary is simply a consequence of a change in approach, but it is, therefore, also a valuable indicator of the latter.

II. MYSTAGOGY
Among the various sacramental theologies, there is one in particular, known as "mystagogy," that seeks to give a theological explanation not only of the sacramental fact, but of each rite making up the liturgical celebration.

The Church has always had explanations of its liturgical celebrations. Only at the end of the fourth century, however, did the explanation take on the truly distinctive form of mystagogical catechesis. The phenomenon is an extremely interesting one. Its chief representatives are Ambrose of Milan, Cyril (or, more probably, John) of Jerusalem, John Chrysostom, and Theodore of Mopsuestia.

The mystagogical homilies of these men are themselves liturgical entities, not only because they are homilies, but also and above all because of their purpose, which is to explain to the neophytes, or newly baptized, the meaning and nature of the liturgical actions in which they have participated: baptism and the Eucharist.[1]

It is difficult to say why this literary and liturgical phenomenon should have appeared precisely at the end of the fourth century. Suffice it to say here that this seems to have been the fact. It is true that Basil, for example, has left us a homily on baptism, but he provides no evidence to suggest a regular practice of mystagogical catechesis. The rise of the phenomenon at this point in history should not, however, surprise us when we consider that this was a period of major innovations in liturgical practice. We need think only of the rites for the reconciliation of heretics, the final (postbaptismal) anointing that was to become our "confirmation," and, lastly, the development of the anaphora of the Antiochene type as found in the mystagogical homilies of Theodore of Mopsuestia[2] and Cyril of Jerusalem.[3]

Let me offer a hypothesis that would explain the rise of mystagogy at that historical point; it may have been Canon 46 of the Council of Laodicea[4] that gave rise to the interesting type of Christian instruction that we see embodied in the literary genre known as the mystagogical homily. The council in fact ordered that the baptized were to study the faith thoroughly[5] and "give it back" (the *redditio* or recital of the creed) on Holy Thursday.[6] Just as Canon 48 of this council[7] gave rise to the postbaptismal anointing, so Canon 46[8] may have given rise to the idea of mystagogical instructions or catecheses.

If we accept this hypothesis, fragile as it is, it would explain why so many examples of mystagogical catecheses, very similar among themselves, came into being in such a short period of time. This is especially true if we take into account the fact that as far as the mystagogical catecheses are concerned, this magical period at the end of the fourth century has no parallels in preceding periods, much less in those that followed.

III. SCOPE AND LIMITS OF THE PRESENT STUDY

Any piece of research must first of all be a collection of data that is then to be interpreted. My first effort will be, therefore, to present clearly our information regarding mystagogy, so that a correct interpretation of it will emerge from the data themselves and not be imposed from outside on the basis of preconceived theories.

This does not mean, of course, that I shall ignore the work already done by others. My interpretation of the texts of Ambrose, for example, will take as its point of departure the results achieved by G. Francesconi in a work to which I owe a great deal.[9] His study of the sacramental vocabulary of Ambrose[10] is the foundation to which I refer as taken for granted in my own researches. On the other hand, when I come to Theodore of Mopsuestia, I am obliged to undertake a more direct analysis, since there are no studies by others on which I could rely and thus save myself the labor. This is true especially of Theodore's homilies on the Eucharist, inasmuch as the problem arises here of reconstructing the twofold structure of the anaphora in the Eucharist on which he is commenting.[11]

Analysis of these texts and those of John Chrysostom and Cyril of Jerusalem shows that mystagogy is a way of theologizing that these Fathers at the end of the fourth century apply to instruction on the sacraments of initiation. But another very important fact also emerges from the inquiry, namely, that when these Fathers of the Church are confronted with the problem of sacramental realism, they are no longer satisfied to stick with biblical typology. That is, they regard biblical typology as inadequate to explain the realism that marks the sacraments. To use a somewhat riddling expression, I would say that in this respect, these Fathers anticipate their descendants.

Does it follow from my analysis that there must have been a period when typology was regarded as a sufficient criterion for asserting the realism of the sacraments? No, I cannot say that it follows. I can indeed say that there are clues pointing in that direction, but I must add that the clues may be interpreted differently; I must therefore conclude that no sure answer is possible without a thorough study of mystagogy prior to the end of the fourth century.

When I claim that at certain points these Fathers anticipate their descendants, I mean that at certain moments, mystagogical theology already makes room for another way of viewing the sacraments, a way fairly like our own. The loss of the typological dimension effects a distancing from the biblical data and opens the way to the "theology of the mysteries," which claims to be a better way of describing sacramental realism, namely, as the "presence" of the saving event in the liturgical rite. I may cite as one example how Theodore, as a direct consequence of the loss of biblical typology,[12] asserts the *ritual* death and *ritual* resurrection of Christ as a way of saving sacramental realism. But the theology of the mysteries, though latent in the texts with which I shall be dealing, did not formally emerge until a later time.

I may say in conclusion that in these specific areas, the theology contained in the mystagogical catecheses already foreshadows the theology of later ages and has links with our own in particular. For contemporary theology displays two characteristics: difficulty in accepting the biblical perspective and, in an attempt to overcome this drawback, a retrieval of the theology of the mysteries. Both of these phenomena are directly due to the loss of biblical typology, which was the method at work in mystagogy. This disastrous loss was already beginning to play a role in the mystagogical homilies that I shall be studying here. It follows that the study of these homilies can also help us better understand the contemporary situation in liturgical theology.

CHAPTER ONE

General Questions

I. MEANING OF THE TERM "MYSTAGOGY"

Nowadays, the term "mystagogy" signifies catechetical instruction on the sacraments, with special reference to the sacraments of Christian initiation and to the deeper spiritual meaning of the liturgical rites. The broader sense of mystagogy as meaning simply "explanation of liturgical rites" dates from the beginning of the Byzantine period. It is on the basis of this broader meaning that mystagogy is applied to every type of liturgical celebration, including priestly ordination and the anointing of the sick.

The word mystagogy derives from the Greek verb *mueō*,[1] which was always used in a sacral context and meant "to teach a doctrine" and therefore "to initiate into the mysteries." *Mystagogia* was thus always closely connected with *mystērion, mystikos,* and *mystēs,* as has been well brought out in schematic form by T. Federici.[2]

Among the Greek Fathers, mystagogy has several meanings:

"In addition to the general sense of 'initiation into the mysteries,' two main meanings can be distinguished: first, 'performance of a sacred action' and in particular the celebration of the sacraments of initiation, that is, baptism and the Eucharist; second, 'oral or written explanation' of the mystery hidden in the scriptures and celebrated in the liturgy."[3]

In Cyril of Alexandria, Pseudo-Dionysius the Areopagite, and Maximus the Confessor, mystagogy means the performance of a sacred action; in Theodore of Studios, it means the liturgical celebration; in the writings of Origen and Chrysostom, it means Christian initiation in general. In Epiphanius, Gregory of Nazianzus, and Gregory of Nyssa, it also means initiation to the

1

Eucharist. In both the Antiochene and the Alexandrian Fathers, it means the oral or written explanation of the mystery hidden in the Scriptures and celebrated in the liturgy. In Cyril of Alexandria, Diodorus of Tarsus, and Origen, for example, it means the explanation of the spiritual sense of the Scriptures; it can also have the broader meaning of an explanation of the figures contained in the Old Testament and fulfilled in the New, or of the eschatological realities announced by the Church (as in Eusebius, Cyril of Alexandria, and Maximus the Confessor).[4]

II. MYSTAGOGICAL CATECHESIS OR MYSTAGOGICAL THEOLOGY?

A. The Problem

History has passed mystagogy on to us in the form of *homilies* addressed to catechumens or neophytes, or in *commentaries* on the liturgy with a strong emphasis on the spiritual meaning. For this reason, we spontaneously tend to regard mystagogy as belonging to the realm of either catechesis or spirituality.

In the first interpretation, mystagogy ends up being regarded as simply one of the many ways by which a homilist adapts himself to an audience that is not yet capable of a deeper understanding of the mystery and therefore requires a very lively kind of instruction, one without much theological meat in it lest this uselessly burden the hearers. As a result, description of the biblical figures would play a large part and the narrative method would take precedence over doctrinal, systematic, and more properly speculative considerations.

In the second interpretation, greater emphasis is placed on requirements more specific to spirituality; I am referring to the need of symbols in order to give expression to the taste for spiritual things, which must be represented in the figurative mode. To this end, the homilist has recourse to episodes from the Old Testament; these, being more accessible, make it possible for the experience of the divine and of spiritual realities (which in themselves are inexpressible) to acquire a kind of material consistency and thereby the concreteness of what is visible and tangible.

2

In both interpretations, mystagogy loses its own proper status and is, as it were, located within specialized experiences (initiation or greater spiritual understanding) that owe their existence to the specific situation of the group in question rather than to the very nature of the object being explained, namely, the liturgical celebration.

Mystagogy would then have its origin not in the Church as such and be her understanding (*epignōsis, theōria*) and explanation (*historia*) of the mystery, but rather in the special experience of limited groups (initiates and contemplatives). It would, therefore, not be *the* way of interpreting the liturgical celebration, but simply *one* particular way arising from the limited situation of some.

Careful study of the mystagogical writings that have come down to us shows that mystagogy has its own special method of developing an understanding of the mystery. The method, which never changes, is applied to the entire field or liturgical action, a term that here includes what we may call the "ontological content" of the sacraments. The mystagogical method is seen as capable of bringing to light and explaining even contents that are theological in the true and proper sense; the method does not have to be modified or forced for this purpose.

If I can successfully prove this claim, I can conclude that mystagogy is not to be regarded as belonging solely to the sphere of catechesis or spiritual theology, but is rather a true and proper theology: a liturgical theology.

B. Some Examples
(a) Nicholas Cabasilas is known as the author of an important mystagogy that was, and still is, influential in both East and West. J. Gouillard has compared him with some Fathers of the Church who also authored mystagogies (Cyril of Jerusalem, Maximus the Confessor, and others) and has concluded: "Our author had predecessors, but he eclipsed them all; at the same time his work caused the inspiration of his imitators to run dry."[5]

Cabasilas is evidently a man of lofty spirituality; his work is in the full and proper sense a faithfilled contemplation. For a sample of his spiritual riches, one need only read the pages he devotes to sanctification.[6] Here is J. Gouillard's summary appraisal of the work: "The *Commentary* is not the exercise of a pedantic theologian who stands remote from his object; it is the spiritual exercise of a devout man who is involved with his object."[7]

But Cabasilas is not only a spiritual writer, for his interests are theological in the full sense of the term. For example, he displays outstanding theological competence when he deals with the problem of the eucharistic consecration and discourses on the relation between the epiclesis and the account of institution[8] and on the nature of the eucharistic sacrifice.[9] This last case is especially interesting, for in his lengthy and solid work on the Eucharist, M. de la Taille, S.J., formulates a theory of the eucharistic sacrifice that is practically identical with that of Cabasilas,[10] whereas H. Boüessé, O.P., is so convinced of the soundness of Cabasilas' teaching that he compares it with the decrees of Trent and is able to take it over and present it as consistent with Catholic teaching.[11]

These responses were truly surprising at a time when Catholic theology was not displaying any great ecumenical openness. At any rate, the judgment of J. Gouillard stands: "Cabasilas is the only Byzantine theologian to propose a speculative analysis that can be called 'Scholastic'[12] of the eucharistic sacrifice."[13]

(b) In Ambrose, too, we find the same combination of theological competence with spiritual riches. A careful examination allows me to claim that while this combination is due ultimately to the author's faith, it derives proximately from the special character of the mystagogical method.

Ambrose, too, develops a true and proper theology in his mystagogical writings and, like Cabasilas, deals at length with the eucharistic consecration.[14] In order to explain the transformation of the bread and wine into the body and blood of Christ, he appeals to the creative omnipotence of the divine word and then, like Cabasilas, goes on to personal reflections that are not found in the sources used by each of the two men.[15]

The only problem with illustrating the spiritual dimension in Ambrose's mystagogy is one of choice. Here is an example: means of a verse from the Song of Songs: " 'Let him kiss me with the kisses of his mouth.' Do you wish to apply this to Christ? Nothing is more pleasing. Do you wish to apply it to your own soul? Nothing is sweeter."[16] The theme of the kiss is then continued into the interpretation of the Eucharist: " 'Let him kiss me,' " because after baptism, the believer is clean of all sin and is therefore judged worthy of the heavenly sacrament and is invited to the heavenly banquet: " 'Let him kiss me with the kisses of his mouth.' "[17]

I shall point out here only that it is the mystagogical method itself that allows the faith of the author of a mystagogical explanation to express itself freely and thus bring out the spiritual and saving value of the liturgical action. In order to show more clearly how mystagogy with its typological method directly yields theology, it will be appropriate to look at one aspect among many of Ambrose's baptismal theology. He builds his argument on the story of Naaman, which is told in detail. He gives this story a typological interpretation that leads to a theology of baptism understood as healing and regeneration.

When he comes to the end of the Naaman story, Ambrose asks: "What does it mean?" Here he begins his explanation, which is based on the contrast between "what is seen" and "what is not seen" (a characteristic theme of sacramental theology). He asks the meaning of the Old Testament incident and answers by pointing to the baptismal water, the special properties of which he then lists. The method entails a kind of superposition and identification of two things that are being compared: baptism and the cure of Naaman.[18] It becomes clear that the water of baptism heals precisely because of the Naaman incident, but it is the grace of Christ that makes that incident present and operative in the water of baptism. The grace of Christ in turn is connected with the descent of the Spirit, who consecrates the water. Ambrose goes on to speak of the Spirit and the institution of baptism. Clearly, all these matters are properly theological.

The theme of the Spirit introduces a further factor, which is explained on the basis of another biblical incident: the baptism of Jesus in the Jordan. In describing the baptism of Jesus, Ambrose says: ". . . when our Lord Jesus Christ instituted the rite of baptism."[19] "If then the rite of baptism was instituted for our sake, it is to our faith that the rite is proposed."[20] The reason why the baptism of Christ is seen as an act of institution and the paradigm for our baptism[21] is that the sacraments are thought of as *imitations*: if the Spirit descended on the Jordan in the form of a dove, then he will also descend on the water of our fonts to consecrate it and make it capable of healing.[22]

Circling back, Ambrose returns to the question that concerned him at the beginning of his discussion: the healing efficacy of baptism. Institution by Christ, Trinitarian presence, and gift of the Spirit, who consecrates the water: these are the factors that justify his conclusion about the saving efficacy of baptism.

Now all this is nothing but theology; it is no longer possible to distinguish between a mystagogy of baptism and a theology of baptism. The text of Ambrose makes it clear that theology is directly produced by the consistent typological application of Old Testament passages to the Christian sacraments. Since this is the specific and proper method of Ambrose's mystagogy, it follows that mystagogy as such is theological or, better, a way of doing theology.

C. Conclusion

I am aware that no valid conclusion can be drawn from a couple of examples. I must point out, however, that these examples are only some of the many that could be cited.

They show how mystagogy, while remaining itself, is capable of being developed along properly theological lines. Anyone can continue the investigation and supply other examples that demonstrate this thesis. I may, therefore, conclude that mystagogy is not so much a form of catechesis or spiritual theology as it is a way of doing theology in the true and proper sense of the term. Consequently, we ought to speak of it as *mystagogical theology*. And since theology takes the liturgical celebration as its point of departure, it may be inferred that we are dealing with a theology of the liturgy.

6

A. The Use of Scripture

In the patristic age, there was no standard way of doing theology, if for no other reason than that theology sprang not so much from a felt need of developing a treatise as from the Church's vital needs, which called, depending on circumstances, for a homily or more thorough instruction (catechesis) or the refutation of some heretical position. It seems then that it was pastoral need that forced bishops to become theologians and thus Fathers of the Church.

At the same time, it must be recognized that throughout the patristic period, the use of Scripture was extremely important both in theological discourse and in decisions affecting life. Scripture, both the Old and New Testaments, was the native setting in which the Church of the first centuries lived and worked. The Christian way of using the Old Testament was felt as a problem from the very beginning; the use itself is already visible in the New Testament, which in many passages uses the Old Testament in order to speak of Christ and provide a deeper understanding of the mystery of his person.

"It has been said that the history of dogma is the history of exegesis, since the entire development of Christian doctrine is based on a certain number of scriptural texts that are interpreted in the light of specific needs. The same can be said, however, of every other aspect of the Church's life: its organization, its discipline, its worship, and so on."[23]

The Christian use of the Old Testament is a "problem" because it is not really a simple matter to take an Old Testament passage and apply it directly to Christ or the Church. In fact, "the application of the sacred text to the various purposes of communal life required a deeper grasp of its meaning and value, so that it could then be adapted to needs and tasks which might well have no direct or obvious connection with the given passage."[24]

Without this deeper grasp of the meaning, it is not possible to apply the Old Testament to the realities of the New. It is here precisely that the typological method comes on the scene, its pur-

7

pose being the understanding of the mystery. In Christianity, the problem of how to interpret the Old Testament is especially clear in the question of Christ's person, since the Old Testament must be applicable to Christ and be able to confirm his claims and accredit him. The situation called for a special hermeneutical method.

We must bear in mind, however, that the Jewish world had already faced the problem of Old Testament interpretation and had developed a number of interpretational techniques in the true and proper sense of the term. Among these were *halakah*, or the practical application of the sacred text to the activities of everyday life; and *haggadah*, which found its chief expression in the homily and aimed at the edification of the faithful. There was the *targum*, which was a kind of paraphrase, and the *midrash*, which was a special kind of interpretation that applied the Old Testament to the present by combining various passages. Mention may be made, finally, of the *pesher* (explanation), which served to actualize a biblical text, usually of the prophetic type, by connecting it with the historical experiences of, for example, the Qumran sect or, more generally, of Palestine.[25]

The first Christians were Jews and well acquainted with this actualizing use of the Old Testament. This is evident from the Old Testament citations found throughout the New Testament. At times, these citations are in the form of midrashes, as in the Magnificat; that is, they present new ideas by combining Old Testament passages, each of which suggests others.[26]

It is, however, Paul and the Letter to the Hebrews that give special attention to the use of the Old Testament:

"When Paul reflects on the scriptures [= the Old Testament] in the light of Christ he sees hidden in them the mystery (Rom 16:25; 1 Cor 2:1) which only the lifegiving spirit, and not the letter that kills, can reveal (2 Cor 3:6). When read in this perspective, the old Law acquires a new dimension. . . . The Law was written for us, says Paul a propos of Dt 25:4."[27]

Paul and Hebrews even reflect a theorization of the interpretative method in their use of the idea of *typos* and their interpreta-

8

tion of Old Testament figures.[28] But the gospel of John also uses the same exegetical method when speaking of the brazen serpent and the Passover lamb.

All these Pauline and Johannine figures are the real origin of mystagogical interpretation of the liturgical celebration. The Old and New Testament texts on which mystagogical interpretations are built have their principal predecessor, and therefore their legitimation, in this Pauline and Johannine typology.[29]

B. Typology and Mystagogy

I have shown how mystagogy is a "theology"; I must now explain its main activity: the use of Scripture and especially of the Old Testament. The problem faced in mystagogy is how to apply the Scriptures to the mystery being celebrated. Anyone familiar with the history of biblical exegesis knows that the Alexandrian and Antiochene schools used different methods: the Alexandrian school went in for allegory, whereas the Antiochene school stressed the literal meaning. But things are really not that simple and the difference not that clear-cut, since both schools practiced the typological method and at this level ended up resembling each other more than scholars are disposed to allow.

Both schools practiced mystagogy and the exegetical method characteristic of each was reflected in this practice; as a result, the differences between the respective mystagogies are much less considerable[30] than might appear at a first reading of the texts.

Typology is of great interest at this point, since "the application of this method to the Scriptures is called spiritual exegesis, whereas its application to the liturgy is called mystagogy."[31] By way of example, I may cite the opening of Origen's fifth homily on Numbers,[32] since "an analysis of the vocabulary of this passage shows in fact that the terms he uses in speaking of liturgical initiation are the same as he uses in the explanation of the scriptures."[33]

It follows that the problem of mystagogy must always be seen as closely connected with the problem of biblical typology. Only a satisfactory answer to questions concerning biblical typology will make possible a correct approach to mystagogical theology.

C. Typology and Allegory

"The hermeneutical procedure which Paul and the other New Testament writers use in their spiritual interpretation of the Law is allegorical in kind, inasmuch as it discovers another meaning beyond the immediate, literal meaning of the passage under consideration. The usual word Paul uses in explaining the connection between the two meanings is *typos*, that is, form, figure, symbol, prefiguration (Rom 5:14; 1 Cor 10:4; etc.). But in Galatians 4:24, when speaking of the sons of Hagar and Sarah as prefigurations of Jews and Christians respectively, he says: 'These things are said allegorically (atina estin allegoroumena),' showing that he regards *typos* as synonymous with *allegoria*. As we shall see, this way of interpreting the Old Testament, which was to have a very prosperous future and become the authentic Christian way of reading the Old Testament, is described by modern scholars as 'typology' or 'typological interpretation,' in deference to Pauline terminology. The ancients themselves described it as the 'spiritual' or 'mystical' interpretation of scripture."[34]

In this hermeneutical approach, ancient happenings speak of present day events, since they have their fulfillment in Christ; consequently, their true interpretation comes from Christ and therefore from the today of the New Testament. This method does not give priority to the New Testament over the Old or to the Old over the New; it requires both to be continually referred each to the other. The interpretation is a very dynamic one and consists in keeping the two Testaments constantly interrelated in a kind of continual superposition of each on the other. It is from this *relationship* that understanding of the mystery flows.

"Although the early exegetes sometimes express reservations about the use of allegory and its derivatives, they do not distinguish between allegory and typology and regard spiritual interpretation as a mode of allegorical interpretation."[35] We moderns, on the other hand, distinguish carefully between allegory and typology. The distinction may be expressed in the words of Melito of Sardis, who when positing the theoretical principle of the relation between the Old and New Testaments, differentiates between a correspondence of *texts*, which occurs at the level of meaning, and a correspondence of *events*, which occurs at the level of historical saving realities: "What is said[36] is parable, what happens is prefiguration."[37]

If the *written text* of the Old Testament is interpreted as referring and corresponding to New Testament realities, then the Old Testament *events* likewise refer and correspond to the same realities by reason of their meaning. But the texts are not the events; the process by which the texts correspond can be called allegory, whereas the process by which the events correspond can be called typology. It follows that allegory has to do with the meaning of a text, whereas typology has to do with the realization or fulfillment of a saving event. The passage cited from Melito makes the distinction very accurately, since "parable" is always used when speaking of the interpretation of a text and not of the salvific meaning of Old Testament events; these correspond to and have their "truth" in New Testament events.[38]

This distinction between texts and events is extremely important, since it allows us to recover typology while avoiding the serious problems attendant on the allegorical interpretation of Scripture. Based as it is on comparison and evocation, allegory quickly proves to be a procedure that is uncontrollable because it follows no sure and objective criteria. Subjectivism is the only objective criterion at work in allegory. R. Bornert expresses himself in terms such as I have just been using and, following J. Daniélou, tries to clarify as follows the difference between typology and allegory:

"Biblical and liturgical typology explains the scriptures or comments on the rites in function of the objective correspondence that exists between the several phases of salvation history. The typology may be prophetic and announce the eschatological future, or it may be commemorative and show how the past is fulfilled. Allegory, on the contrary, interprets the scriptures and the liturgy without paying any attention to the real relations that exist between the successive stages of the divine economy. Typology has an objective historical basis. Allegory, on the other hand, abstracts from the *analogy* between the different phases of the one divine plan and sets up arbitrary innovations. . . . In spiritual exegesis and in mystagogy that which depends on typology remains permanently valid; that which belongs to allegory is transitory."[39]

The statement is a very accurate one and, as far as concepts are concerned, quite clear. On the other hand, it is extremely difficult to distinguish in a patristic passage between the elements that depend on an allegorical method and those that depend on a typological method.[40] J. Daniélou was correct in saying that "what is proper to the Alexandrians is not typology but allegory,"[41] but it must be added that for the Alexandrians, allegorizing was their way of practicing typology. This was due not so much to the specific exegetical method used by the Alexandrians as it was to the inherent closeness between typology and allegory and to the objective difficulty of practicing typology without falling into allegory. The problem is especially clear in those Fathers who were not Alexandrians[42] and yet practiced typology in such a way that they ended up quite frequently in allegory.

The catechetical homilies of Theodore of Mopsuestia are a splendid example of the work of the Antiochene school.[43] This school kept its distance from allegory and practiced a primarily literal exegesis. This means that in its mystagogy, it deliberately ignored the figures of the Old Testament.[44] In fact, it regarded the liturgical celebration primarily as an *image* of the economy that reached its climax and fulfillment in Christ. The rites symbolize the main stages of this economy, and Theodore is thus the first to propose a parallelism between the events of the passion and the rites of the Eucharist, turning the latter into a kind of dramatization.[45]

In the final analysis, this typology likewise uses allegory but applies it to the liturgical rites; in this way, it differs from the Alexandrians, who applied the allegorical approach chiefly to the Old Testament figures. If the Antiochene school was nonetheless successful in maintaining a distinction between mystagogy and allegory, this means only that the distinction made before between typology and allegory is not so easily reduced to practice.

This entire problem of the difference between typology and allegory had a direct impact on the various mystagogical treatises, as can be seen in the work of so great a mystagogue as St. Maximus the Confessor.

The allegorical method would later be extensively used in the *explicationes Missae* (explanations of the Mass) and the great commentaries on the liturgy that saw the light in the Latin Middle Ages. It would be applied either in drawing parallels between the Old Testament figures and the liturgy or in viewing the liturgical rites as a kind of dramatization of the events of Christ's passion.

The allegory in these great commentaries often deteriorates and presents us with arbitrary and groundless interpretations. Our rejection of allegory prevents us, however, from seeing that these commentaries (for example, the *Liber officialis* of Amalarius of Metz[46]) are true and proper mystagogical treatises, even if the balance between typology and allegory is unfortunately often upset to the great advantage of the latter. If we ask why mystagogical catechesis and mystagogical commentary have for practical purposes disappeared from the contemporary Roman Church, we must recognize that the reason is the excessive part played by allegory in the medieval treatises and in the devotional books that they inspired in the modern era. Allegory has historically been the death of mystagogy.

CHAPTER TWO

Ambrose of Milan

In order to speak correctly of mystagogy, one must start from
mystagogy as it really existed, that is, from a specific, concrete
mystagogical work. Otherwise one risks building an arbitrary
theory. I have chosen to begin my discussion of mystagogy with
Ambrose and his two works *De sacramentis* and *De mysteriis*, the
former probably written about 380–390 and the latter between
387 and 391.[1] At the outset, I must call the reader's attention to
G. Francesconi's excellent study of the sacramental vocabulary of
Ambrose[2]; were it not for this book with its extensive documentation and many stimulating insights, it would indeed be difficult
to make one's way in this difficult area.

I. THE HISTORY OF SALVATION AND ITS VOCABULARY
In Ambrose's view, God's salvation is mediated to us through
the history of the world, a history whose various stages he discovers in the Scriptures,[3] as, indeed, do Hilary, Origen, and
even Philo.[4] The final stage will be eternity. In Virgil's vision,
history had as its goal the building of the Roman Empire; Ambrose transposes this conception into a Christian setting, so that
for him "the religious history of the world advances toward and
builds the Christian empire. But he conceives of this progress in
rather negative terms: it is because each stage is a failure that it
calls for a next stage."[5]

The successive stages are ordered toward a single goal: Jesus
Christ. But for Ambrose, "the historical evolution of the world
remains secondary. . . . He is less interested in the stages of the
history of salvation than in the stages of the soul's journey to
God."[6] This explains why "he almost never looks at the historical
meaning of biblical events and things, but sees them rather as

symbolic reminders of other, usually moral, realities: ideas, virtues, and so on."[7]

Since this is Ambrose's perspective, it is easy to understand why he is more interested in the unity of God's saving work than in its pluriformity.

"This very history, then, is a mystery in Ambrose's eyes. Within it God is at work *in mysterio*. If, then, we are to grasp his action, which is the guiding thread of events, we must move beyond figures, beyond external signs, and read the 'deeper meaning' hidden in events. Openness and docility to God at work *in mysterio* is, as we shall see, a characteristic of faith. Meanwhile, every event of human history that is told in the scriptures can itself be, in Ambrose's eyes, a mystery pregnant with the divine plan for the human race."[8]

In all his writings, but especially in his mystagogical works, Ambrose emphasizes the close connection between three things: the Old Testament, the New Testament, and the liturgical rites of the Church. The means he uses for this purpose are (1) his exegetical method, and (2) the meanings of a certain number of words: *mysterium, sacramentum, figura, umbra, forma, typus, imago, species,* and *similitudo.* Nor is any very clear distinction made between the two tools. In fact, there is really only a single procedure, since even when used in a sacramental context, the words I have listed retain the meanings they had in their original use in, biblical interpretation.

A further point to be kept in mind is that the several words listed are not synonyms of one another, even though the meaning of each partially overlaps that of the others. It would be a serious mistake to let this objective proximity of meanings lull us into thinking that the words are simply interchangeable synonyms, all expressing the idea of *sacramentality*.[9]

In the works of Ambrose, this entire vocabulary is applied to three kinds of things. In the first place, it signifies the relation between Old Testament and New Testament realities; its purpose in this context is to ensure the unity of the history of salvation through the two Testaments. The vocabulary is used, next, to signify the relation of unity between the order of creation and the order of salvation. Most importantly, however, it is used to indicate the unity and identity of the salvation that comes to us in the sacraments with the salvation that is made objectively real in history.[10] The function of the words is thus to establish a relation of unity and identity between two correlative things, while at the same time ensuring that each of them retains its specific nature and is not simply reduced to the other.

The vocabulary thus described is identically the vocabulary proper to biblical typology. It consists of a series of technical terms that make possible the typological interpretation of the Scriptures.

A. *Mystery* (Mysterium)

"The typological method properly consists in showing the unity of the divine plan by pointing out the parallelism between events. . . . Typology unifies past, present, and future."[11] *Mysterium*, therefore, "is for Ambrose predominantly a category with which to read and interpret the scriptures; the search for the *mysterium* ensures that the scriptures are not reduced to a simple listing of 'facts.' . . . Discovery of the *mysterium* brings the realization that God has a single plan which shows itself as a history of salvation."[12]

B. *Figure* (Figura)

An analogous claim must be made for *figura*: "A figure is therefore not reducible to a simple historical datum: it is not, for example, the exodus either as a brute fact or in some idealized understanding of it; rather, the factual episode is grasped as an event in which a religious interpretation reveals a liberating presence of God, a presence that is mysterious but nonetheless real enough to play a determining role in a history."[13]

Mysterium and *figura* are not synonyms. In fact,

"*Figura* sets up a dynamic relationship between the Old Testament and the New, a relationship which is first of all of a general kind. The role of *figura* is to provide a key for understanding these two historical stages and their meaning. The concept of

16

figura seeks to prevent each of the two being taken in isolation
and show each as requiring the other. . . . *Figura* points to a historical precedent that only today can be fully understood."[14]

For this very reason, *figura* can be combined with *mysterium*:

"The expressions *mysterium, in figura* or *figura mysterii*, which oc-
cur often in Ambrose, emphasize the mediational and revelatory
function of a *figura. Figura* refers to historical realities, but insofar
as they carry a salvific meaning. It designates historical realities
to the extent that they play a part in a movement of revelation
and emit an echo that looks beyond them and carries history
forward toward its fulfillment."[15]

Mysterium and *figura* are, therefore, not completely overlapping
terms, since *mysterium* signifies that historical realities are in fact
manifestations of the salvation given by God, while *figura* also
brings out the connection of the various mysteries among themselves and with their ultimate fulfillment. *Figura* calls for, and
already contains within itself, a complementary term, namely
veritas (truth), without which it would be incomplete and even
unintelligible.[16] In other words, *figura* calls attention to the
evolutive and dynamic character of the history of salvation: "it
locates historical events within a movement from the less to the
more complete."[17]

In conclusion:

"*Figura* makes it possible to see history as searching for and
teaching its own meaning. . . . A figure directs the mind forward. Given this perspective, it is understandable that *figura*
should express the totality of history in relation to its definitive
meaning (its fulfillment) and, at the same time movement of the
historical process toward its completion. The movement is less a
movement of the figure than a movement within it; in other
words, a constitutive element in the very idea of figure is that it
is caught up in a movement toward fulfillment and completion. . . . Consequently, the *figura–veritas* relation cannot be understood as a relation between a prior and a posterior; the 'truth'
does not come after the figure; a figure is not something false.
Rather we are dealing with two levels of truth."[18]

C. Shadow (Umbra)

Whereas *figura* can also be applied to New Testament realities in relation to their eschatological fulfillment, *umbra*[19] applies only to Old Testament realities.

"*Umbra* essentially describes the Old Testament phase in its relation to the New Testament and the Church and to the eschatological age. . . . [The present] casts its shadow before it in the past, so that the past acquired meaning and value precisely from the fact that it was not self-contained but was to have a fulfillment."[20]

Consequently, "history, beginning with the past, is a shadow that promises a reality. . . . *Umbra* is therefore a technical term describing the Old Testament past in its relation to Christ and the Church."[21]

D. Appearance (Species)

This term is related to the preceding; it can also designate the same realities that are described as *figura, imago,* and *similitudo,* but the connotation here is quite different. "*Species* describes a reality in terms of what it shows externally, by its appearance. The truth of the reality depends therefore on the content behind the *species.*"[22] "External aspect" is by far the most common meaning of *species,*[23] even though "*species* also occurs in Ambrose with a precise technical meaning, since it is used in the sense of 'prefiguration' to designate realities in the history of salvation."[24]

The "appearance" or "external aspect" of a thing is a way of participating in the thing's truth, although it does not exhaust that truth. Therefore, the contrast of *species* and *veritas* is not to be understood as the antithesis between false and true, but is to be interpreted dialectically: the present in relation to the future is provisional and relative.

"*Species* is a historico-typological category; that is, it expresses a relation between a past and a present (the Church), a relation based essentially on external aspects that are alike and therefore suggest one another."[25] This phenomenon allows Ambrose to cite a large number of passages from the Bible, solely because a certain external similiarity exists. He is able to make a heavily allegorical use of typology precisely because of the "external aspect" meaning of the term *species* that belongs in the area of typology and serves also to indicate the relation between the Old Testament and the realities of the New. In this case, the biblical passages speak no longer of events but of ideas. All this has a direct impact on mystagogy, since *species* designates the sacraments inasmuch as they are visible and tangible.

E. *Image* (Imago)

In all of Ambrose's thinking, the term *imago* implies revelation; through images, human beings have access to what would otherwise be inaccessible. In this perspective, *imago* is first and foremost a christological concept, since in Christ, the invisible God reveals himself to us.

But if the term *imago* is to function in this way, it must have an additional meaning that makes it irreducible to *species*. *Imago* signifies the ontological relation between the image and the imaged. It can be said to have this signification in Ambrose, since "from the idea of the Son as *imago* he not infrequently deduces and asserts the equality between Father and Son as, for example, in *Exam* I, 19."[26] Nor is *imago*, used in this way, an isolated concept; rather it is carefully stated[27] theological datum that perhaps reflects Platonic influences, since in his view, an "image" does in fact *participate* in the reality it images.

Ambrose is not the only one to understand "image" in this way, for the concept is widespread among the Greek Fathers:

"The description given of Christ in Colossians 1:15—'image of the invisible God'—may seem contradictory in modern logic: How can what is invisible have an image? As a matter of fact, the thought in Colossians 1:15 becomes intelligible only when connected with the conception the ancients had of the world. In this conception, an image is not simply a functional representation of an object and understood as such by the human mind. It can also be a radiation or visible manifestation of the essence of a thing, as such, can involve a participation (*metochē*) in the substance of that object. Consequently, far from being a mere datum of consciousness and as it were torn away from the reality, an *imago* participates in the real and is even truly the reality itself. Therefore the term *eikōn* does not mean only a weak reflection or, as it were, a deformed copy of an object, but rather the projection into visibility of the object's innermost essence."[28]

For Ambrose, the way in which one thing becomes "like" (*ad imaginem*) another is imitation. This is true of Christian life as a whole,[29] but it is true above all of the sacramental celebration,[30] since it is baptism that forms the image of God in Christians. Any further discussion of the point requires that we turn now to the term *similitudo*, which is complementary to *imago*.

F. Likeness (Similitudo)

Perhaps because of Genesis 1:26, *imago* and *similitudo* are regarded as complementary terms.[31] In Ambrose, *imago* carries ontological implications, whereas *similitudo* is the very definition of sacramentality, both for baptism[32] and for the Eucharist.[33] The concept of *similitudo* is completely traditional. Its use in the Anaphora of Serapion[34] shows that the original meaning of the term is the baptismal "likeness" found in Romans 6:5; this was then applied to the Eucharist, since the Eucharist is a "likeness of his death." Ambrose use of the term in the *De sacramentis* and the *De mysteriis* is fully identical with this, as far as vocabulary goes.

"Likeness," as well as "image," is connected with imitation[35] and is used by Ambrose in a comparable way to express Christ's equality with God:

"We may therefore maintain that Ambrose makes christological use of the concept of *similitudo* in his effort to understand and give human expression to the mystery of Christ: his consubstantiality with the Father and, simultaneously, his human dimension, whereby he is a sign of the presence of God in the world of human beings. In that context, then, I consider the concept to be 'sacramental.' "[36]

The meaning is that Christ possesses equality with God because he is the image of God, and he is the *imago* because he is the *similitudo*.[37]

I may therefore conclude that *similitudo* is very close in meaning to *imago* but not identical with it. If asked what "likeness" adds to "image," I can only answer: concreteness. In giving this answer, I am falling back on the underlying Greek term, *homoiōma*, which in the Scriptures has a very precise technical meaning that continues to make its presence felt in the Fathers.[38] I would say, then, that in the semantic area covered by the paired concepts, *imago* and *similitudo*, the latter more clearly points to sacramentality as such. In a "sacrament," Ambrose distinguishes between what is accessible to sense perception and what is invisible.[39] It is here that sacramentality is located, and it is this that he calls *similitudo*—something that cannot be seen but can only be learned from the Scriptures.[40]

G. *Type* (Typus)

In keeping with the logic at work in Ambrose's vocabulary, *typus* is never used of a *sacramentum* nor (in Francesconi's judgment) are there any passages in which *typus* is used directly of prefigurations of the Eucharist.[41] According to the use most widely found in his writings, *typus* signifies figurative realities in the history of salvation; but he also uses the term in allegory.

"As a category in the history of salvation *typus* is used of the negative form [of some reality] as contrasted with its positive form, that is, its full form or fulfillment. A *typus* is not false, however, but simply provisional; it designates a figural reality in relation to its fulfillment. It has real historical existence (if the *typus* is an event or a person), but beyond it a deeper meaning can be glimpsed. Understanding it in this way, I regard it as a historical sacramental concept; it points to historical realities insofar as they are carriers of the *mysterium*."[42]

For practical purposes, *typus* is identical with *figura* and *forma* (two Latin words used to translate the Pauline *typos*).

H. *Sacrament* (Sacramentum)

Sacramentum is objectively close to *mysterium*, inasmuch as both are categories for interpreting the history of salvation and both are used in dealing with the sacraments and in mystagogical teaching. "Ambrose finds many *sacramenta* in biblical history; that is to say, God's plan is mediated through many sensible realities (persons and events) which, precisely because they are visible, become 'signs' of a deeper reality. In these contexts *sacramentum* is a focal point for the tension of the past toward Christ."[43]

Despite what the words just cited might suggest, a "sacrament" is not the same as a "figure," for it also applies to New Testament realities and even to Christ and his redeeming cross:

"The cross of Christ, then, is the *sacramentum* of our salvation. Various prefigurations are here fulfilled; like Joseph with his brothers, Christ 'has delivered us from shame by the sacrament of the Lord's cross'; Jonah was a pale figure of Christ, 'who fulfilled that figure by the sacrament of his death'; the three hundred chosen by Gideon to do battle against the enemy (Jgs 7:6) foretell in figure that 'by the sacrament of the cross the world is to be delivered from the attack of far greater enemies'; in the psalms 'the Savior begins to reveal increasingly the sacraments of his passion,' since what is prophetically announced there is fulfilled in the gospel. The cross of Christ gives meaning to that entire history; indeed it was already figuratively signified by the wood which Moses threw into the bitter water (Ex 15:22–25)."[44]

But if we inquire more closely into what is specific to *sacramentum*, we are compelled to say that its primary meaning is "sign," that is, the reality designated such by human beings, but understood as the locus and medium of God's saving action. This description already gives us a glimpse of the element that most completely distinguishes *sacramentum* from *mysterium*. Here is the conclusion Francesconi reaches in his study: "Both designate prophetic signs in ancient history. But in light of my brief survey I think it must be said that *sacramentum* emphasizes more the external element that manifests the interior *mysterium*. . . . This difference is suggested by the occasional use of the two words in combination (*mysterii sacramentum*)."[45]

The difference emerges very clearly in Ambrose's mystagogical catecheses:

"Circumstances now urge me to speak of the mysteries and to explain the meaning (*rationem*) of the sacraments. If I had decided to refer to them before baptism, when you were not yet initiated, I would rightly have been judged a traitor (*prodidisse*) rather than a transmitter (*tradidisse*). Furthermore, the light of the mysteries makes its way into persons more effectively if they are not expecting it than if an instruction has preceded it."[46]

B. Botte pinpoints the difference very clearly when he writes: "*Mysteria* are here distinguished from *sacramenta*. The latter are the sacred rites, the former the deeper meaning of the scriptures."[47]

II. THE MYSTAGOGY OF ST. AMBROSE
In discussing the sacramental vocabulary of Ambrose, I reserved the term *sacramentum* to the end because it allows me to move directly into a theological examination of his mystagogy.

The passage I cited a couple of paragraphs back (at n. 46) is from the beginning of the *De mysteriis*. In it, Ambrose says that he intends to explain the mysteries and the *rationem* of the sacraments. Why does he say "*ratio* of the sacraments" and not just "sacraments" (as he does "mysteries")? Is there a difference between "sacraments" and "meaning of the sacraments"? Yes, there is.

The *mysterium* is salvation, that is, the deeper content of history insofar as history is a series of saving events; and this content is now made available to human beings through the *sacramentum* or liturgical celebration. The *ratio sacramentorum* is the meaning of the *sacramentum* or liturgical rite, namely, the connection of the sacrament with the *mysterium* or, in a word, its sacramentality. In some passages, Ambrose uses a special word to signify this connection: *similitudo* (with the meaning the word has when he uses it for the Eucharist).

"But perhaps you will say: 'I do not see the appearance of blood.' But it [the wine] is the likeness [or symbol] of the blood. Just as you have received the likeness [or symbol] of the death, so too you drink the likeness [or symbol] of the blood, in order that there may be no disgust provoked by flowing blood and yet the price of redemption may have its effect. You know (*didicisti*), therefore, that what you receive is the body of Christ."[48]

The "likeness" is not the visible element of the sacrament; the word for the external or visible element is *species*, to which, in fact, "likeness" is opposed. The "likeness" is rather the invisible element of the sacrament and can be known only through instruction (*didicisti*).

The phrase *ratio sacramentorum*, which is the object of mystagogy, has an interesting parallel in Origen, in whom, as in Ambrose, we find an identity between exegetical method and mystagogical method. As for Ambrose, who must "explain the *ratio sacramentorum*," so for Origen

"liturgical ceremonies contain a *ratio* which can be revealed (*patere*), explained (*explicare*), and reached by the understanding (*adsequi*). It is probable that in his Latin version Rufinus translated *logos* as *ratio*. Among its many meanings, the word *logos*, when applied to the mystery, signifies the intelligibility of the latter. . . . We may infer by analogy that the *ratio* of liturgical ceremonies expresses the intelligibility of the mystery which they contain. . . . Origen's sacramental and liturgical mystagogy is, therefore, not so much an initiation into the mystery of the liturgy as it is an introduction to the one mystery with the liturgy as point of departure."[49]

St. Maximus the Confessor inherits the same conception and makes it the basis of his mystagogy.[50] Pseudo-Dionysius, too, inherits the same perspective from Origen; in the Areopagite, this perspective can in fact be formulated in a way very like that which we find in Ambrose. *Theōria*, which is a means of union with God, has two points of departure:

"The two points of departure are scripture and the sacramental rites. We contemplate the mysteries in the scriptures through sensible symbols, and we reach the divine archetypes of the sacraments through their visible manifestations. . . . In Pseudo-Dionysius, as in Origen, sacramental *theōria* and scriptural *theōria* are closely connected with one another."[51]

24

I conclude, therefore, that the thinking of Origen and Maximus can help us understand Ambrose's distinction as a key element in his mystagogical thought. Given this objective similarity between the three writers, I accept the hypothesis that Maximus' definition of mystagogy is valid for Ambrose as well: the purpose of mystagogy is to introduce the Christian to knowledge (*gnōsis*) of the mystery.[52]

Such is my hypothesis. It remains only to see whether Ambrose does in fact understand mystagogy as an initiation, via the liturgy, into the mystery of salvation that has taken place in history, or, to put it in other words, as an initiation into the liturgical rites understood as themselves embodying the mystery.

A. *Celebrating the Mystery of the Opening* (Aperitionis celebrantes mysterium)

Ambrose speaks to the neophytes of the rite of "opening (*aperitio*)," which he had celebrated with them; he even reminds them of the liturgical formula he had used.[53] In this context, he refers to the rite both as *sacramentum* and as *mysterium*. Are the two words simply synonyms, or do they still reflect the distinction that he has made only a few lines earlier?

The answer is to be found in what immediately follows. Continuing his explanation of the sacrament, Ambrose cites the episode of the deaf-mute healed by Jesus and speaks of it as a *mysterium*[54]; and, in fact, the incident is an event in the history of salvation as reported in the Scriptures. It is to be noted that he establishes an ontological identity between the rite of the Church and the action that Jesus performs on the deaf-mute. This assertion of identity is justified by biblical typology, that is, by the hermeneutical method used in the Scriptures and expressed in the technical terms that we saw a bit earlier.

A study of this vocabulary shows that the events comprising the history of salvation are objectively bound together to form a coherent whole; there is a movement from the lesser to the greater, from sketch to full reality, terminating finally in the revelation proper to the eschaton. As a result, the various stages in the history of salvation refer to one another and are mirrored each in the others in a kind of ontological correspondence. This makes it possible to take the characteristics and attributes of one reality or event and predicate them of another that corresponds to it. Thus, the characteristics of the ritual action can be predicated of the historical event, and the characteristics of the latter can in turn be applied to the liturgical celebration. The two events that are thus brought into reciprocal relation by means of biblical typology end up constituting a single reality in which each merges with the other in a kind of *communicatio idiomatum*.

This is the kind of operation that Ambrose performs when he describes the gospel episode as a "celebration" (a typically liturgical term) and speaks of what Christ did as "this *mysterium*,"[55] or, in other words, as the very thing that the Church is celebrating. If there is no objection to saying that the reality and characteristics of the sacramental rite project their shadow back upon the gospel episode, then there can be no difficulty in predicating of the Church's rite the term *mysterium*, which describes events in the history of salvation. Just as the former procedure does not do away with the difference between the rite of the *Ephphetha* and the cure of the deaf-mute, neither does the application of *mysterium* to the sacramental rite do away with the distinction Ambrose has made at the beginning of his treatise.

B. *How Ancient This Mystery Is* (Quam vetus mysterium est)
When Ambrose comes to speak of the Holy Spirit effectively acting in baptism, he appeals for corroboration to the effectiveness with which the Holy Spirit acted in the Old Testament. In Genesis 1:2, he finds the Spirit hovering over the water; with the aid of this typology, he concludes to the presence and action of the Spirit in baptism. We must bear in mind that the chief characteristic of typology is the superposition of one datum on another— in this case, the Old Testament event and the sacramental action—so that one may pass from one to the other in either direction: what holds for the first holds for the second as well, and vice versa. As a result, Ambrose is able to locate the mystery of baptism at the beginning of the world: "Consider, however, how ancient this mystery is that was prefigured at the very beginning of the world."[56]

Here the baptismal rite is clearly described as a mystery and not as a sacrament. The choice of words is easily explained by the fact that baptism, even if only in its prefigured stage, really belongs to the Old Testament and, more specifically, to the event that is the creation of the world. It is because baptism belongs there that Ambrose can argue to the presence of the Spirit, which he asserts very resolutely and realistically. The argument ends with a rhetorical question: "You see the water, you see the wood, you perceive the dove: can you doubt the mystery?"[57] If the presence and effective action of the Spirit in the baptismal rite are the *deeper meaning* of the event in Genesis, it becomes necessary to describe the sacrament of baptism as a *mysterium*: all the more so since it is not something peculiar to our times, but is of immense antiquity, being part of the event that occurred at the beginning of world history.

C. It Is a Mystery and a Sanctifying Action (Mysterium est et sanctificatio)

The rite of the washing of feet, which was part of the baptismal rite at Milan even though Rome followed a different practice, was challenged by some who saw in the gesture a manifestation of humility and hospitality and claimed that it had no place in the liturgy of baptism: "It should not be part of the *mysterium*, of baptism, of rebirth."[58]

The parallelism of the three words makes it clear that *mysterium* is the rite of baptism; this being the case, we might have expected *sacramentum* to be used instead of *mysterium*. In his appraisal of the washing of feet, Ambrose contrasts humiliation (gesture of humility) with sanctification (sanctifying action).[59] In order to prove that the washing of the feet sanctifies, he does not analyze the rite of the Church, but turns instead to the episode in the gospel of John (13:4ff.) that is the foundation of the Church's practice. Then, with the sanctifying power of the gesture established, he argues that if it sanctifies, it is a *mysterium* and therefore has every right to be part of baptism: "Hear, then, the proof that it is a mystery and a sanctifying action: 'If I do not wash your feet, you have no part in me' (Jn 13:8)."[60]

The citation from John refers not only to a manifestation of humility, but also to an action that sanctifies,[61] for "to have part" in Jesus is to be in communion with him. Ambrose can therefore conclude that in the gospel, the washing of the feet is a sanctifying action; as such it will also be a *mysterium*, since he has linked these two concepts.

The parallel passage in the *De mysteriis* argues even more clearly, since after studying the action of Jesus, it describes it as a *mysterium*: "Peter did not grasp the mystery and therefore refused the service."[62] Ambrose goes on then to explain in what the *mysterium* consists: since the serpent bit the foot of human beings, their feet must be washed in baptism in order to remove inherited sins. The washing is therefore absolutely necessary[63] and possesses a sacramentality of its own, just as baptism proper does.[64]

The ultimate justification of the rite is found in a passage in the gospel: when Peter objects, Jesus answers: "He who is washed need only wash his feet and he is completely clean."[65] We see here once again how Ambrose's thought moves from the liturgy to the gospel and back again without any break in continuity: the words in the gospel are applied to the liturgical rite, and the sacramentality of the baptismal rite is applied to the New Testament episode. He is following the exegetical method of typology in which two elements are interrelated and reduced to unity.

Conclusion: the application of the term *mysterium* to the gospel episode of the washing of feet is completely consistent. Ambrose needs to prove only one point: that in the gospel, the washing of feet sanctifies. This element of the historical action reported in Scripture carries over to its liturgical celebration; no further proof is needed that this is so.

Ambrose does not need to prove that the washing of feet sanctifies when performed in the liturgy. The typological interpretation of what is said in Scripture enables him to develop a theology that, if valid for the archetype, will also be valid for every liturgical reactualization of that action.

D. Consecrated by the Mystery of the Cross (Crucis mysterio consecrata)

Under this rubric, I turn to the episode of the bitter water that became sweet when Moses threw a piece of wood into it (Ex 15:22–25). With the aid of typology, the water of Marah is seen as identical with the water of baptism that becomes lifegiving only after it has been transformed. In his act of throwing the wood into the water of Marah, Moses is regarded as acting prophetically; as a result, the Old Testament episode becomes a figure of the fact that in baptism, the water becomes sanctifying only when joined to the cross. The action of Moses is a baptism in the true and proper sense, though only in the figural stage.

The realism of the typology is such that Ambrose can base an *a posteriori* argument on it: "Therefore if the power of baptism was so great even in the figural stage (*in figura*), how much greater is the power of baptism in its true self (*in veritate*)?"[66]

In the section of the *De sacramentis* from which this citation is taken, Ambrose uses the term *sacramentum*,[67] whereas in the parallel section of the *De mysteriis*, he speaks rather of *mysterium*.[68] But the parallelism is not complete, since the "mystery of the cross" that consecrates the water may well be the historical event of the cross of Christ, for the phrase "mention of the Lord's cross" ("praedicatio dominicae crucis"), which occurs before and again after the words about the "mystery of the cross," refers to the ritual of baptism. The meaning would be: the mystery of the cross consecrates the water because the latter receives the "mention of the Lord's cross," which is a part of the rite. The parallel passage in the *De sacramentis* can be interpreted in like manner, even though it contains a clearer emphasis on the sacrament, which is placed in parallel to the cross of Christ by having the same verb govern both objects: when the water receives the "heavenly sacrament," it also receives the cross of Christ ("sed ubi crucem Christ, ubi acceperit caeleste sacramentum, incipit esse dulcis").

I do not claim that Ambrose is bent on respecting at any cost the distinction between "mystery" and "sacrament"; it is nonetheless interesting to note that in his mystagogy, this distinction is more important than it might at first seem, even if the *De sacramentis* seems less carefully written in this respect than the *De mysteriis*. The distinction remains firmly set in Ambrose's mind and, even if not always respected at the level of terminology, it continues to influence all his writings; indeed, it can even be used as a hermeneutical criterion of texts.

E. This Is That Great Mystery (Hoc est illud magnum mysterium)
In concluding his explanation of the episode of Naaman the Syrian, which had been read that day (2 Kgs 5:1–14), Ambrose again introduces a point that is especially important in his mystagogy: the opposition between seen and unseen. He attributes to the newly baptized the doubts and questions of Naaman and concludes that the water is efficacious solely due to the Spirit. The efficacy that Naaman experienced is a guarantee that the baptismal water is likewise efficacious.[69] He explains that the theme of the opposition between the seen and the unseen had been introduced earlier in order to keep the neophytes from believing, as Naaman did, only in what they can see.[70]

In other words, Ambrose wishes to prevent "what is seen" from being confused with "that great mystery"; it follows from this that the *mysterium* consists precisely in what is *unseen*. If in the celebration of the sacrament, the *mysterium* is the invisible aspect that is brought to pass by the Spirit[71] and is opposed to the sign of water, which has "been seen daily," then we can draw the following conclusion: Ambrose is here setting forth a theology in which the distinction between *sacramentum* and *mysterium* is a necessity, even if this necessity is not immediately evident at the level of terminology. His is a typological theology that carries us beyond the visible data of the baptismal rite.

Modern liturgical theology likewise develops its thought by starting from the "visible" datum of gesture and prayer in order to reach the "invisible" element of the sacrament. This, however, is not the same procedure as is used by Ambrose, since today the "visible" element is located in the sacramental rite itself, whereas Ambrose identifies it with the Old Testament figures that lie behind the sacrament. In fact, Ambrose accomplishes this operation by using not the prayers and rites of the sacrament he has celebrated, but the scriptural verses describing the Naaman episode.

It is clear that these are two different ways of conceiving sacramental theology even if, as we shall see in a moment, they are not as far apart as they may seem. Although the scriptural verses recounting the Naaman episode are not part of Ambrose's baptismal rite, they complement it due to typology. In fact, they belong to the sacrament when the latter takes on another mode of being: the figural, which it has in the Old Testament episode to which reference is made.[72]

F. Sacrament of Baptism—Mystery of Rebirth (Baptismatis sacramentum—Regenerationis mysterium)
As far as vocabulary is concerned, the words "if you remove one of these [water, blood, Spirit], there is no sacrament of baptism" are perfectly parallel to "Likewise, without water there is no mystery of rebirth."[73] I think nonetheless that the distinction between *sacramentum* and *mysterium* is part of the theology Ambrose is expounding.

He says that in baptism there are three witnesses: water, blood, and the Spirit; in baptism, these three are one. To begin with, we must observe three levels of testimony: the water is an element in the visible rite; the blood stands for the event of the cross; the Spirit is Christ's invisible gift. The three levels are different: one is ritual, one historical, and one spiritual. Ambrose continues his commentary by asserting that if any one of three is lacking, there is no longer the sacrament of baptism. This general principle is then given two concrete applications. Without the cross of Christ, the water is only the everyday element and lacks sacramental value ("sine ullo sacramenti valore"); without the water and with only the cross of Christ at hand, human beings are still catechumens, that is, they have not received the mystery of salvation.[74] *Mysterium*, therefore, refers to the invisible content that is the fruit of the sacramental action. This passage once again manifests the distinction made at the beginning of the *De mysteriis*.

G. *They Handed Down This Mystery to Us* (Hoc nobis mysterium tradiderunt)

Ambrose compares the prophet Elijah with the priests who celebrate the liturgy of the Church. If, he says, we esteem Elijah, then we ought to esteem at least as much the apostles Peter and Paul who have handed down these mysteries to us.[75] A few lines later ("ubi ecclesia est, ubi mysteria sunt"), we have the same sacramental meaning. *Mysterium* here is certainly a synonym of *sacramentum* in the sense of a ritual celebration.

H. *Let Us Establish the Truth of the Mystery* (Adstruamus mysterii veritatem)

The subject of this passage is the transformation of the bread and wine into the body and blood of Christ. After presenting a theology of consecration based on the omnipotence of God's word, Ambrose develops an approach of his own, based on the parallelism between Eucharist and Incarnation: "But why do we appeal to arguments? Let us use his examples and by means of the mysteries of the incarnation establish the truth of the mystery."[76]

The "mysteries of the incarnation" are the events that occurred in connection with the birth of Christ, events that display characteristics that surpass the powers of nature. In this context, "mysteries of the incarnation" refers not so much to the mystery of the incarnation as a saving event, as it does to the overall mysteriousness of the Incarnation. "Truth of the mystery" here means not the fulfillment of past events in their reactualization today, but rather the truth, in the modern sense of the word, of the eucharistic mystery. "Mystery" here corresponds perfectly to "sacrament."

In this final text on eucharistic doctrine, we have Ambrose's thinking not simply insofar as it represents the tradition, but also insofar as it contains his personal contribution. It is a kind of thinking that postdates him, so to speak, and already points ahead to medieval realism.

I have offered sufficient evidence that the distinction between mystery and sacrament is important in Ambrose's theology, even though the terminology fluctuates. In the final text just discussed, it is possible to see that he can ignore the distinction at the key point in the argument; here he uses "mystery" and "sacrament" with the meaning's they will have after him. While the *De mysteriis* uses both *exemplum* and *mysterium*,[77] the parallel passage in the *De sacramentis*[78] does not use *mysterium* but only *exemplum*; we may, therefore, suppose that this is the key concept in Ambrose's mind.

I. Conclusion

In this analysis of Ambrosian texts, we have seen how he carefully formulates a distinction between *mysterium* and *sacramentum* and how this distinction remains present and influences his theology even when it is not clearly made at the level of vocabulary. But in the last text that I cited, we saw that when he wants to explain the eucharistic consecration in a more relevant and profound way, he departs from the typological method and as a result understands *mysterium* in a way that is incompatible with the distinction between *mysterium* and *sacramentum* with which he began.

Ambrose is a man of tradition. Tradition is valuable to him; he accepts it, makes it his own, becomes imbued with it, and faithfully preserves it. The distinction between *mysterium* and *sacramentum* is therefore truly a part of his theology and his deeper thought, even if it is perhaps already historically outmoded. Indeed, Ambrose himself even helps to speed up the process whereby it becomes outmoded; in fact, the new thinking later to be found in Scholasticism is already present in him. Nonetheless, even if he is not completely consistent with himself, he makes conscious and deliberate use of the distinction.

Let me conclude by stating my acceptance of the hypothesis that I formulated at the beginning of this section: as for Origen and Maximus the Confessor, so for Ambrose, the purpose of mystagogy is to lead the believer to a knowledge of the mystery (in the sense already explained). Mystagogy is an initiation, via the liturgical celebration, into the saving mystery that took place in history.

The point can be made with greater precision: Ambrose does not construct a biblical theology of the sacrament; rather he constructs a biblical theology of the event recorded in Scripture that lies behind the celebration and is its objective foundation and archetype.

In short: Ambrose's mystagogy is a theology of the archetype and only by derivation a theology of the sacrament. This claim is amply supported by the data analyzed before, even if I have had to acknowledge that in the final text I cited, there is also present a theology that focuses directly on the sacrament without passing through the theology of the archetype.[79]

The conclusion of this section confirms what emerged earlier, in Section I, from an analysis of the sacramental vocabulary of Ambrose. Just as the sacramental vocabulary is the vocabulary of biblical typology applied to the sacraments, so the teaching on the sacraments is simply the biblical teaching on the archetype that is contained in Scripture and applied to, and typologically identified with, the Church's celebration.

III. THE TYPOLOGICAL APPLICATION, OR SACRAMENTALITY

A. Correspondence, Superimposition, Identity
Typology is a hermeneutical method that is essential for the Christian reading of the Scriptures, for it ensures the unity of the two Testaments. By means of typology, the two become a single discourse and a single drama in which Christ is the protagonist: "The peculiarity of the typological method consists precisely in this, that through the parallelism of events it brings to light the unity of the divine plan. . . . Typology unites past, present, and future."[80]

As Christ belongs also to the period preceding the New Testament, so he belongs also to the time after the New Testament. In the first case, the problem that arises is solved by means of typology; the same holds for the second case and explains discourse on the sacraments and more generally on the liturgy. It becomes clear that the hermeneutical method is in the service of the doctrinal issue: the presence of Christ in the events of the Old Testament.[81]

I must now study some passages in the *De sacramentis* and the *De mysteriis* in order to show more clearly how typology brings to light the unity between Christ's presence in the Scriptures and his presence in the celebrations of the Church.

In Ambrosian typology, we are dealing with a procedure that makes use of superimpositions. On the high priest of the Old Testament is superimposed the "priest" who once each year leads the candidates for baptism into the baptistery. The baptistery itself is superimposed on the "second [innermost] tent."

I have used the word "superimposition" because it reflects Ambrose's literary procedure; if, however, we ask what the precise point of the method is, or what relation is being asserted between Old Testament event and New Testament event, we must speak no longer of "superimposition" but of "identification." Here is one example: the rod of Aaron is put in relation to the baptized: just as the withered rod flowered again, so the baptized, who were withered, have begun to flower again in the water of baptism. Now, the rod of Aaron belongs to the Old Testament tent, not to the baptistery; nonetheless, in Ambrose's eyes, the rod of Aaron flowers in the baptistery: "What is the point of this? It is that you may realize that it is into the second tent that the priest has led you—the tent into which the high priest was accustomed to enter once a year, that is, the baptistery in which the rod of Aaron flowered."[82]

In the play of typology, it is possible to superimpose the Old Testament datum on the New Testament datum, because the former is identified with the latter; the former lives on and finds new expression in the latter. The New Testament datum becomes a hermeneutical criterion for reading the Old Testament; it also reactualizes the latter at a higher level of effectiveness; it becomes its *veritas*. The passage I am analyzing ends by citing Psalm 1:3 ("planted by streams of water") in explanation of the fact that the baptized are no longer "dry sticks," but have begun to bear fruit.

Another passage shows us the same typological procedure being applied to baptism, which is explained in light of the Naaman episode, this being told at length. At the end of the story, Ambrose asks: "What then does this mean?" He then begins his explanation, which is based on the opposition between seen and unseen. He asks what the meaning of the Old Testament incident is and answers by pointing to the water of baptism, whose specific properties he lists. The method used implies a superimposition and even a kind of identification of the two things that have been brought together: baptism and the cure of Naaman: "You saw the water, but not all water heals; only that water heals which contains the grace of Christ."[83] It follows that the episode of Naaman is the reason why the water of baptism is seen to be healing.

The incident takes effect in the water of baptism because of the grace of Christ, and the latter in turn is connected with the descent of the Spirit who consecrates this water. This further factor is explained in terms of the baptism of Jesus in the Jordan, which is described by saying: "When our Lord Jesus Christ instituted the rite of baptism. . . . "[84] "If then the rite of baptism was instituted for our sake, it is to our faith that the rite is proposed."[85] This view must have been traditional since Ambrose uses the same expressions elsewhere.[86] Since the sacraments are thought of an "imitations," the baptism of Christ is seen as the institution and paradigm of our baptism: if the Spirit descended on the Jordan in the form of a dove, he will also descend upon the water of our fonts in order to consecrate it and make it capable of healing.[87]

Ambrose formally raises the problem of the correspondence of these two rites: the baptism of Jesus in the Jordan and the baptism celebrated in the Church. He asks why Christ descended into the Jordan first and the Spirit second, whereas in the rite and practice of baptism, the water is first consecrated by the descent of the Spirit and only then does the candidate descend into the font.[88] His concern with this problem makes it clear that the doctrine of *similitudo* is applied to the sacraments in an extremely realistic way and also that the *similitudo* is not external of ritual. The *similitudo* exists even where the two rites differ. *Similitudo* is an ontological category that applies not to the visible elements of the sacramental rite, but to what is invisible.

After discussing Naaman, Ambrose continues his baptismal discourse by taking a point from the reading of the previous day: the episode of the pool into which the angel descended in order to stir the water so that the first person to enter it would be cured of every infirmity.[89] In Ambrose's eyes, the angel who descends into the water is a figure of Christ. The answer to his rhetorical question about the reason for this identification is based on a conception from the very earliest christology: "Why an angel? Because he is the 'angel of great counsel' " [Is 9:6 LXX].[90]

More importantly, Ambrose supposes that the neophytes are astonished and ask themselves why the water is not moved now: " 'Why is the water not moved now?' Here is the explanation: Signs are for unbelievers, faith for believers"[91]

The two cases are seen as identical, so much so that the neophytes are surprised not to see the water of the baptismal font being moved as the water of the pool of Bethzatha had been. This parallelism or, better, this identity does not refer to the order of external details, for it is based on a strict typological interpretation: the angel, a figure of Christ, descended into the pool; the objective content of baptism is the passion of Christ, in which human beings are saved.

From this it follows that due to the play of typology, there is a true and proper identification between the elements of the *figura* and of the *veritas*. The question about the nonmovement of the baptismal water presupposes an identification for all intents and purposes or what we would call an identity at the ontological level. The argument ends with Ambrose pointing out the preeminence of the Church over the Old Testament because in the case of the pool, only the first person to enter was cured, whereas in baptism, all who go down into the font are saved.[92]

As a result of this identification that typology establishes between parallel episodes, the elements of the Old Testaments event can be predicated of the Church's celebration, and vice versa. Here is an example: the efficacy proper to baptism is also predicated of its *figura*, for the bitter water becomes sweet because Moses throws a piece of wood into it; this wood is effective, however, because it in turn is a *figura* of Christ's passion. It can, therefore, be said that the bitter water becomes sweet because of Christ's passion.

In Ambrose's eyes, the *figura* is a true and proper baptism, even though the *veritas* is much more effective: "Bitter, then, is the water, but when it receives the cross of Christ, the heavenly sacrament, it begins to be sweet and pleasant. And rightly sweet because the offense is cast out. If, then, the power of baptisms is so great in the figure, how much greater must be the power of baptism in truth?"[93] At one point, therefore, when Ambrose is summing up the various figures he has been explaining, he calls all of them "baptism": "There, then, you have one baptism and in the flood another. You have a third kind of baptism when our fathers were baptized in the Red Sea. You have a fourth in the pool when the water was stirred."[94]

I may conclude, then, that typology, and therefore mystagogy, brings out the connection between the saving events of the Old Testament, the New Testament, and the Church's life; this connection is a relationship of true and proper identity.[95] The events correspond, are superimposed, and are seen as identical, even though it must immediately be added that the *veritas* surpasses the *figura* in perfection, without, however, rendering it outmoded and useless.[96]

The explanation of the figures concerns also the content proper to baptism, namely, the grace of the sacrament. In order that the baptized may realize the importance of the grace they have received, Ambrose makes use of figures and argues on the basis of typology: "The holy prophet David saw this grace in figure and desired it. Do you wish to know what he desired? Listen to him once again: 'Sprinkle me with hyssop and I shall be cleansed. You will wash me and I shall become whiter than snow.' "[97] The element of figure allows the psalm to speak of baptismal grace.

If David as a prophet saw *this* baptismal grace that is now being celebrated in the Church and if Psalm 50(51):9 is speaking of this grace, then we must say that the permanent value of the Old Testament is due to its being a prophecy or, better, a *figura* (to use Ambrose's term here) of the New Testament. It follows that when read by Christians, the Old Testament ends up being stripped of its own autonomous coherence by the New Testament. Consequently, when the present-day reality of salvation is described by citations from the Old Testament, the reading does not accommodate the Old Testament text, but gives it its true and proper meaning.

B. Jewish Sacraments and Christian Sacraments

We have already seen that the possibility of superimposition and ontological identification is due to the correspondence between the events of the Old Testament, those of the New, and those of the Church. All this might suggest that the process is based on an excessive allegorism, but this is not the case with Ambrose.

In making this claim, I must appeal to a new consideration that Ambrose expresses by saying that the Christian sacraments are older than the Jewish sacraments.[98] He proves this by locating the institution of the Christian sacraments in the Old Testament. Such a statement shows us how realistic his typological conception of things is; his analysis of figures is situated in the world not of allegory but of fact, for it possesses an ontological density so great that he can set his argument in the sphere of history and thus prove the temporal priority of one people over another:

"At that time God rained down manna from heaven on the complaining Jews. For you, however, the figure came earlier, in the time of Abraham, when he assembled three hundred and eighteen servants, went in pursuit of his enemies, and rescued his nephew from captivity. For, when he returned victorious, Melchizedek the priest came to meet him and offered bread and wine. Who had the bread and wine? Not Abraham. Who, then, had them? Melchizedek. He then is the author of the sacraments."[99]

The figural element, by reason of which the sacraments of the New Testament are present in the Old Testament, causes the Old Testament episode that prefigures them to be regarded as the action by which the sacraments themselves are instituted. We have already seen Ambrose's conclusion: the Christian sacraments are older than the Jewish sacraments. From this, it is but a step to saying that the Christian people is older than the Jewish people: "Know that the Christian people began before the Jewish people did; we were there, however, through predestination, they in name."[100]

We saw, a few lines earlier, that Melchizedek was the "author of the sacraments." This evidently creates a problem with regard to the role of Christ in the institution of the sacraments. Ambrose answers the difficulty by appealing to Hebrews 7:3 and establishing a figural parallel between Christ and Melchizedek:

"Melchizedek was, he says, 'without father, without mother, without genealogy, having no beginning of days or end of life . . . like to the Son of God.' The Son of God is born without a mother in his heavenly birth, because he is born of God the Father alone. On the other hand he was born without a father when he was born of the virgin. . . . Like in all things to the Son of God, Melchizedek was also a priest, for Christ too is a priest to whom it is said: 'You are a priest forever, according to the order of Melchizedek' " [Ps 109:4; Heb 7:17].[101]

Ambrose takes the word *similis* ("*like* in all things . . . ") from the Letter to the Hebrews, but he gives it an ontological density that appears to be lacking in his source. He uses this "likeness" as the basis for arguing to a certain identity of the two persons, Christ and Melchizedek; in fact, he is able to draw the following conclusion: "Who, then, is the author of the sacraments, but the Lord Jesus? It is from heaven that these sacraments came, for the plan at work in them is entirely from heaven. It is truly a great and divine miracle that God should rain down manna from heaven for the people and that the people should eat without toiling."[102]

The "likeness" that binds Melchizedek and Jesus to each other permits Ambrose to call both the "author of the sacraments." Nor is there any difficulty in his doing so since these two persons are not really two but one. The bond between them is "likeness," that is, a set of relations that in typology represents identity.

The realism of "figure" becomes very clear in Ambrose's discussion of Melchizedek. "Figure" and "truth" interpenetrate, so that the "figure" can be said to be present in the "truth" and the "truth" in the "figure." In order to avoid the concept of "presence," which can be equivocal, I shall say that the "figure" participates in the "truth," or that the "figure" is one way in which the "truth" exists, even if this way be different in form and embody a lower degree of being. Therefore: because of the participation, there is a real identity of essence between "figure" and "truth"; at the same time, however, the two are different because the "truth" is superior to the "figure." Here is how Ambrose puts it:

"Where are those who say that the Son of God is a temporal being? Melchizedek is said to have had neither beginning nor end of days. If Melchizedek had no beginning of days, can Christ have had one? But the figure cannot be greater than the truth. You see, therefore, that he [Christ] is 'first and last' [Rv 1:17]: first because he is the author of all things, last not because he will come to an end but because he completes everything."[103]

We moderns have difficulty with this figural identification of Melchizedek and Christ; in fact, the identification may even seem doctrinally suspect because of the uniqueness of the divine sonship and the redemptive incarnation. We would be unjust to Ambrose if we thought he was following a suspect path. How then are the data to be interpreted? Must we reduce the figurality of Melchizedek to a simple external reminder and evocation of Christ? Certainly not. The concept of "figure," while leaving, and therefore displaying, a certain difference, expresses a real, ontological identification between the two realities that are related as figure and truth.

Ambrose is thoroughly aware of all this. Thus, we find him carrying the argument a step further. Just at the right moment, he asks who and what Melchizedek is. After looking at the data, he turns to Revelation 1:17 and 22:13, applies the expression "first and last" to him, and concludes that he cannot have been a mere human being. There could be no better way of bringing of the realism of "figures": if a human being is a figure of Christ, then he or she cannot be a mere human being, but rather must be said in some way to have neither beginning nor end, any more than Christ does. From all this, it follows that Melchizedek achieves his full identity only in Christ: "Do you not recognize what he is? Can a human being be king of justice when he is barely just? Can he be king of peace when he is barely at peace?"[104]

For this reason, there is no difficulty in predicating "author of the sacraments" indifferently of Melchzedek or of Christ; because of the figural relationship between these two, there is but a single author. Ambrose can therefore say that Christians today receive a sacrament that belongs to Melchizedek: "The sacrament you have received is not a human but a divine gift, brought by him who blessed Abraham, our father in faith, whose grace and actions you admire."[105]

In this context, there is another passage that may appropriately be cited.[106] Speaking of Psalm 22(23), Ambrose supposes that David wrote it as the fruit of his figural experience of the Eucharist and that this is why the Church can interpret it typologically and apply it to the Eucharist. He gives expression to this conception when he comments on Christians approaching the altar for eucharistic communion: "You drew near, then, to the altar, you received the body of Christ. Learn once more what sacraments you received. Listen to what holy David says. For in the spirit he foresaw these mysteries and rejoiced and said that nothing was lacking to him. Why so? Because those who have received the body of Christ will never hunger again."[107]

In Ambrose's eyes, no difficulty is created by the fact that David preceded Christ, for it was "in the spirit" that David "foresaw" the celebration of these mysteries. He regards this participation "in the spirit" as utterly real; anyone who had such a sacramental experience was not in any way deprived by comparison with the faithful who come after Christ.

If David wrote the psalm with his eye on the Eucharist, we must conclude that the typological perspective of the text is part of the author's explicit intention. If we adopt this viewpoint, then typology does not simply supply us with the "fuller meaning" (*sensus plenior*) of the passage; rather it gives us the meaning of the text as such, that is, the "only" meaning intended by the author or what we would call the "literal sense." In other words: because David foresaw the Eucharist "in the spirit," he decided to write a psalm that would speak of the Eucharist.[108] On the basis of this passage, we must say that Ambrose includes in eucharistic typology not only the external aspects—table and cup— but also the theological content of the bodily passion and eternal divinity of Christ, which he reads as the themes of redemption and creation. To put it differently, the entire passage cited from Psalm 22 describes the Eucharist.

If David wanted for nothing, the reason is that those who are nourished by the body of Christ will not hunger for ever. David, therefore, had the opportunity to communicate sacramentally in the body of Christ, even if only "in the spirit"; but the restriction "in the spirit" in no way diminishes the realism of David's "communion." This follows from the very "sacramental" nature of the eucharistic communion of Christians; Ambrose can therefore propose David as a model for the behavior of Christians who approach the sacrament.

C. Conclusion
It follows from this lengthy discussion that the biblical typology used in commenting on liturgical actions provides an explanation and a "sufficient reason" for a doctrine of the sacraments as both "realistic" and "efficacious." But typology applied to the liturgy is simply mystagogy, as I explained earlier. Mystagogy is, therefore, simply a form of sacramental theology or, more accurately, of liturgical theology and is able fully to explain and ensure the efficacy of liturgical actions, since this efficacy is identical with that of the events in the history of salvation. This efficacy is combined with extreme realism, since the realism of the sacraments is the same as that which the events themselves had when they occurred in the history of salvation.

Our theologies today are exposed to a danger unknown to mystagogy: the danger that the sacramental celebration may end up being a duplicate of the historical saving event. Since mystagogical theology is based on the archetypal event as narrated in Scripture, it will never end up as an alternative sacramental theology or a sacramental theology that is in competition with the theology of salvation history.

Identity and diversity: this is the essence of typological comparison.

One point left unexplained, at least in Ambrose, is how and why this "figural" identity exists between the archetype and its celebration. Perhaps the explanation is to be found in the singleness of the divine plan of salvation, inasmuch as "revelation of the *mysterium* is in reality an event that is being accomplished throughout the history narrated by the scriptures."[109] I suggest as a hypothesis that the theology of the sacraments as "likenesses" is present in Ambrose as something that he has inherited from the tradition but has not fully understood.

Another undeniable excellence of mystagogy and the typological method is the close connection between word[110] and sacrament, or between Scripture and celebration, and therefore between faith (which grows) and rite. Such a theological system locates the sacraments in the history of salvation, which remains intact in its historical dimension without being duplicated.

It remains to be seen whether the theological and spiritual riches in the typology of Ambrose are due to his particular typological method, which makes such abundant use of the Old Testament, or are also possible when other hermeneutical methods are used.

CHAPTER THREE

Theodore of Mopsuestia

I. THE CATECHECTICAL HOMILIES OF THEODORE

It is not easy to date with any accuracy the catechetical homilies of Theodore of Mopsuestia that I shall be discussing in this chapter. They were probably delivered after 383 and before 392. The current view is that they were delivered at Antioch,[1] but it is more likely that they were delivered at Tarsus or Mopsuestia, since the liturgy on which they comment is not the one which Theodore's contemporary, John Chrysostom, shows being celebrated at Antioch.[2]

There are seventeen homilies in ms. Mingana syr. 561,[3] which has been edited by Raymond M. Tonneau and Robert Devreesse. The manuscript itself clearly divides them into two blocks, for there is this note at the end of the tenth homily[4]: "End of the writing down of the ten homilies on the explanation of the creed by His Excellency Mar Theodore, friend of Christ, bishop, and interpreter of the divine writings."[5] Immediately after, the eleventh homily bears this title: "By your power, our Lord Jesus Christ, we begin to write down the explanation of the mysteries by the same blessed Mar Theodore. Lord, help me and enable me to reach the end."[6] This title is followed by one homily on the Our Father, three on baptism, and two on the Mass.

In the Syriac tradition, these two sets of homilies are two distinct works. Distinct does not, of course, mean unrelated, since at the beginning of Homily 11 (on the Our Father), Theodore himself refers to the preceding homilies on the Creed. The ancient witnesses to this work of Theodore give the same division into two series[7]; in A. Mingana's opinion,[8] the Syriac translation must have been made by two different individuals at two different times, with the second series being translated some years after the first.[9]

This division into two sets of homilies justifies and explains my decision to study Theodore's mystagogy on the basis not of all the catechetical homilies, but of those only of the second series, that is, the homilies on the Our Father, baptism, and the Eucharist; these in fact are the more pertinent to my purpose.[10]

II. QUESTIONS OF VOCABULARY

"Syriac has but a single word to express the ideas of sacrament, mystery, and figure."[11] The word is *raza*, which perfectly translates the Greek *mystērion*. The person who translated the sixteen homilies from Greek into Syriac realized that in the Greek text of Theodore, the vocabulary of the sacraments played an important role; he therefore decided to keep the Greek terminology and simply transliterate it into Syriac. As a result, while "mystery" is systematically translated as *raza*, the words *eikōn* (image) and *typos* (type or figure, and so on) are simply transliterated. "Sign" is rendered by the Syriac word *'ata*, and the Greek *schēma* (= *species*) is transliterated.[12]

Here are some examples of passages in which the vocabulary is important.

A. *Figure, Sign, Mystery*
Of baptism, Theodore says:

"There are, then, signs (*'ata*) and mysteries (*raza*) which we accomplish through water; and once again we are renewed and formed according to the operation of the Spirit that is accomplished in it [the water]. Thanks to it, by means of the sacrament, as in a figure (*'ak dbtapsa*), we gain these (blessings): we who obtain baptism and who in the world to come will all receive in full truth an ineffable renewal of our nature."[13]

Since the expression "signs (*'ata*) and mysteries (*raza*)" is here parallel to "in a figure" (*'ak dbtapsa*), it might be thought that Theodore sees no difference between these several words. But this is not the case: as the homily proceeds, it becomes clear that

46

"figure" (*'ak dbiapsa*) has a different meaning than *typos*. Within the sphere of *possession* of the blessings of redemption, the term "figure" serves to distinguish the historical sacramental phase from the definitive and eschatological phase.

B. *The Use of* Typos *and the Problem of the Words Signifying Sacramentality*

In the patristic period, the vocabulary of sacramental theology seems to be of two kinds:

1. The first kind is identical with the one we use today and expresses sacramentality in a single word (for example, mystery or sacrament, and so on). The single word conveys both the outward aspect (the sacrament as sensible) and the deeper dimension or invisible content of the sacrament.

2. In order to express sacramentality successfully, the second kind of vocabulary needs two interconnected words. There are, for example, such pairs as "image–truth" and "type–antitype." If I am to explain this more clearly, I must run the risk of oversimplifying it. In this kind of theology, one of the two terms is suited to designating the historical saving events as described in Scripture, while the other is suited to designating the liturgical celebration.

This schematic division is very useful from a strictly theoretical standpoint and is therefore regarded as valid; but it is valid only from this standpoint. In practice, the concrete use of sacramental vocabulary in the works of the Fathers is not controlled *a priori* by this rigid scheme; on the contrary, it fluctuates greatly and its uses are intertwined. In some texts of Ambrose, for example, even the terms "mystery" and "sacrament" seem to belong to this kind of sacramental theology that requires two correlative terms. This becomes clear not only in various passages,[14] but even in the formula "sacrament of the mysteries" and its converse, "mystery of the sacraments."

Theodore uses the vocabulary of this archaic sacramental theology,[15] but he uses it differently. When he speaks of the sacraments, he always uses a single word, as we do today; he uses all the words, but he always uses only one of them, never a pair. He already represents, therefore, what I described before as the first of the two kinds of sacramental vocabulary.

This appears quite clearly in all his catechetical homilies. He uses chiefly "mystery" or "type" (*typos*). Of special interest is his use of the latter, which is especially suited to evoke immediately its correlative: "antitype." And yet "antitype" is completely absent from his catechetical homilies, whether as a Greek word transliterated into Syriac or as a Greek word whose translation into Syriac can be documented. When used to express the "event–sacramental rite" relation, neither "type" nor "mystery" is ever correlated with a second term.

At the same time, however, the problem of the relation between a sacrament and the event of which it is a sacrament continually arises, first and foremost as a theological problem and then, by derivation, as a problem of terminology. In any case, the theological problem is unavoidable, even when considered apart from the terminological problem. Theodore does not evade it and in one passage clearly resolves it by calling the sacrament a "type" and the historical event "truth."

I must caution that this use of the two terms seems to be an *ad hoc* solution and that Theodore does not give the two words the meaning that marks, for example, the "image–truth" pair. In fact, it is not clear whether in this passage he is attending to the underlying problem of sacramental theology. My own opinion is that he is simply using a vocabulary developed prior to his time, one with which he is familiar but whose theological implications he does not realize. Here is the passage:

"Therefore, just as the true new birth is that which we await from the resurrection, while the new birth which we accomplish in baptism is one in type and symbol, so the true food of immortality is that which we hope to receive and which we will then truly have by a gift of the Holy Spirit, while at present it is as it were in type that we are nourished with an immortal food which we have, whether in type or thanks to types, by the grace of the Holy Spirit."[16]

In Theodore's language, "type" and "mystery" are often used as synonyms. At times, however, as in the following passage, theological necessity compels him to give them two different meanings, with "type," like "sign," designating the visible aspect, and "mystery" designating either the deeper reality or the rite as a whole (comprising both the visible aspect and the deeper reality):

"According to the statement of blessed Paul [1 Cor 11:26], they were to mingle with the sacramental types [= the wine of the Eucharist] the same thing [= water] that had to be mixed for us with the gift of holy baptism whereby, as we believe, we receive the new birth in type. Such, then, is the power of the mystery and such are the types and signs of the mystery, both food and drink."[17]

III. THE PURPOSE OF THE *CATECHETICAL HOMILIES*

The lengthy exposition of the Creed established by the 318 Fathers would have been sufficient for the instruction of catechumens; they would thereby have been formed to a broadly and deeply based faith that was solidly anchored in the Christian dogma of the two Councils of Nicaea and Constantinople.[18] The homilies on the mysteries have a further purpose.

Theodore's intention in them is certainly to imbue the catechumens with a profoundly existential and spiritual outlook, as R. Devreesse says,[19] but this alone is not enough to explain the existence of these homilies.[20] There is in fact a specific reason why he preached these homilies on the mysteries: to explain the rites of baptism and the Eucharist on a strictly theological basis. Such a basis obviously could not be supplied by explaining the Creed.

Nor may we say that the homilies on the Creed give us Christian doctrine, while those on the mysteries give us mystagogy, understood as the spiritual and inspiring aspect of doctrine.[21] This solution cannot explain the data. As I said in Chapter One, mystagogy is a way of doing theology (that is, sacramental theology) using a specific method. As we shall see, this description holds for Theodore's mystagogy. It is precisely herein that we find the explanation of the homilies of the second series, which

49

differ from those of the first not because of any greater spirituality but because of a different content. How is it possible to say
that for Theodore, too, mystagogy is a way of doing theology?
The answer must come from an examination of the purpose he
sets himself in these homilies.[22]

A. Homily on the Lord's Prayer
At the beginning of the homily on the Our Father, Theodore
explicitly states its purpose: "to say everything necessary about
the prayer handed down by our Lord."[23] In Theodore's view, the
prayer has primarily a moral meaning. He sees this interpretation as based on Scripture:

"After saying 'Go, teach all nations, and baptize them in the
name of the Father and of the Son and of the Holy Spirit,' our
Lord added: 'and teach them to observe all that I command
you.'[24] He said this in order to show that in addition to accepting
religious and orthodox doctrine we must be careful to make our
lives accord with the divine commandments. For this reason
they joined to the words of the Creed a prayer which contains
an adequate teaching on morals: the prayer which our Lord put
in a few words and gave to his disciples."[25]

Theodore does not restrict the application of our Lord's words to
the Our Father; rather his words state a general principle that
holds for all prayers: "Every prayer, whatever it be, is a teaching
about life for those who devote themselves to their duty."[26] This
point is then developed on the basis of the text of the Our Father until it becomes a theory in the true and full sense: "Our
Lord used these few words as though to tell us that prayer does
not consist of words but of habits, love, and dedication to what
is good. . . . Prayer should be offered with conduct in view: if it
is not right to do something, neither is it right to ask for it."[27]
The conclusion from this principle is: "Therefore authentic
prayer is moral uprightness, love for God, and zeal for what
pleases him."[28]

Given this fundamental interpretation, a homily commenting on
the text of the Our Father cannot but be a moral teaching aimed
at having one's manner of life correspond to what one asks in

prayer. In other words, the homily gives a "theology of life" and has a specific content worthy of what Jesus taught us to ask of God. Theodore continues his homily by commenting on the Our Father, making frequent use of biblical passages that explain the prayer's meaning, from which in turn moral instruction is derived.

We must not think that Theodore succumbs to a simplistic kind of moralizing; he is not capable of that. His approach to morality is strictly theological and based on ultimate realities, namely, the life proper to the world to come. Here is how he sums up: "(Our Lord) orders those who believe in him to apply themselves to good works and conduct themselves in a heavenly manner, to scorn all the things of this world and endeavor, as far as possible, to model[29] themselves on those of the world to come."[30] Clearly, then, the purpose of the homily is to give a theology of prayer that is also a theology of life.

B. Homilies on the Mysteries

Theodore also states his purpose in preaching the five homilies on the mysteries: to convey an understanding of the mysteries being celebrated. The homily on the eucharistic food has for its purpose "that you may understand what it is and accurately grasp its greatness."[31] His purpose then is understanding of the sacrament and its value.

This understanding is not an end in itself, but ought to lead to an understanding of the reason for the sacrament. Here is one passage: "It is right that from now on you receive teaching on what happens in the sacrament itself, for if you learn the reason why it exists, you will have an excellent grasp of a doctrine that is of no little importance."[32]

Other passages can only confirm this perspective. It applies to the sacrament as such, that is, as a whole, and to each of the rites or ceremonies that make it up: "When, therefore, through the exorcisms you have escaped from servitude to the usurper and by reciting the Creed have taken on awesome commitments to God, then you present yourself for the sacrament itself. But in what manner? That is what you must learn."[33]

Theodore here makes it clear that he ascribes a specific effect to each of the rites mentioned. The exorcisms are a judgment upon the devil and have for their purpose to deliver human beings from the power of the demon. The recitation of the Creed has power to commit human beings to God. "Awesome" (or "terrible") is an adjective typical of discourse on the sacraments; its application here to the commitments assumed in relation to God implies that these commitments are marked by the realism and efficacy proper to the sacraments.

In conclusion: Theodore supposes that the exorcisms and the recitation of the Creed possess the same efficacy as the sacraments themselves, although he never applies the word "mystery" to these rites; he reserves that term for baptism in the true and proper sense. It follows from all this that theological explanation of the mystery may have for its object either the mystery itself or one of the rites composing it, and still remain a true and proper theology of the mystery.

The reason why a person approaches the mystery is expressed by the signs and ceremonies that describe the content of the sacrament itself. In Theodore's eyes, there is (a) a content of the sacrament as such, which coincides with a particular point in the rite; and there is (b) a content proper to each of the rite. The content of each of the rites making up the mystery does not duplicate but rather brings into view all that is implicit in the sacrament proper: "This, then, is why we approach the mystery wherein we perform signs that dispel the evils from which we have been delivered beyond all hope and that give us a share in the new and magnificent blessings which have their source in our Lord the Christ."

Here baptism is described according to the two things it effects: (a) deliverance from evil, and (b) participation in the messianic blessings. The beginning of this paragraph, then, tells us that the reason why we approach the sacrament is to obtain redemption. Theodore therefore ends the paragraph by saying: "It is time now to tell you the reason for each (of the ceremonies) performed."[34]

Theodore thus adopts an ontological perspective that is capable of bringing to light what each part of the liturgical rite is in itself, independently of the overall action of which it is a part. Perhaps my word "ontological" is not completely accurate, but, for lack of anything better, I use it to point out that as Theodore looks at each element of the liturgy, his primary interest is in "What is it?" rather than in the function that the element has in the rite as a whole.

The conclusion to be drawn is that despite the danger of falling into allegory, in Theodore as in Ambrose, the explanation of each part of the liturgy must be described as a "theology of a mystery." There is another passage that is worth our reading here because it can show that the author of the homilies had a properly theological intention. Here is how he explains the theology of a mystery:

"Every mystery points in signs and symbols to things invisible and ineffable. A manifestation and explanation of these signs and symbols is required if those who present themselves are to experience the power of the mysteries. If all that occurred was these actions, any discourse would be superfluous; the sight of them would be enough to make plain to us each thing that occurs. But since the sacrament contains signs of what will take place or has already taken place, a discourse is needed that will explain the meaning of the signs and mysteries."[35]

Theodore here derives the need of a mystagogical catechesis from the very definition of a sacrament. It is true, of course, that the invisible and ineffable realities of which the sacrament is a sign remain invisible and ineffable even in the celebration. This idea is present in Ambrose, too, for we do not find Ambrose positing any "likeness" (similitudo) between the sacramental sign and the reality of which it is the sacrament. We are probably dealing here with a traditional idea that Theodore simply repeats, since in the catechesis on the Mass, his thinking seems to be different. If sacramentality belongs to the invisible element, it follows that mystagogy is not simply an explanation of the sacrament in its visible unfolding, but is a true and proper theology of the mystery and capable of grasping the deepest reality of the sacrament.

There is now but one further little step to be taken: we must inquire into the pastoral fruitfulness of mystagogy. I showed before that the purpose of these homilies is to give an understanding and theological explanation of the mystery, both as a whole and in the individual parts or rites that make it up. I must turn now to the fact that the ultimate reason for the mystery itself is the salvation of the believers who participate in it. It follows that if the object of mystagogy is the mystery in all its fullness, then mystagogy must also take up the theme of salvation, since the mystery is in the service of salvation. But how is it to do this? Here is how Theodore explains it:

"But since the time for the mystery has come, when by God's favor you are going to receive a participation in holy baptism, I must now, as the order (*taxis*)[36] requires, explain to you the power of the sacrament and of the (ceremonies) that make it up and tell you why each of them is performed, so that having learned what the cause of all of them is you may receive with profound love that which will take place."[37]

It is important to understand this passage properly. Mystagogy is effective and fruitful because, in Theodore's view, knowledge of the purpose and power of the mysteries is in the service of the love with which one approaches them. The bishop with his personal witness plays a role in this dynamic movement. He must manage to convey to the faithful how salvation can be attained by those who participate in the sacrament. But how can he communicate such an experience except by first living it himself and then giving testimony of it to the other faithful? By means of his own total commitment of faith, the mystagogue must manage to bear witness to the importance and value of what is experienced in the sacraments, that is, the salvation and redemption that they bring and that will be complete only in the last times.

C. Conclusion
The purpose of mystagogy for Theodore is to instill an understanding of the power and purpose of the mystery, whether this be taken globally or in the individual units of ritual that make it

54

up. By its nature, the mystery tends to lead the participating faithful to salvation. It follows that knowledge of the mystery at its deepest level must lead the faithful to so intense and lively a participation that the mystery is enabled to achieve its ultimate purpose: the communication of salvation. In this way, mystagogy becomes part of the dynamic movement of the mystery itself.

IV. MYSTAGOGY AND ALLEGORY

Theodore was a disciple of Diodorus of Tarsus and is regarded as a principal representative of the Antiochene school. By reason of its literalism in interpreting Scripture, the Antiochene school has been strongly contrasted with the Alexandrian school, which has been criticized for an excessive use of allegory. But some nuances must be introduced into this sharp distinction between literal and allegorical interpretation, for as a matter of fact, the Antiochene school was not focused exclusively on the literal meaning. Beginning with an essay of A. Vaccari,[38] there has been a tendency to play down the importance of the difference between the Alexandrians and the Antiochenes,[39] on the grounds that the Antiochenes too use allegorical interpretation when the biblical text itself points clearly in this direction.

There is a further factor that in fact brings the two methods of interpretation, the Alexandrian and the Antiochene, closer than they may at first glance seem to be; I am referring to typology. Typology is applied both to biblical interpretation, especially when there is question of the relation between the Old and New Testaments, and to the interpretation of liturgical rites, both in themselves and in their relation to Scripture. I shall leave aside the question of biblical typology in the school of Antioch and shall discuss only the typology that emerges in the interpretation of the sacraments.

When we turn to the liturgical typology of Theodore, we must first note that the interpretation of some liturgical rites is based exclusively on allegory,[40] which is applied in a massive and systematic way. A look at a few examples will shed light on Theodore's method of interpretation.

A. The Vision of Isaiah

If we would like to see a good demonstration of Theodore's ability to engage in allegory, we should study the theme of *fear* as expressed in the vision of Isaiah that is remembered in the celebration of the Eucharist:

"The seraphim took the burning coal, not with his hand but with tongs. This vision shows that even those spirits fear to approach the mysteries without some intermediary. In your case, it is the pontiff who with his hand gives you the mysteries, saying: 'The body of Christ.' Even he, however, does not think himself worthy to take and give such gifts; for in place of tongs he has the spiritual grace which he receives to make him a pontiff and which makes him bold enough to give such gifts."[41]

This text is valuable to us because it shows allegory being used in Theodore's typology. The incident of the tongs enables him to infer that even the seraphim are afraid to approach the holy mysteries. The point that interests me here is that the tongs served the seraphim in laying hold of the burning coal, not of the sacred mysteries; in liturgical typology, however, the burning coal and the mysteries interpenetrate each other and form a single reality. From the viewpoint of typology, then, the burning coal becomes a "participation" in the mysteries.[42] The tongs, or intermediary, is the pontiff. The pontiff in turn needs tongs of his own, and this takes the form of the spiritual grace of being a pontiff or, in our language today, the sacrament of orders. At this point, fear ceases and is replaced by confidence.

B. Eucharistic Communion

The ritually prescribed manner of receiving communion becomes an occasion for reflecting on the interior attitude of the communicant. This attitude arises out of the gestures performed. According to the directive in the ritual, "then each of us draws near, eyes lowered and both hands outstretched."[43] With this directive as his starting point, Theodore builds a commentary on the two prescribed actions. The commentary moves forward along two lines: (1) simple amplification, and (2) allegory.

Here is an amplification dictated by his pastoral outlook: "By looking down [the faithful] pay a kind of debt that is appropriate for adoration; they thereby make a kind of profession of faith that they are receiving the body of the King, of him who becomes Lord of all through union with the divine nature and is also adored as Lord by all creation."[44]

Here, on the other hand, is a passage in which allegory already plays a part: the hands themselves become the leading actor in the scene and are thus offered as a model of the reverent behavior the person should adopt:

"And by the fact that his two hands are equally extended, he truly acknowledges the greatness of the gift he is about to receive. 'One extends the right hand to receive the oblation that is being given, but under it one places the left' (Ritual), and thereby one shows great reverence. If the right hand is extended at a higher level, it is extended in order to receive the royal body; the other hand supports and guides its sister and companion, not regarding it as demeaning to play the part of a servant to the other, which is equal to it in dignity—and this because of the royal body which it carries."

C. *The Vestments*
In Theodore's allegorical scheme, even the sacred ornaments and vestments have significance. Here is the meaning of the orarion: "But when you have been marked you spread on your head an (orarion of) linen, which is the sign of the state of freedom to which you have now been called."[45]

Theodore spreads himself even more when he describes the vestments of the pontiff, which are signs of eschatological realities. The splendid vestment that the pontiff wears is a sign of the newness of the world to which the baptized are going. It is splendid, signifying the splendor of the other life; it is light, signifying the delicacy and grace of that other world.[46] The garments of the newly baptized have the same eschatological meaning, but their character follows the logic of the liturgical sign. Since salvation is not yet complete but is of the sacramental order, a splendid garment is indeed called for.

" 'But as soon as you ascend from there, you put on a wholly resplendent garment' (Ritual). This garment is the sign of the shining, resplendent world and the kind of life and conduct into which you have passed through the types. When, however, you really receive the resurrection and are clad in immortality and incorruptibility, you will no longer need such garments. Now, since you are not yet truly there and have received those things in mysteries and types, you need garments; you don those that manifest the sweet state in which you now are by means of types and in which you will truly live when the time comes."[47]

But the garments are also functional and awaken reverential fear and love, "with the result that the novelty of the garment makes you realize the excellence of this (rite)."[48] We can therefore say also that allegory has a didactic function.

The vestments of deacons are also the subject of commentary; they are, however, not related directly to the eschatological blessings, but only to the angelic liturgy. These vestments are strictly functional in regard to the sacramentality of the ministry, since they express the sublimity of the heavenly liturgy and are of a higher order than the person who wears them: "They also have an adornment that befits the reality, for their external garb is more sublime than they."[49] In view of the deacon's liturgical function, his vestments are also related to the passion of Christ.

D. Baptismal Actions

Theodore gives an allegorical interpretation of many liturgical actions. I shall look at only two of them. During the baptismal rites, the baptizands kneel. This action is interpreted as a sign of the situation in which the baptizands presently find themselves, namely, enslavement to the devil.[50] Theodore's thinking is that kneeling for prayer is part of the exorcisms; therefore, the action must express the theology of the rite of exorcism, which sees this rite as a condemnation of the demon and deliverance of the baptizand from servitude. Kneeling, therefore, is a reminder of the state of servitude in which human beings lived before being delivered from the demon.

For the baptismal immersion, the baptizands bow their heads. The pontiff places a hand on the head of each and guides it under the water; in this position, the baptizands cannot help keeping their heads bowed. At the third invocation, when no further immersion is to follow, they raise their heads. The bowing and raising is a functional action, but Theodore also finds a symbolical interpretation for it: the bowed head represents an implicit, tacit "Amen" to the Trinitarian invocation.[51]

V. THE RELATION BETWEEN THE SACRAMENTS AND NATURAL REALITIES

Theodore says that there are two stages in taking care of newborn children. They are first wrapped in swaddling clothes. These represent the baptismal instructions received by the newly baptized. In the second stage, they receive "the natural food which is proper and suited to them."[52] The baptized go through an analogous stage, for they too receive food suited to them, namely, the Eucharist. Christian initiation thus shows an analogy to a human being's first birth, inasmuch as this initiation includes in its ritual structure baptism, instruction, and Eucharist.

The analogy reflects a definitely allegorical approach to initiation. The relation between baptism and the Eucharist is analogous to the relation between birth and food: birth gives existence and food gives continued existence. In fact, when food is lacking, the being decays.

The relation between birth through resurrection and birth through baptism also serves as a basis for showing the need of a sacramental food: "Since it is by means of types and signs that we are now born in baptism, we must also receive—again in types—a food geared to what we have become, so that we will continue in our existence."[53] A sacramental food exists, therefore, because there has been a sacramental birth. From this, we can infer that in Theodore's catechetical instruction, the "necessity" of the Eucharist flows from the very nature of this sacrament's relation to baptism.

But the argument does not end here. On the basis of what he sees in the natural world, Theodore points out that every animal born of another animal receives food from the body of its progenitor. This is the food suited to the animal. The same holds at the sacramental level: "We too, therefore, who in a type have received divine grace, must also receive food from the other world, just as we have received our birth from there."[54]

Theodore makes an explicit theoretical principle of the relation between natural realities and the sacramental organism. The logic of sacramental typology is dictated by an analogy with the things of the natural world: "The nature of signs and types must accord with this present state, wherein we receive food in types."[55] Baptism is administered with water, an element fundamental to all life "to the point that without water we cannot even make bread."[56] The same applies to the eucharistic elements: "We receive bread and wine mixed with water because these are the foods that are chiefly suited in this life and that keep us in existence."[57]

In his homilies, Theodore has a habit of repeating the same things several times over, but this has one advantage: all the repetitions enable us to gain a sure understanding of his thought. If a point is repeated three or four times in different contexts, the point cannot be said to be incidental and insufficiently thought out. Let us follow Theodore, therefore, as he repeats what he has to say about the bread and wine: the bread and wine are the elements used in the Eucharist because the Eucharist is food, and bread and wine are the essential foods for our present life. He therefore calls them "suited." This term then, in the case of both baptism and the Eucharist, indicates that there is a relation with what sustains us in our biological life: "In this world we are sufficiently sustained by types suited to us, and it is these that are necessary for keeping us alive."[58] And again, even more clearly: "Here then is why he gives us the bread and the cup: because it is by means of food and drink that we continue in life here below."[59]

VI. THE EUCHARIST AS TYPE OF THE PASSION

Theodore devotes a good deal of space to this theme; his homilies faithfully reflect the theology of the Ritual and very effectively explain the matter.

A. The Passion in Relation to the Angelic Liturgy

Although Theodore's theology displays a strong sacramental realism, as we shall see further on, his explanation of the Eucharist as mystery of the Lord's death is completely allegorical. In my opinion, this is because he draws his inspiration from the Ritual: a fact that brings home to us the authority that the Ritual enjoyed.

In the two homilies on the Mass, the Eucharist is clearly divided into three main parts: (1) the prothesis, (2) the anaphora, and (3) the rites of communion.[50] An allegorical explanation is given for each part: in the prothesis, there is an image of the passion; in the anaphora, we have the offering of the oblation and thus an image of the heavenly liturgy, and, at the epiclesis, an image of the resurrection; in the communion rites, we have an image of the Lord's resurrection.

Theodore's method is descriptive. Starting with what is visible, he urges the faithful to imagine in their hearts the scene of the passion as this occurred historically. The main actors in the prothesis are the deacons, who for functional and not symbolic reasons prepare the altar for the celebration. They solemnly bring the bread and wine to the altar, place them on it, and remain near it. It is on these steps in the rite that Theodore bases his commentary on the Eucharist as type of the Lord's passion.

When we turn to *Homily* 15, 26, we find ourselves in the midst of a full-blown liturgical allegory. Every point in the rite has its equivalent in the event being commemorated: the gifts are Christ, even though we are still at the prothesis and the anaphora has not yet begun; the deacons are the angels; the altar is the tomb of Christ; the laying of the bread on the altar is the burial; the altar cloths are the wrappings in which Christ was buried. In addition: the deacons wear sumptuous vestments, as is appropriate for the burial of a great person; when they use their fans to move the air over the body of Christ, they are doing something typical of the funeral wake of important people, the intention being that nothing may come to rest on the body; the actions of the deacons thus show the grandeur of this particular body. The presence of the angels at the empty tomb, which is documented from the gospel story, is the basis for the sacramental importance assigned to the presence of the deacons in the liturgy for the deposition of the bread on the altar.

We cannot claim that this obvious allegorization is to be interpreted simply as a "dramatization" after the manner of a sacred play. No, Theodore's typology has already been transformed into allegory, although it has not yet lost the sacramental realism proper to typology. It will be worth our while to look more closely at the sacramental realism that Theodore assigns to the prothesis as a type of the passion: "And when they have brought (the particle of bread), they place it on the holy alter for the completion of the passion. We believe therefore that he (Christ) is now laid in a kind of tomb when he is placed on the altar and that he has already undergone the passion."[61] And again: "And when we see the oblation on the altar—as though some one after death had been laid in a kind of tomb—recollection then fills all present because what has taken place is awesome for all."[62]

Theodore contemplates two moments in the passion of Christ, deriving them from the Ritual that is cited at the beginning of the homily: "We must now look upon Christ as he is being led out and goes to his passion and as, at another moment, he is once again extended on the altar for us, in order to be sacrificed."[63] These two events are put in a direct relation to the rites performed by the deacons during the liturgy, for it is the deacons who carry the offerings to the altar and who then remain near it; in other words, they carry the body of Christ to the tomb and then they keep watch. The realism of the liturgy depends for Theodore on the fact that the sacrament is an image of the angelic liturgy. The liturgy celebrated by human beings is true if and insofar as it participates in the heavenly liturgy. This is the theological principle on the basis of which Theodore assigns sacramental realism to the prothesis as a memorial of the Lord's passion; the same principle marks the Ritual.

In the liturgy of the prothesis, the role of the deacons is to represent the angels. Indeed, the liturgy being celebrated is a true liturgy because it is an imitation of the angelic liturgy. The argument expounded in the homily has an undeniable logic of its own; at the same time, an explanation is given of the way in which the angelic liturgy celebrates the passion of Christ.

The deacons stand at the altar "in remembrance of those [the angels] who came and stood by throughout the passion and death of our Lord."[64] "To us who are instructed by the divine scripture it is evident that there were angels at the tomb."[65] But their role was not limited to "remaining there in honor of him who had died." The duty of the angels at the empty tomb was to reveal the resurrection to the women, and it is this action that is expressly described as "angelic liturgy." For it is in the resurrection that "the renewal of the entire creation" originates.[66] The action of the angels was therefore an extremely important event in the economy of redemption. That is why Theodore regards it as so important that there should be in the eucharistic action an image (eikōn) of the angelic liturgy at the tomb.

The representational character of the liturgy as an imitation of the angelic liturgy has a twofold value. In relation to the angelic liturgy, this representational character serves to ensure the truth and realism of the Church's liturgy. In relation to the faithful, it serves to guarantee the possibility of fruitful participation in virtue of their interior activity.

In fact, it is the types that Christians see in the liturgy that inspire them to think of Christ in his passion. They must exercise imagination and reason so that, starting from what is seen in the liturgy, they can represent to themselves the corresponding actions of Christ:

"By means of the types 'we must now look upon Christ as he is led out and goes to his passion and as, at another moment, he is once again extended on the altar for us, in order to be sacrificed' (Ritual). When, in fact, the oblation that will be offered comes forth in the sacred vessels—on the patens and in the chalices—you must think that our Lord the Christ is coming forth and being led to his passion."[67]

This passage very accurately describes the representational function of the types. But the representational function is not exercised at a purely external level, since it remains connected with and based on sacramentality. This is clear from the fact that all the elements that do not enjoy a sacramental "presence" are expressly excluded from the representation. See, for example, the commentary on the entrance of the gifts that the deacons will be placing on the altar. Since it was the Jews who brought Christ to his death, we might think that the deacon would represent the Jews. Not so: "He does not come forth led by the Jews; for it is not permitted, it is not licit, that there be any evil likeness in the types of our life and our salvation; rather these are (types) that lead us to those *invisibly serving powers* who were also present and carrying out their ministry when the saving passion was being accomplished."[68] This sentence makes it very clear that the type, even if constituted such by a process of allegorical representation, is endowed with sacramental realism and efficacy by reason of its relation to the angelic liturgy.

With regard to the liturgy of the Church, which is constructed in the image of the angelic liturgy, we must draw two conclusions: (1) allegorical representation is not opposed to the sacramental realism associated with typology, but is even fully consonant with it; and (2) the fruitful participation of the faithful depends on the interior activity in which they imagine and interiorly represent to themselves the successive events of the passions. Imaginative and representational activity is consonant with the nature of the liturgy since the latter is essentially image and representation.

Consequently, the prothesis as type of the passion is not to be interpreted as a dramatization comparable to a sacred play; rather, by reason of the typology at work, it is to be regarded as belonging to the sphere of sacramentality proper: the prothesis is the moment of the sacramental death of Jesus.

B. The Passion in Relation to the Bread and Wine

Although the prothesis is a type of the passion by reason of its relation to the angelic liturgy, we must not forget that the eucharistic celebration is essentially constituted by the bread and wine. What, then, is the relation between the passion and the bread and wine? Theodore reflects on all this and is in a position to give a good answer that fits into his theological system. As natural elements, bread and wine help to give life. But the passion of Jesus is also a vehicle of life. Therefore, there is a positive correspondence between the bread and wine, on the one hand, and the passion of Christ, on the other. In this way, Theodore establishes a *bond* between these two, and we know that the *bond of likeness* is at the basis of all typology.

But Theodore goes beyond this simple recognition of a bond of likeness. He applies his exegetical method and refuses to settle for just any bond; he will accept only the bond guaranteed by the text. In our case, it is the words of Jesus himself that are presented as the bond. Jesus says that the bread is his body and that the cup contains his blood; the meaning of the bread and wine is determined not by the natural typology of food, but by the typology of the passion: "This then is why he also hands down the bread and cup: because it is by means of food and drink that we continue in our life here below. But he calls the bread his body and the cup his blood, because suffering affects the body and grinds it and causes the blood to flow. These two (body and blood) in which the passion is accomplished he makes the type of food and drink."[69]

The referent of the bread and wine, then, is the body and blood of Christ that undergo the passion.[70] The typological relation between the body and blood and the "food and drink" serves to "manifest the life that continues in immortality."[71] Since the function of the passion is to give life,[72] it follows that the passion cannot be looked at in isolation or by itself; it must always be accompanied by the resurrection, which in Theodore's soteriology is the way of reaching the eschatological blessings. Since, in fact, we live in history and have not yet reached the ultimate realities, the Eucharist gives us life as something future and therefore as an object of hope: "It is while waiting to receive

65

it [the life that continues in immortality] that we partake of this sacrament through which, we believe, we have a firm hope of those blessings to come."[73]

While it is true that the passion is the vehicle of the eschatological blessings and is therefore inseparable from the resurrection,[74] it is no less true that, in direct dependence on Pauline thought, Theodore sees the eucharistic celebration in direct relation to the passion as to its primary object.[75] He clearly asserts this view when speaking of the Eucharist as a sacrifice. The sacrifice has already been accomplished and we have already seen the greatness of the gift "which had already been shown in advance to the prophet." The sacrifice is that which Christ carried out in his passion, and "we are commanded to perform the memorial" of that sacrifice "in this liturgy now set before us." The greatness of the sacrifice is reflected in the liturgical action; the liturgy is therefore so exalted that we must lower our eyes to the ground and stand with great respect, since "we cannot even look at this liturgy, so sublime is it."[76]

Within this development on the attitude of reverential fear that is to be maintained during the liturgy, another justification is given for using the words of the invisible powers: "We use the awesome words of the invisible powers in order to show the greatness of the mercy that has been poured out on us beyond our expectation."[77]

VII. THE EUCHARIST AS TYPE OF THE RESURRECTION

In his discussion of the passion, Theodore argued in two ways: one was connected with the allegorical reading of the prothesis, and the other with the interpretation of the bread and wine. Despite any links one might try to establish between them, these two approaches are quite distinct and independent of one another, as though they belonged to two different "theological areas." In an analogous manner, the resurrection is treated in two different ways that are difficult to interrelate. One focuses on the epiclesis and on the relation between the resurrection of Christ and the bread and wine; the other engages in an analysis of certain actions that are seen as allegorical interpretations and types of the resurrection.

66

A. The Communion Rites as Types of the Resurrection

Theodore has shown how the deacons and the rites of the prothesis are a type of the passion. On the other hand, the death of Christ points to his resurrection, as we saw before. It follows that the Eucharist as type of the passion should also be able to show us the resurrection. But I shall let Theodore speak:

"Because of this [the death of Christ] they [the faithful] must gaze with recollection and awe on what is occurring, and also because at this moment, by reason of the awesome 'liturgy' that is being accomplished according to the rules of the priesthood,[78] it is fitting that our Lord the Christ should arise, proclaiming to all a participation in the ineffable blessings. This is why in the oblation we recall the death of our Lord: because it proclaims the resurrection and the ineffable blessings."[79]

It is easy enough to state as a principle that "the Lord should arise," but it is not easy to find an action in the liturgical celebration that is capable of being a type of the resurrection. When Theodore wished to identify the "sign" of the passion in the prothesis, he made extensive use of allegorical interpretation. He does the same now and manages to find a type of the resurrection in the communion rites. His argument is: the separation of the body from the blood is a way of signifying death; therefore, the reunification of the bread and wine, however done, meets all the requirements needed for it to serve as a type of the resurrection.

Theodore finds a first image of the resurrection in the act of signing. After the pontiff makes a sign of the cross with the bread over the blood and with the blood over the bread, he takes the two

"and joins them, bringing them together again, in order to show all thereby that although they are two, they are nonetheless one in power and are the memorial of the death and passion which the body of our Lord (underwent) when his blood was shed on the cross for us all—all of which the pontiff does by making the sign of the cross, bringing them together, and commingling them."[80]

The explanation is given immediately: the body forms a single whole with its blood; such was the case with the body of Christ before his passion. The words spoken over the bread at the Last Supper serve Theodore for describing the passion, and the words spoken over the cup for bringing out the length and violence of the passion, during which a great deal of blood was shed.[81] Therefore, the bread and cup were "given" by Jesus as a revelation of the passion.

The one to whom they were "given" is the Church, which therefore uses "the two," that is, the bread and the cup, in the same way: "We too, according to this tradition, rightly place the two on the altar in order to reveal what took place, so that it may be known that these two are one in power because they belong to that which alone underwent the passion, that is, the flesh of our Lord, whose blood was also shed."[82]

The argument is not very clear. More importantly, we must admit that in addition to difficulty in the argument, there is also a difficulty in the liturgical gesture, which does not appear very well suited to be a type of the resurrection. True enough, the bread is brought close to the cup and the cup to the bread, and a sign of the cross is traced with the one over the other. This bringing together of the two is already, in a way, uniting of the body and blood, so that the embracing unity is shown. But the two are still separate. The sign is still incomplete.

We must therefore recognize that the analysis thus far yields only an inchoative sign of unity and must be completed. The completion will be added by the liturgical gesture that follows immediately. Continuing with his reading of the Ritual and his commentary on it, Theodore goes on to say: " 'For this reason it is a rule [= liturgical regulation] that the lifegiving bread be placed little by little in the chalice' (Ritual) in order to show that (the body and blood) are inseparable, that they are one in power, and that they give one and the same grace to those who receive them."[83] The sign of the resurrection is the unity between bread and wine, a unity effected by using the one to make the sign of the cross over the other, but also, and above all, by placing the bread in the chalice containing the eucharistic wine.

At this point in Theodore's commentary, we might think that the identification of the type of the resurrection is now complete, an identification based on the union of the bread with the wine. But within the perspective he has adopted, Theodore finds still another gesture that is capable of revealing the resurrection, namely, the breaking of the bread: "The pontiff breaks the bread, not just in any manner, but, because Christ our Lord, after the resurrection from the dead, showed himself to all his followers."[84] But how did the risen Lord show himself? He showed himself in the sign of a meal[85] or, more accurately, in "the breaking of bread."[86] In Theodore's interpretation, "this was in order to show himself to them as risen and to manifest the resurrection which had taken place and to proclaim that they too would be associated in these magnificent blessings."[87] In Theodore's view, therefore, the eucharistic rite of breaking bread is also a type of the resurrection.

In conclusion: each of the three rites that follow upon the "offering of the oblation"[88] is interpreted as a sign of the resurrection: the signing and the placing of the bread in the chalice, on grounds of the unity of Christ's body before the passion; the breaking of the bread, on grounds of the Scripture. As the prothesis was a sign of Christ's death, so the rites preceding communion are a sign of the resurrection. But there is a difference between the two cases: allegorical interpretation of the prothesis was linked to sacramental realism because these rites were an imitation of the angelic liturgy, which served as a model whose imitation ensured sacramentality. In the second case, however, no explicit element is said to be a source of sacramentality.

We must acknowledge, however, that such an element exists and that Theodore has referred to it earlier. When he spoke of the sacrament as a "food suited to us," he showed the suitability by drawing an analogy with nature[89]; thus the rite of signing and putting the bread in the cup is based on an analogy with nature that requires that a body be one. As for the third sign, the breaking of the bread, here again there is a strong guarantee of sacramentality, for this gesture "imitates" one used by Jesus himself to reveal his resurrection. It can be said, I think, that "imitation" of a gesture of Jesus is almost on the same level as "imitation" of the angelic liturgy. But Theodore never expresses this idea or explicitly thematizes it; I have to say, therefore, that here I am offering an interpretation of Theodore based on the internal consistency of his ideas, rather than giving his formally expressed thought.

From what we have seen thus far, it is legitimate to conclude that these three gestures, which are a type of the resurrection, have sacramental value as much as the prothesis did. Still to be explained is the function of the offering of the oblation[90] and, above all, the function of the epiclesis, which, as we shall see in a moment, is presented as the key moment in the manifestation of the resurrection. But, in the final analysis, Theodore does not seem to have fully mastered the kind of sacramental theology that pushes the ideas of "likeness" and "imitation" into the realm of allegory, which is the basis of ancient typology.

B. Epiclesis, Holy Spirit, Resurrection

The eucharistic prayer, or anaphora, contains a text known as the "epiclesis," which is an invocation that the Holy Spirit may descend on the faithful and the gifts.[91] There is one point in Theodore's thinking in this area that is of great interest: he makes the epiclesis a manifestation of the resurrection of Christ's body.[92] When the epiclesis is pronounced, it is united to the bread, which is the body of Christ, and in this way, the Holy Spirit manifests the resurrection. In the sequence of actions that make up the liturgy, this is the moment of Christ's resurrection, which is the source of grace for the faithful.

But let me appeal directly to the Ritual: "Next, it is appropriate that in virtue of these (liturgical) actions our Lord the Christ should rise from among the dead and pour out his grace on all of us."[93] This sentence comes between mention of the *Sanctus* and mention of the epiclesis, which, according to the Ritual, is a prayer referring solely to the faithful and not to the sacred gifts. Theodore's commentary goes notably beyond what is said in the Ritual. In fact, it brings out fully the action of the Holy Spirit: the body of Christ was mortal and became immortal through the resurrection.[94] It follows from this that if the bread and wine are to be seen as a memorial of immortality, they must receive the Holy Spirit,[95] who is the cause of Christ's resurrection.

Here is Theodore repeating what the Ritual says and commenting on it: " 'Next, it is necessary that in virtue of these (liturgical) actions our Lord the Christ should rise from among the dead and pour out his grace on all of us.' This can happen only through the coming of the grace of the Holy Spirit."[96] Theodore's focus is entirely on the Holy Spirit and his efficacious action in the sacrament, whereas this concern does not appear in the Ritual recorded at the beginning of the homily. On the other hand, Theodore bases the sacramental importance of the Spirit on his importance in the resurrection of Christ.[97] Since the resurrection of Christ is the work of the Spirit and since the gifts, after and because of the prothesis, are a type of Christ's death, the Spirit must also be at work in the sacrament and bring about the resurrection.

It is clear that this entire way of proceeding depends on a much fully developed Trinitarian theology than we saw at work in the commentary on the rites of signing, putting the bread in the chalice, and breaking the bread. Two different theologies are being used that bear witness to two different ways of handling the problem of sacramental realism and efficacy.

C. The Eucharist as Remission of Sins

As in dealing with the passion and the resurrection, so too in dealing with the theme of the Eucharist as remission of sins, Theodore uses two different methods. These two conceptions are interwoven in all of the passages in which he comments on the Eucharist. The first comes from the words of Jesus at the Last Supper, and the second comes from the theology that sees our liturgy as related to the angelic liturgy. The two methods are even clearer in the discussion of the Eucharist as remission of sins. The solution of the problem is based first on the Lord's words[98] and then on Isaiah's vision of the angelic liturgy.[99] We must, however, be cautious about giving the name "angelic liturgy" to the episode of the seraphim purifying the prophet's lips with a burning coal. It would be more accurate to speak of a typological reading of the Old Testament for the purpose of explaining the eucharistic mystery. But then the angelic liturgy is not identical with the heavenly liturgy and the attainment of the eschatological blessings.

VIII. THE HEAVENLY LITURGY

In his catechetical homilies, Theodore frequently appeals to the heavenly liturgy, which, in his view, the Church's liturgy imitates. In any explanation, then, of Theodore's conception of the sacraments, it is important to find out what he understands by "heavenly liturgy."

In the biblical and earliest patristic traditions, the theological theme of imitation does not refer solely to externals but concerns the innermost being; in other words, imitation is of the ontological order. Imitation, therefore, makes one like the object imitated, but does so by means of a real change in being. Those who imitate Christ undergo a profound transformation of their being and become ontologically like[100] Christ.[101] Were we to attempt to express this idea in modern theological categories, we would have to say that "imitation" effects a "real presence."[102] If the faithful imitate Christ, he is present in them. The situation is not different when we turn to the liturgical rites, for these too are what they imitate. This is the only way of explaining the earliest vocabulary of worship: a liturgical action is a "likeness"[103] (we today would say a "sacrament") because it is an imitation.[104]

In Theodore's view, the liturgy on earth is an imitation of the heavenly liturgy. Now, if he held the concept of imitation that I explained before, it would follow that because of the "imitation," the angelic liturgy is present in the liturgy of the Church. Or, to put it more accurately: that the liturgy of the Church is a participation in the angelic liturgy. But this is in fact not the case in Theodore; the concept of "imitation" that I explained before is completely absent from his thinking, even though he asserts that the earthly liturgy is a "type" of the heavenly liturgy. He has already abandoned the early patristic idea of the liturgy as a "participation" (an idea still held by John Chrysostom).

72

A. The Concept of Redemption

In Theodore's view, Christ's death was caused by the demon, who has control of things earthly; but the death of Christ in turn rescues human beings from the power of Satan. This is possible because God condemns the devil on account of his depraved ill will toward Christ and the human race. The power of the devil over human beings is shown in death, which is the fruit of sin. God actually effects the rescue of human beings from the devil's power by raising Christ: "Then he raised our Lord the Christ from the dead, made him immortal and unchangeable, and caused him to ascend to heaven. Then he set the enjoyment of the gifts before the entire (human) race, so that the demon would no longer have the least occasion for harming us."[105] This passage makes Theodore's theology of redemption very clear.

Redemption is described in terms of the gift of immortality that is given to human beings. The demon does not resign himself to this situation and asks in regard to it: "And is he [Adam and the human race] now to be immortal, which is something beyond his nature?"[106] But Theodore does not make redemption consist solely in the gift of immortality. He puts immortality in its proper context, that is, in the one place where it can truly exist, namely, the context of the eschaton. Christ

"rescued the human race from the power of the demons; he delivered us from that enslavement and captivity and placed us under his own authoritative hand: 'he ascended on high,' says (the scripture), 'and led captivity captive' (Ps 67[68]:18), (whence) he showed the new world to come and the marvelous life of that which is called 'the heavenly Jerusalem,' where Christ our Lord has established his kingdom that does not pass away."[107]

These passages make it clear that Christ effected redemption in two stages, an earthly and a heavenly. In the first, the demon brings about the Lord's death; in the second, through his resurrection, Christ manifests to human beings the gift of the eschatological blessings, namely, immortality and immutability. The gift of life thus belongs essentially to the heavenly phase of redemption. It follows that for Theodore, redemption is essentially eschatological.

The importance of the "ascension to heaven" is fully explained only when the theology of salvation is conceived in an essentially eschatological way. Consider how Theodore interprets the baptismal rites as vehicles of redemption. The exorcisms, he says, are an expression of our struggle with the devil[108] and tell of his being condemned by God so that he will no longer make bold to approach the newly baptized.[109] The profession of faith is also interpreted in eschatological terms. This faith must remain constantly firm, because it alone brings us to baptism: ". . . Father and Son and Holy Spirit, regarding whom you were instructed in the Creed, and whose invocation brought you the joy of this inscription which is a participation in the heavenly blessings."[110]

The same themes are present both in the explanation of redemption and in this explanation of the baptismal rites. The clear thematic parallelism is reason for thinking that the eschatological character of the sacraments derives not from a particular sacramental theology, but from the doctrine of redemption.

B. Sacrament and Salvation

In other passages, too, Theodore links baptism with the theme of redemption, understood as abrogation of the decree of death and possession of the eschatological blessings. In this perspective, these blessings are, of course, possessed "in hope"; redemption will be complete only at the end of time. In all this, Theodore is following the Scriptures:

"This is why blessed Paul also says: 'We who were baptized into Jesus Christ were baptized into his death. We were buried with him in baptism so as to die, in order that as Jesus Christ rose from the dead for the glorification of his Father, so we too might lead a new life' (Rom 6:3–4). As a matter of fact, in the past, and before the coming of Christ, death by a divine judgment lorded it over us as sovereign, and its bonds were utterly unbreakable. Powerful indeed was the hold it had on us. But because our Lord Jesus Christ died and rose, he changed this decree and broke the power of death.

"As a result, the death of those who believe in Christ is henceforth like a prolonged sleep, as blessed Paul says: 'Now Christ is risen from the dead and has become the firstfruits of those who sleep' (1 Cor 15:20). 'Those who sleep' is his description of those who have died since the resurrection of Christ, because they will rise and strip off death through resurrection.

"Therefore, it is because Christ our Lord has destroyed the power of death by his own resurrection that (Paul) says: 'We who were baptized into Jesus Christ were baptized into his death' (Rom 6:3); we know that death has already been done away with by our Lord the Christ. It is in this faith that we approach him and are baptized, because we want to share henceforth in his death, in the hope of participating in the same (blessings, namely): to rise from the dead in the same way he rose. That is why, when I am baptized, immersing my head, it is the death of our Lord the Christ that I receive, and his burial that I desire to lay hold of; and thereby I truly confess also the resurrection of our Lord; while when I come out of the water, I regard myself as already risen in a kind of type."[111]

The signing with the cross in baptism is also seen in an eschatological perspective: "You received the consignation, a sign that you have been chosen for an ineffable service; it is to heaven that you are called."[112] In baptism, God is invoked, and the invocation has the effect of establishing a certain contact with the divine nature that gains eschatological blessings for the human person:

"It is while invoking it [the divine nature] that we are baptized; it is also through it that we expect to receive those blessings which are now given in type; and (it is through it) also that we shall continue to enjoy those blessings to come when we really rise, immortal and immutable by nature, from among the dead, and become heirs and sharers in the dwelling and citizenship of heaven."[113]

The same type of argument, indeed the almost identical argument, is also found in the first homily on the Mass. Due to the resurrection that the Holy Spirit brought about, the body of

Christ became immortal. The sacrament effects something similar, for in the eucharistic celebration, the coming of the Spirit works the transformation of the bread into the body of Christ, which is enlivened by the Spirit, becomes immortal, and rises. In Theodore's theology, redemption consists in the bestowal of immortality; the Eucharist can give salvation because when the faithful participate in the immortal body of Christ, they participate in the eschatological gift of immortality. But now we must read Theodore while keeping in mind his treatment of the epiclesis, which I sketched before: "It was not by its own nature that even the body of Christ possessed immortality and the power to grant immortality; rather it is the Holy Spirit who gave it to him, and it is through resurrection from the dead that he received union with the divine nature and became immortal and a cause of immortality for others."[114]

It is clear from this that the eschatological aspect of the sacrament is due not to "imitation" of the heavenly liturgy, but to the redemptive content of the sacrament or, in other words, to its ability to save, which in turn is a fruit of the immortal body of the risen Christ, truly present in the sacrament. In introducing his discussion of this point, Theodore says that "when giving the bread he (Christ) did not say 'This is the type of my body,' but 'This is my body.' "[115] The conclusion: since the body of Christ was made immortal through the resurrection and became an eschatological reality, it follows that as a result of sacramental realism, the fruits of the Eucharist will likewise be essentially eschatological realities.

For this reason, even the way in which the faithful participate interiorly will be described in eschatological terms. Thus, Theodore comments on the exhortation to "lift up your minds" by saying that what we do is "a memorial of the sacrifice and death of our Lord Jesus Christ, who suffered and rose for us, was united to the divine nature, is seated at God's right hand, and is in heaven."[116] If he is in heaven, the only appropriate attitude for us is to direct our minds to God: "We too therefore must direct thither the gaze of our soul and, by means of this memorial, transport our heart thither."[117]

The resurrection is the first of the eschatological gifts that are the fruit of redemption. Moreover, the resurrection has a specific function in relation to sin, for as a result of it, human nature becomes completely immutable and therefore loses the capacity for sinning.[118] Other eschatological gifts are: existence in the image of God; dwelling in heaven with knowledge of our Lord[119]; impassibility[120]; immortality and immutability of soul[121]; and incorruptibility and spirituality of body.[122] All these gifts are the work of the Holy Spirit, who brings about a new birth. Furthermore: (1) by God's will, human beings are meant to be in heaven because that is where Christ is; (2) heaven is characterized by freedom; and (3) human beings participate in the great glory of reigning with Christ.[123]

In summary, it can be said that the source of our salvation is the economy brought to fulfillment in Christ. How does this economy generate salvation in us? Christ was the first to be taken up from among us and "the first to receive this transformation from the divine nature." Since all this has already taken place in him, he has also become the one who gains these eternal blessings for us. The faithful must therefore approach the holy mysteries in order to enter into contact with the "divine nature" of Christ. By means, then, of these various "types" and "signs," "we believe we already possess those same realities."[124] In other words, salvation consists in receiving from Christ what he himself first received because of his divine nature: the resurrection from the dead that is the source of immortality.

Even though these realities exist only in heaven, they are already given in some manner in the sacraments that the faithful now receive. The liturgy thus becomes a privileged moment for putting human beings in contact with the final gifts; they must display now, in anticipation, the characteristics that those blessings will bestow. With this in mind, Theodore expressly refers to the Scriptures, citing Matthew 22:29–30 and Luke 20:36, where it is said that human beings "will be like the angels" and "are children of God, being children of the resurrection."[125] We may conclude that because the worship of the Church has an eschatological content, that is, bestows the blessings to come, it must be thought of as related to the heavenly liturgy.

C. *The Angelic Liturgy and the* Sanctus

It is above all in commenting on the eucharistic anaphora that Theodore has occasion to discuss the angelic liturgy. In his step-by-step commentary, he comes to the *Sanctus* or praise given by the angels. At this point, the earthly liturgy depends on the biblical description of the angelic praise, which God revealed to human beings through the prophet Isaiah. Human beings praise God as the angels do:

"To this divine nature, which exists from all eternity, all creation and first and foremost the invisible powers offer praise and glorification at every moment. He (the bishop) mentions, out of all these, the seraphim who raise to God the praise which the prophet Isaiah learned of by divine revelation and which he passed on in the scriptures, the very same praise which we who are gathered say in a loud voice; thus we too say the very same thing that the invisible natures say: 'Holy, holy, holy, Lord God Sabaoth, whose praises fill heaven and earth' (Is 6:3)."[126]

The *Sanctus* prayer is said in union with the invisible powers and in a kind of imitation of them: "We have the same intention as they, and we make a confession similar to theirs."[127] This prayer is a prayer of praise of God and is offered "to render our worship to God."[128]

In these passages, the earthly liturgy is not thought of as a participation, in the ontological sense of the word, in the angelic liturgy. Rather, because of the eschatological connotations of Christ's redemptive work, the praise offered and confession made by human beings is similar to that of the angels. It is therefore redemption in Christ that enables human beings to join with the angelic choirs in celebrating the praise of God, and not the other way around: "for this too we are enabled to do by the economy (brought to fulfillment) by Christ our Lord: to become immortal and incorruptible and to offer our worship along with the invisible powers, when, as the Apostle says, 'we shall be caught up in the clouds to meet the Lord in the air, and so we shall always be with the Lord' (1 Thes 4:17)" (*ibid.*).

Theodore's idea of salvation is strongly eschatological in character, and this is the ultimate reason why human beings can join the invisible powers in praising God. It should be noted that the entire argument is based on two citations from Scripture: 1 Thessalonians 4:17 and Luke 20:36, and that since these provide the starting point for the argument, they also show the way to an understanding of Theodore's discussion of the *Sanctus*. With regard to the angelic liturgy, therefore, we may conclude only that the earthly liturgy of the *Sanctus* is inspired by it and is celebrated in accompaniment with it: nothing more. The real ontological foundation of the praise of God that human beings sing in the *Sanctus* is Christ himself and not the angelic liturgy.

Strong emphasis is laid on the point that the *Sanctus* was revealed to Isaiah in a vision that Scripture has passed on to us. The angelic liturgy, which is too sublime for human beings, was revealed to him. It was revealed to him that the angelic powers stand there in great fear and reverence; that is why they lower their gaze and cover their feet and faces with their wings. Also revealed to him was the doctrine of the Trinity as expressed in the threefold "Holy," while the unity of God was revealed to him in the one "Lord" who is addressed. Theodore speaks expressly of three persons, thus developing his exegesis along strictly dogmatic lines. Holiness and eternity are attributes peculiar to the divinity, whereas creatures are holy only by God's gift.

But the commentary on the *Sanctus* conveys a theology of the sacraments as well as theology of the Trinity. For Isaiah, the heavenly vision of the seraphim singing the threefold "Holy" is a revelation of the economy with all it contains:

"When he saw this awesome revelation, which was a manifestation of the economy (brought to fulfillment) by Christ our Lord— by reason of which the entire universe was necessarily filled with praise of God and had to learn the mystery of the Trinity and receive instruction, the profession, and baptism in the name of the Father and of the Son and of the Holy Spirit—to make this known the seraphim cried aloud this song: 'Holy, holy, holy (is) the Lord, whose praises fill heaven and earth' (Is 6:3)."[129]

The attitude of the prophet in response to all this is one of great fear, for he knows his own human weakness, being "full of sin and uncleanness." Because of this awareness, one of the seraphim takes a burning coal, puts it to the prophet's lips, and purifies them. Theodore cites the angel's words: " 'Behold, this has touched your lips; let your guilt pass away and your sins be forgiven' (Is 6:7)."

Theodore must still explain how Isaiah's case can be applied to the eucharistic liturgy of the Church. Here is how he makes the connection: "On the altar there were burning coals, a revelation of the mystery that was to be passed on to us. The coal was at first black and cold, but when it was put in the fire, it became luminous and hot."

What happens to the coal is a paradigm of what happens in the sacred mysteries.[130] The connection between the two is ensured by some points they have in common: (1) both bestow the forgiveness of sins; (2) both are connected with the altar; (3) both are transformed[131]; (4) both are carried to the lips; (5) both inspire fear.[132] (6) Still another point in common can be seen in the image of fire that is like a bridge between the burning coals and the Spirit: "If we apply ourselves to becoming like him,[133] it is certain beyond doubt that the grace of the Holy Spirit will help us to do good and, like the fire that burns up thorns, will completely cover all our sins."[134] Theodore's conclusion is categorical: As we are certain that the seraphim purified the prophet, so we are to be certain that "by communion in the holy mysteries our debts are completely covered, provided that we repent and that we suffer and feel compunction in our hearts because of our sins."[135]

Theodore uses the incident in Isaiah in order to make a theological point about the eucharistic mystery: its ability to forgive sins. We must not underestimate the fact that in the final analysis, Theodore's argument is biblical in character. He brings to light the theological content of the Eucharist by means of a typological reading of an incident in the Old Testament. The vision of Isaiah is a paradigm for, and explains, the eucharistic celebration, as though it were the archetype of the latter.

Theodore thus applies the classical method of typological interpretation of the sacraments, and, in fact, we see the boundary between Old Testament and New Testament realities being lost.

The Trinitarian interpretation of the *Sanctus* in the anaphora is projected back into the Old Testament as the correct reading of Isaiah's vision.[136] But Theodore applies the principle in the Antiochene manner, not the Alexandrian; he requires the presence of an objective connection, and the text itself supplies him with this. Because the anaphora contains the threefold "Holy" and because this originates in Isaiah, Theodore can take over the Old Testament passage and use it as the basis for some points in his own eucharistic theology.

All this shows us that the idea of the earthly liturgy being a participation in the angelic liturgy has been reorganized. Theodore never confuses the eschatological character of the liturgy with the theme of participation in the angelic liturgy. The former is strongly emphasized and depends on the salvific nature of the sacraments; the latter, though clearly present, is seen in a more nuanced way.

D. Life in the Image of Heaven

The logic of the eschatological gifts controls not only the liturgical celebration, but the living of life. This subject is handled under the heading of how to be worthy of the sacrament; we today would put it under the rubric of the relation between liturgy and life.

After commenting on eucharistic communion, Theodore has a section on Christian life, which can, if modeled on the eschatological gifts, make us worthy of the mysteries. In this perspective, the unmarried state is seen as an imitation of heaven and to be preferred. Here the theme of eschatology brings the theology of life into close association with the theology of the mystery, since the latter too is conceived of in relation to the blessings of the eschaton.

Here is Theodore's argument: he asks the faithful to behave in a manner conformed to the content of the mysteries, a content comprising the eschatological gifts; it follows that the faithful should live like angels. The argument is based on a passage of Scripture,[137] although this refers only to not marrying. The theme of living like angels, on the other hand, comes from the general setting of Theodore's theology. He knows, of course, that he is on difficult ground here; in fact, it would be easy to put him on the spot by asking whether only the unmarried can be imitators of heaven. He is aware of the problem and answers that married people too can live in imitation of heaven, since married people too participate in the mysteries that are an imitation of the heavenly liturgy.[138]

He shows, however, that he has not fully mastered the theme, for, after urging that the married too should live in imitation of heaven, he observes that in heaven there will be no marrying or eating or drinking. From this fact, a conclusion necessarily follows:

"Therefore it is fitting that those also who are married should try as best they can to imitate the world to come. That is what blessed Paul tells us: 'Henceforth let those who have wives live as though they had them not, and those who mourn as though they were not mourning, and those who buy as though they did not possess, those who rejoice in their possessions as though they did not rejoice, and those who have dealings with this world as though this world were not outside justice: for the figure of this world is passing away' (1 Cor 7:29–31)."[139]

But the ultimate explanation is to be found in the fact that this world is only a "figure" (schēma), whereas the world to come will endure for ever.[140]

In any case, married or not, those who participate in the holy mysteries must necessarily base their lives on the heavenly model: "Such, then, it is necessary and fitting that we become, once we have been nourished with sacramental food and have set our sights on that for hope of which we participate in the holy (mysteries)."[141]

E. *The Actions of Jesus as Types*
If the earthly liturgy is not celebrated as an image of the heavenly liturgy, then the heavenly liturgy cannot be defined as the archetype of the earthly liturgy. But since the archetype is in some way present and hidden in the "image" of it that is cele-

brated by the Church, it follows that the earthly liturgy does not have for its content the content of the heavenly liturgy.

There are passages in Theodore that seem to point in this direction, both in regard to the supposed archetypal role of the heavenly liturgy and in regard to the events that do stand at the origin of the Church's celebration. Thus the baptism of Jesus in the Jordan would be the archetype of our baptismal celebration, and the Last Supper of Jesus would be the archetype of our eucharistic celebration.

"Even our Lord the Christ, before his resurrection from the dead, was seen to receive baptism from John the Baptist in the river Jordan, for the purpose of serving in advance as the type (= model) of the present baptism which by his grace we are to receive. For, 'since he was the first-born from among the dead,' as blessed Paul says, 'in order that he might be first in all things' (Col 1:18), it was not only in the reality of the resurrection that he willed to be first for you, but also in its type. It was for this reason that he accepted to be baptized by John (the Baptist), and therein sketched in advance the type of the grace of this baptism which you are going to receive, so that in this respect too he might become your head."[142]

The statement that the baptism of Jesus is the model of ours is one that Theodore does not make simply in passing. He repeats it in number 23 of this same homily: "But he was baptized with our baptism, and thereby presented its type (= model) in advance. Therefore he also received the Holy Spirit, who appeared to descend in the form of a dove and remained upon him, as the evangelist says."[143]

The function of a "model," expressed in the word "type," is not reducible to a purely external analogy. It involves the true presence of the archetype in the image, that is, in the liturgy that we celebrate. We may therefore say that the use of the term "type," with all the ontological density it connotes, is completely appropriate. Here is a passage in proof:

"You must therefore realize that you are baptized with the baptism with which our Lord the Christ was baptized in his flesh;

that is why you are baptized 'in the name of the Father and of the Son and the Holy Spirit,' because this kind (of baptism) was already sketched out (= was present in a rough-draft state) in the events themselves, in this way, in type."[144]

The problem is more complex in the case of the Eucharist. As a matter of fact, Theodore's main concern is to explain effectively the relation between the eucharistic sacrifice and the sacrifice accomplished by Jesus in his passion, and not so much the relation between the Last Supper and our celebration of the Eucharist. He does, however, describe the account of the Last Supper as "the handing on of the mysteries,"[145] which means that the institution is being understood as the *giving of a model*. But this "model" is not to be thought of as a purely external ritual pattern, for a *model* or *archetype* has an ontological function.[146] Here is Theodore again: "(Christ) gave us this mystery. . . . When about to go forward to his passion, he handed it over to disciples."[147]

What Jesus did at the Last Supper is looked upon as a "model" that he himself handed on to the Church; so true is this that Theodore can say: "Now that the liturgy is adequately carried out, in accordance with the tradition of our Lord, the memorial of whose death and resurrection it is. . . . "[148] The passage goes on to speak of the breaking of the bread as an action imitating that of Christ; in other words, the bread is broken because Christ broke the bread when he handed on the model to be imitated.

It must be said again very emphatically that Theodore does not think of the model as a purely external action, as if we were to act out a mime in accordance with rubrical notations; no, the action of Christ is to be imitated in its deeper content as well. According to Theodore, then, what is to be imitated in breaking the bread is the Lord's act of giving himself for all: "The bishop therefore breaks the bread as he (our Lord) first broke it[149] in his manifestations; at times he appeared to this person, at times to that; and it happened that he also appeared to a large number of people together, so that all could approach him."[150] Therefore, the action imitating that of Christ is complete, but this is not yet enough, since when we perform it, we must imitate the deeper reality that Christ gave it.

A conclusion may be drawn from all this, namely, that the liturgical celebration is an "imitation" of an archetype to which reference must be made. That archetype is the actions of Christ. I must add, however, that the theme, though important, is not given any extensive treatment. It is not treated on the same scale as the content of the sacrament, that is, the gift of the eschatological blessings. It can be said that for Theodore, the theme of the "archetype" is a "recessive" trait of his theology, whereas the theme of the "content" of the sacrament is a "developed" trait.

Let me turn to a final passage that shows how the "eschatological blessings" and especially the heavenly liturgy can be so much at the center of Theodore's treatment that they seem to be the "archetype" of which the liturgy is an imitation. The sacrifice, he says, is such because it is a memorial of the true sacrifice, that is, the Lord's passion; but it must also be a figure of heavenly realities, which means that it contains these in some way: "Since it is the signs of heavenly reality that he accomplishes in type, this sacrifice must likewise be a manifestation of it; and the bishop performs a kind of image (*eikōn*) of the liturgy that takes place in heaven."[151] The priestly action performed in the liturgy has for its function to manifest heavenly realities. But the heavenly realities in question are the "heavenly liturgy"; this, however, is not a true and proper archetype, but only the "content" of the sacrament that must be manifested because of the principle of sacramental efficacy.

IX. SACRAMENTAL REALISM

Theodore's entire treatment of the sacraments is marked by realism, and the sacramental vocabulary he uses always shows a clear ontological density. In this context he makes use of an interesting theological principle: every function that is part of a sacrament derives from the nature of the sacrament, which must, therefore, have the same characteristics as the function. If we are to understand Theodore's sacramental realism, we must always keep in mind this principle that unites the nature and the effect of the sacrament in a single interpretative scheme. The principle holds for both baptism and the Eucharist. Its application to the eucharistic food yields the statement that if the sacramental food is a vehicle of the gift of immortality, then it must itself be immortal.

Theodore sets great store by his unitary vision of baptism and Eucharist; these two sacraments are always seen as being administered one after the other. They are, as it were, two stages in a single organic vision: baptism is birth and the Eucharist is food.

The broadest framework in which these sacraments are located is provided by the eschatological perspective, which in turn is developed in terms of Paul's teaching on the Church as the body of Christ. But in Theodore, the scriptural basis for this teaching is not one of the classic Pauline verses on the Church as the body of Christ; it is a text from the Letter to the Hebrews that describes Christians as children of God.

Theodore's argument depicts Christ as a nursing mother, undertaking to give food to her children. The food is the Eucharist. "In holy baptism he [Christ] gave us a new birth and thereby made us his own body, his own flesh, his first-born—as it is written: 'Here am I and the children God has given to me' (Heb 2:13)— and with the kind of love a natural mother has he takes care to feed us with his own body."[152] This passage shows: (1) the close continuity between baptism and the Eucharist and (2) the conception of the Eucharist as a "strengthening" of baptism. But Theodore's argument is not yet complete, for he has not yet described the role of the Holy Spirit and the eschatological fruit of the Eucharist.

Let me now move on to Theodore's sacramental realism as he formulates it in connection with baptism: "Consequently, since these things are in figures and in signs, (and desiring) to show that we are not using empty signs but realities which we confess and unhesitatingly desire, he [Paul] says: 'If we have grown together with him in likeness to his death, we shall also (in likeness) to his resurrection' (Rom 6:5)." Sacramental realism is here derived directly from the Scriptures, in keeping with the best typological tradition. Theodore then concludes that the content of the sacrament is the saving event that took place in history:

86

"From the excellence of what is to be he shows that the grandeur of the types is worthy of belief. Now the figure of these things is baptism: such is the work of the Holy Spirit."[153]

The fruit of baptism is no less realistic:

". . . so that you die and rise with Christ; so that you are henceforth born to a new life; so that you bring to fulfillment the type of this true second birth; so that, drawn by these signs, you come to participate in their reality. . . . Great is the sacrament that takes place, awesome the excellence of the signs. It is worthy of belief and will certainly grant us to participate in the (blessings) that are to come."[154]

The power at work in the sacrament is the Holy Spirit. It is he who ensures the realism and saving efficacy of the sacrament, for the water is not capable by itself of producing these effects. Therefore, Theodore continues his train of thought by speaking of the sanctification of the baptismal water, which is effected by the coming of the Spirit. " 'You then descend into the water which has been consecrated by the blessing of the bishop' (Ritual). The water in which you are baptized is certainly no longer ordinary water; it is the water of a second birth, and it cannot become this except by the coming of the Holy Spirit."[155] Theodore's sacramental realism is so great it compels us to suppose a real transformation of the baptismal water; then this water will be capable of serving as a womb in which a new birth takes place.

The realism is no less marked in the Eucharist. As baptism brings a new birth through the conferral of future gifts, so the Eucharist feeds the faithful through the conferral of those future gifts.

The bread and chalice enable us to eat the body and blood of Christ, which are the food of immortality.[156] Theodore's reasoning is of great interest because he looks at the bread not only in christological terms, but also in pneumatological terms: the bread and the chalice also give us the Holy Spirit, the bearer of eschatological gifts. In summary, we can say that for Theodore, the bread and the chalice are the body and blood of Christ and that these are our food. Since the body of Christ is risen, it is immortal, and, consequently, his body and blood are food that gives immortality.

Theodore regularly says that the bread and wine are changed into the body and blood of Christ by the coming of the Spirit. He expressly refers to the Spirit in, for example, the following passage: "What is presented is ordinary bread and wine, but by the coming of the Spirit they are changed into the body and blood and thereby transformed so as to have the power of being a spiritual and immortal food."[157] And again: "For one is the bread and one the body of Christ our Lord, into whom the bread that has been presented is changed; the bread receives such a change solely because of the coming of the Holy Spirit."[158]

In the past, the Holy Spirit effected the resurrection of Christ's body; it follows that now, when he descends on the sacred gifts at the moment of the epiclesis, he again effects the resurrection of Christ's body. Another effect of the epiclesis is the change of the gifts into the body and blood of Christ. After the epiclesis, the bread and wine appear to be truly the body and blood of Christ and therefore a memorial of immortality:

"Now again, in the same way, when the Holy Spirit comes, there is a kind of anointing by the supervenient grace, an anointing which, in my opinion, is received by the bread and wine that have been presented. For this reason we believe them to be the body and blood of Christ: immortal, incorruptible, impassible, and immutable by nature, just as the body of our Lord is as a result of the resurrection."[159]

The commentary on the story of the Last Supper provides another occasion for stating at length that the bread and wine are the body and blood of the Lord. The words of the account of institution have the same explanatory function in the anaphora that they have in the gospel stories of the Last Supper. Their function is to proclaim what the bread and wine are: "When, then, the pontiff says that this (bread and wine) are the body and blood of Christ, he clearly shows that they have become this by the coming of the Holy Spirit and that by his operation they have become immortal—for the body of our Lord, when it was anointed and received the Spirit, also clearly showed itself to be such."

Theodore supposes that at the moment of communion, the faithful, by their attitude of adoration, are making a true and proper profession of faith in the "eucharistic presence." They should consider, he suggests, that the gesture of extending their hands to receive the body of Christ is one signifying adoration: "They thereby make a kind of profession of faith that they are receiving the body of the King, of him who became Lord of all through union with the divine nature."[160]

Theodore's commentary is based on the fact that the faithful are fed on the body and blood of Christ; this is the central point on which everything depends. His concern is to explain in what this feeding consists. His words make it clear that we are far removed from any "physicism."[161] As a matter of fact, he locates the feeding in the area of affectivity: "He gives himself to each of us so that we may receive and embrace him with all our strength and show our love for him as much as each of us pleases. In this way the body and blood of our Lord truly nourish us and make us look forward to our transformation into a nature that is immortal and incorruptible."[162]

The sentiments the faithful should cultivate at this moment are not derived from the liturgical texts but from consideration of the content of the sacrament, that is, the body of Christ: "Now, by means of these remembrances, by means of these symbols and signs that have been accomplished, with sweetness and great joy we draw near as it were to Christ our Lord risen from the dead; and according to our ability we embrace him sweetly because we see that he is risen from the dead and also because we hope to reach a share in the resurrection."[163] But we must look with a good deal of reserve on this expansion of the affective response. In itself, this attitude of the faithful would be more in place in dealing with the Lord when he lived on earth—a human being among human beings as a result of the incarnation—than now in the sacrament. This excessive realism is even clearer in passages to which I now turn.

The communion formula, "The Holy One to the holy," is in Theodore's eyes the very definition of the sacrament, and it also brings out fully the intensely realistic strain in his teaching on the sacraments. It is in that perspective that we must understand the difference between the original communion formula: "Holy things [that is, the holy mysteries] to the holy," and Theodore's interpretation of it: "The Holy One [that is, Christ] to the holy." The shift is effected by changing the neuter plural form (*hagia*) of the objective for "holy" to the masculine singular form (*hagios*). In effect, Theodore completely identifies the sacrament with its content, Christ.

Other examples of Theodore's sacramental realism allow us without hesitation to describe it as "exaggerated."

The same strong realism marks the eucharistic action as commemoration of the Lord's passion; nowadays, we would say that Theodore looks upon the Eucharist as a "sacrament of the Lord's passion." He overdoes things and falls into an "exaggerated realism," in the proper sense of the phrase, that leads him to speak of a *new* immolation of Christ. We must ask why he accepts these really excessive formulations; the answer, I think, is that he lacks the theological categories that would enable him to assert a "sacramental realism" without going to the extreme of a "duplication" of Christ's action. Here is a very clear passage:

"Now all of us, in every place, at all times and continually, celebrate the memorial of that sacrifice, for every time we eat this bread and drink this cup we celebrate the memorial of the Lord's death until he comes. . . . Now he himself is once again immolated by means of these types; so that when by faith we look with our eyes on these remembrances which are now accomplished, we are led to see that he dies again, rises, and ascends to heaven—exactly what formerly took place for us."[164]

In a passage such as this, the problem obviously arises of how the uniqueness of the saving events, as described in the Letter to the Hebrews, is to be reconciled with sacramental realism; in Theodore, sacramental realism wins out. One point: the final part of the passage just cited makes clear how bent Theodore is on finding the moment in the eucharistic liturgy that is a type of

Christ's death and then the moment that is a type of the resurrection.

There is further proof of the realistic way in which Theodore views the presence of heavenly realities in the liturgy. He speaks of the interior activity of the faithful during the liturgy; today we would speak of "active participation." He sees this as connected with the presence of heavenly realities, and indeed he derives it from this presence. Here is the passage: "Every time the liturgy of this awesome sacrifice is performed . . . we must think of ourselves in our imagination as people present in heaven; by faith we sketch in our minds a vision of heavenly realities."[165]

The text shows that the liturgy is a likeness of heavenly realities, but also that it is a likeness that cannot be seen but only believed; consequently, the likeness emerges within us by means of an interior activity that consists in imagining the things of heaven. The liturgy contains these realities; therefore, we ought to imagine them. From this, we can infer that in Theodore as in Ambrose, "likeness" refers to the sacramentality[166] of the liturgy, not to what is seen and experienced by the senses in the liturgical rite. In other words, the passage shows that the liturgy is a likeness of heavenly realities, not because it represents them in kind of dramatization, but because it contains them invisibly. For this reason, believers do not see with their bodily eyes a likeness of the liturgy to things heavenly, but only believe it by faith. That is why they must represent them imaginatively in the course of the liturgy.

What is said in this passage is not a remark thrown off in passing, but rather is part of the programmatic definition of a sacrament that Theodore gives at the beginning of his mystagogical homilies:

"Every mystery points in signs and symbols to things invisible and ineffable. A manifestation and explanation of these signs and symbols is required if those present are to experience the power of the mysteries. . . . But since the sacrament contains signs of what will take place or has already taken place, a discourse is needed that will explain the meaning of the signs and mysteries."[167]

Taking as he does this strong position on sacramental realism, Theodore could not but run into problems. These already crop up at the level of the terminology he uses for sacramentality, namely, "mystery" and "type" These terms have too narrow a meaning to allow him to manage all the liturgical phenomena on which he must comment. Here is an example: the word "type" is applied to every element of the celebration: to the prothesis as well as to the breaking of the bread; to the deacons and vestments as well as to the bread and wine; to the Last Supper as well as to the *Sanctus*. It is not possible to think that sacramental realism can be the same in the case of the bread and wine as in the case of the prothesis. Theodore is not naive; he is fully aware of the inconsistency, but he must limit himself to pointing it out[168] and offering consideration very like those we have already seen in Ambrose.

Like Ambrose, Theodore explains the "sacramentality" of the bread and wine by opposing *type* to *reality*.

"At the moment of giving the bread he did not say 'This is the type of my body,' but 'This is my body,' and in like manner the chalice: not 'This is the type of my blood,' but 'This is my blood,' for, now that these (the bread and wine) had received the grace and coming of the Holy Spirit, he wanted us to look no longer at their natural being[169] but to take them as being the body and blood of our Lord."[170]

It is clear that for Theodore, the statement that the bread is the body of Christ is marked by a much greater realism than the statement that the bread is a type of Christ's body.

Although "sacramentality," expressed in the word "type," is a theological category that Theodore recognizes as having a full ontological density, his sacramental realism is nonetheless so strong that he feels the word "type" to be inadequate. In order to reflect Theodore's thinking, we would have to say, in our modern terms, that the bread is the body of Christ and not simply the sacrament of the body of Christ.

The same kind of thinking is familiar to us in the West from the debate over Berengarius.[171] The phenomenon of excessive realism may mark a necessary stage in any sacramental theology that seeks to develop outside the categories of Platonism, however generic the latter may be. Sooner or later, the problem of the relation between a sacrament and the event of which it is a sacrament must emerge and be faced.

X. THE GAP BETWEEN SACRAMENT AND CONTENT

I come now to the final point in my discussion of Theodore. Here I must take up what seems to me to be the most important problem in the work of this great Father of the Church: the relation between sacrament and content, that is, between a sacrament and the reality of which it is the sacrament. Is there a complete identity between the two, or does some difference persist? And if there is a difference, how is this to be reconciled with sacramental realism?

A. Sacrament and Eschatology

This first theme does not raise any special difficulties. Theodore regularly says that the fruit of the sacramental celebration consists in the blessings or gifts of the eschaton.[172] The eschatological gifts are the fruit of the sacrament, and the resurrection, which is the first of these gifts, is the one from which all the others derive. The resurrection is understood in the literal sense, that is, as the end of death and the beginning of new life in the image of the glorified body of Christ. This meaning of the word is so certain in Theodore's mind that he can point to immortality, incorruptibility, and impassibility as fruits of the resurrection. On the other hand, it is utterly clear that no living thing can rise from the dead unless it has first passed through physical death. How is sacramental realism to be harmonized with the eschatological character of the fruits of the sacrament?

Theodore takes up this problem several times; here are some passages.

Baptism is a new birth, but the eschatological nature of that to which we are born raises the question of how really fruitful the baptismal rite is. In fact, how is it possible for human beings to continue living on earth and not yet have died, and nonetheless receive the resurrection from the dead and be living in heaven?

Here is Theodore's position: "You must next advance to baptism itself, in which the types of this new birth are accomplished, for you will receive this second, new birth, which will be effectively manifested at the moment when you rise from the dead and have and once again become that of which death had stripped you."[173] The distinction between the sacrament and the reality of which it is the sacrament is quite clear here. The resurrection is an eschatological gift, and only its sacramental figure is given now.

Theodore goes on to say:

"But at the time appointed for you to be reborn through resurrection, you will effectively possess the resurrection; since at present you have faith in Christ our Lord and await those (gifts), it is necessarily their figures and signs that you receive in this awesome mystery, so that henceforth it is certain that you will participate in those future gifts."[174]

The verb "participate" characterizes the sacramental situation and is contrasted with the eschatological situation; only in the latter will the "blessings" of redemption be possessed as they actually are.

Another passage brings out the work of the Holy Spirit in the dialectical relationship that unites history and eschatology:

"But since this second birth is brought to completion by the action of the Holy Spirit, whom you now receive in the sacrament in the form of an earnest, great is the sacrament that takes place, awesome the perfection of the signs. It is worthy of belief and will certainly grant us a participation in those (blessings) to come. For if it is as an earnest of those blessings to come that we have received the grace of the Holy Spirit, through which also we have now received the use of these sacraments, (then) we shall also expect the enjoyment of those blessings to come. That is why blessed Paul says: 'You have believed in him and have been marked as with a seal by the Spirit of the promise, who is an earnest of our inheritance for the splendor of his glory' (Eph 1:13–14). 'Spirit of the promise' is what he calls the grace given to us here below by the Holy Spirit, because it as a promise of (blessings) to come that we receive this grace. But he (Paul) also speaks of 'an earnest of our inheritance,' because through this we (already) share in those (blessings) to come."[175]

In this passage, Theodore's ideas and vocabulary have their origin in the passage cited from Paul; as a result, a solution of the problem begins to take shape, namely, that what is given to us in the sacrament is a participation, an earnest, a hope, This may not seem like much, but we must consider that it is the Holy Spirit who effects this situation, and that everything the Holy Spirit does is in the highest degree real.[176] When all is said and done, Theodore definitely holds both to the "already," or sacramental realism, and to the "not yet," or fully eschatological character of these gifts.

Another very important passage shows us other terms being used to describe the situation I am discussing. Theodore speaks of "firstfruits" when describing the sacramental phase, and "realities themselves" in describing the eschatological phase:

"In still another passage, then, he says: 'It is God himself who establishes us with you at Christ's side and has anointed us and marked us with a seal and given us the earnest of his Spirit in our hearts' (2 Cor 1:21–22). And elsewhere he says again: 'Now not it (creation) alone, but we too, who have the firstfruits of the Spirit, groan within ourselves and await adoption as children for the redemption of our bodies' (Rom 8:23).

"Here below, I say, it is the 'firstfruits of the Spirit' that we have, for we shall receive the fullness of grace only then when we enjoy the reality itself. He says in fact that 'we await adoption as children for the salvation of our bodies'; this shows that here below we receive a type of adoption as children and that we shall receive filial adoption itself when we are born once again and rise from the dead, becoming at the same time immortal and incorruptible and receiving the complete eradication of our bodily ills. For what he calls 'the salvation of our bodies' is evidently the reception of immortality and incorruptibility, since this in turn is the cause of our bodily ills being completely eradicated.

"Such is the power of holy baptism: it gives you the hope of those (blessings) to come, it offers you a participation in those awaited (gifts); in the types and mysteries of those blessings to come it causes you, through the gift of the Holy Spirit, to receive the firstfruits of them when you are baptized."[177]

The reader may find this rather lengthy passage with its heavy style to be tedious reading. There is no denying, however, that only a reading of the passage in its entirety can show the articulation and movement of Theodore's thought. It is like the movement of a pendulum, for it passes continually from sacrament to ultimate realities and back again. At each passage back and forth, he adds another nuance in the hope of finding a solution, which unfortunately never comes.

Theodore uses "type" and "mystery" as parallel terms in referring to the sacrament of baptism; the sacrament can only give the hope of and participation in future gifts, not the gifts themselves, which continue to be future. The sacraments are "figures and mysteries" of those gifts; they give only their firstfruits. It follows that the sacraments give salvation only in a "rough draft," to use Theodore's term. Salvation in the full sense of the word, that is, salvation in more than a rough draft, will be attained only in the last times through the resurrection. Theodore does not express himself as clearly as this, but I think I am accurately conveying his thought, since he does distinguish clearly between the "type" of "filial adoption," namely, sacramental salvation, and "filial adoption" itself, which will come only after death.

Theodore's sacramental theology is highly realistic. He uses a terminology transmitted to him by the tradition, which, by means of typology, has been able to ensure the full ontological density of the sacraments, while at the same time making them simple "participations" in the realities of which they are the sacraments. In this interpretative approach, it is not possible to identify the sacrament with that of which it is the sacrament. "Sacramental" salvation cannot be simply identified with salvation "itself," that is, with salvation as such, which will come only in the last times. The reality surpasses and transcends the "figure."

If we take all these statements and situate them within a modern theological framework of an Aristotelean-Thomist kind, we will end up emptying them of their content and denying any sacramental realism. On the other hand, if we locate them within the Platonizing culture that permeated the world of the Fathers, we can see how the doctrine of "participation" entailed a full ontological density. Consequently, the use of the concept of participation to explain the relation between a sacrament and that of which it is the sacrament is fully able to ensure sacramental realism, while at the same time maintaining that the reality transcends the type and is not reducible to it.

What is Theodore's position? He has inherited an archaic sacramental vocabulary and the theology that it expresses. He himself, however, is now moving in a different order of ideas and is situated within another cultural horizon that is quite different from the Platonizing culture of the early patristic period.

At the same time, however, at this point in his fourteenth *Homily*, when he is confronting the problem of the sacraments and the reality they contain, he is fully dependent on the traditional approach, even though this has now been outdated; what he says is fully intelligible only within this Platonizing cultural framework.

B. Content or Fruit?

A modern reader may not think highly of these problems that, as it were, cut diagonally across Theodore's sacramental theology, and may not be disposed to pay much attention to them. And, indeed, they do seem to be obsolete and of little relevance to contemporary theology. But in reality, no judgment could be more mistaken. For in every period, the problem of the tension between liturgical celebration and eschatology has remained unresolved, especially at the level of content.

The question to be asked here is this: Are the eschatological gifts the content of the sacrament or its fruit? If they are the content, then they are "really present" in the sacrament. If they are the fruit, then they are not really present.

The answer to the question is given in the principle of sacramental theology, which I explained earlier, namely, that the function of a sacrament derives from its nature. In that exposition, I cited the passage in which Theodore says that the Eucharist is the sacrament of immortality and that, therefore, the Spirit must descend on the bread and wine, transform them into the body and blood of Christ, and thereby give them immortality.[178] For Theodore, then, the eschatological gifts are not simply the fruit of the sacrament, but also its content.

It is obvious that the faithful who approach and participate in the sacraments receive salvation and redemption in an inchoative way; only in the last times will they receive it in its fullness. Thus far there is no problem. The problem begins when we take into account that, unlike the fruit of a sacrament, its content is not subject to the distinction between, "beginning" and "fullness." There are not two redemptive works of Christ, one inchoative and present in the sacraments, the other complete and present in the eschaton.[179] Consequently, it is not possible to apply to the content of the sacrament, namely, the redemptive work of Christ that is "present" in them, the same categories that can be applied to the fruit of the sacraments.

Theodore says very clearly that a sacrament is a sacrament by reason of its relation to the eschatological gifts that are really communicated, even if in a way different from the way in which they will be communicated at the end of time. I take as an example this passage that starts as a commentary on a Pauline text:

" 'We who were baptized into Jesus Christ were baptized into his death' (Rom 6:3); we know that death has already been done away with by our Lord the Christ. It is in this faith that we approach him and are baptized, because we want to share henceforth in his death, in the hope of participating in the same (blessings, namely): to rise from the dead in the same way he rose. That is why, when I am baptized, immersing my head, it is the death of our Lord the Christ that I receive, and his burial that I desire to lay hold of; and thereby I truly confess also the resurrection of our Lord; while when I come out of the water, I regard myself as already risen in a kind of type."[180]

Here is another passage[181] that is the clearest of all in fixing the difference between the sacramental realism of salvation and the "effective" implementation of salvation in the eschatological phase. Theodore begins by saying: "This, then, will effectively take place at the resurrection, whereas it is types and figures that we perform in baptism." At this point, he introduces a citation from Colossians 2:19 that tells us that "we are also called the body of our Lord the Christ"; he does so in order to justify the parallel between what happens in the body of Christ himself, namely, the resurrection, and what will happen in each of who are members of the Church through baptism. We now receive baptism; the resurrection will follow later. This succession of two phases is analogous to what happened in Christ.

"Even our Lord the Christ, before his resurrection from the dead, was seen to receive baptism from John the Baptist in the river Jordan, for the purpose of serving in advance as the type of the present baptism which by his grace we are to receive. For, 'since he was the first-born from among the dead,' as blessed Paul says, 'in order that he might be first in all things' (Col 1:18), it was not only in the reality of the resurrection that he willed to be first for you, but also in its type. It was for this reason that he accepted to be baptized by John (the Baptist), and thereby sketched in advance the type of the grace of this baptism which you are going to receive, so that in this respect too he might become your head."

There can be no doubt that there is a gap, a real difference, between the messianic blessings (which spring from the resurrection) as content of the eschatological phase and as content of the sacraments. In the text just cited, the eschatological phase is described as "reality" and the sacrament as "type." It follows from this that the type is a type because it is a participation in the reality; in this case, participation is not identity.

The situation is even clearer in Theodore's discussion of the Eucharist as sacrifice. In these homilies, we often find the statement that the Eucharist is a sacrifice. The statement is already explicit in the text of the Ritual, which is then further developed in Theodore's commentary: "Above all, you must know this: that what we receive as food is a kind of sacrifice that we carry out."[182]

In his ensuing commentary, Theodore is concerned to safeguard two truths: (a) this sacrifice is not a new sacrifice in relation to Calvary, and (b) the bishop who presides at the liturgical celebration does not carry out a sacrifice of his own. Theodore is hereby stating that the celebration contains nothing new, but is a memorial of the true sacrifice that took place on Calvary.[183]

His point of departure is the recognition that the Eucharist is an action performed as a memorial and narration of the Lord's death. The difficulty he runs up against in arguing to the sacrificial character of the Eucharist is this: while the sacrifice of Christ, by Theodore's own definition, consists in the "true" immolation of which the Eucharist is a memorial, the Eucharist itself is first and foremost a sacrament of future blessings, that is, of the eschatological gifts: "Since it is the signs of the (realities) of heaven that he [the bishop] performs in type, this sacrifice must also be their manifestation."[184]

It is clear that the two things—the immolation and the heavenly blessings—are present in the same way. The bishop: (1) does not carry out a sacrifice of his own, but that of Christ; and (2) this sacrifice must be a sign of the realities of heaven. Also to be taken into account is the fact that sacrifice is identified with immolation and never with resurrection, since resurrection remains linked to the theme of eschatological life. Furthermore, in keeping with customary terminology, "sacrifice" is also a word applied to the holy bread that the faithful eat.[185]

I may therefore conclude that Theodore is aware of the problem of the difference between eschatology and sacrament, not only at the level of the fruits of redemption, but also at the level of redemption as such.

We must be prepared to recognize that once the problem of the relation between eschatology and sacrament was raised, it would inevitably, and quickly, cease to be thus narrowly defined and would reveal its true scope. It would become the problem of the relation between "event" and "sacrament," that is, between "history" (and not just "eschatology") and "sacrament." This broadening of the horizon has already occurred in Theodore himself. He raises the question of the content of the Eucharist in relation to the passion of Christ and, espousing the cause of eucharistic realism, answers that Christ is immolated "anew." In an analogous solution, he also says that the eucharistic bread is the body of Christ and not just its "type."

XI. CONCLUSION

Given the equivalence between redemption and the resurrection of human beings (as a participation in the resurrection of Christ), it is clear that the sacramental phase of redemption has different characteristics than the eschatological phase of the same. The eschatological phase is superior to the sacramental and not reducible to it. The theological problem is thus raised and resolved.

The first step in any solution is not to deny either sacramental realism or the difference between eschatology and sacrament.[186] Theodore proceeds correctly in this respect. In fact, he begins by asserting sacramental realism together with eschatological transcendence; he then turns to the relation between the sacramental and eschatological phases of redemption in order to gain a better understanding of sacramental efficacy.

He is quite familiar with the sacramental vocabulary that he has inherited along the ancient tradition of biblical typology. But he does not seem able to use these in order to build a solution of the problem I have been raising. We might think that the inability is due to an exegetical method that is Antiochene and incapable of working with typology.[187] But this hypothesis cannot be reconciled with the data. For Theodore shows that he is well able, even if in a very limited way, to practice typology both in its strict form and in a broader form that develops at times into very colorful allegory. In this respect, he provides a parallel to Ambrose, who, as we have seen, is a splendid practictioner of both typology and allegory; yet there are cases in which Ambrose, too, shows himself unable to adopt and make fruitful use of typology as a form of sacramental theology that can resolve the problem of the relation between saving event and sacrament.

I should conclude, I think, by offering a more general explanation of the situation. When we study the end of the fourth century, we find ourselves faced with a broader problem than that which shows up in individual authors. We are not dealing simply with the inadequacy or incapacity that may be found in individual Fathers of the Church.

To put the matter in its simplest terms: the end of the fourth century marks the end of a world and its culture. A cultural horizon of a Platonizing kind, with its world-vision based on "participation," is no longer enough. It can no longer serve as an adequate guide to the Fathers, for as they face the problem of sacramental efficacy and realism, they no longer feel that biblical typology applied to the sacramental datum is a sufficient guarantee and protection.

Their interest is focused henceforth on the redemptive content of the sacraments: on what the sacraments are in themselves and on their intrinsic efficacy, rather than on the more or less ontological relation they have with the saving events narrated in the Scriptures. As a result, the vocabulary and theology of typological thought, though able to guarantee the connection between various saving realities that are distant from one another, are no longer capable of giving a satisfactory answer to the problems now being raised. Typology in the strict sense ceases, therefore, to play a role in sacramental theology; the vocabulary of typology and the biblical images associated with them do continue in use, but their meanings are henceforth different and even at odds with the logic of typology.

Let us look at a passage in Theodore that displays this new situation, for in it, the author goes beyond the special meaning that typology had regularly given to the term "truth." He is here relating the sacramental celebration to the event of which it is the sacrament, namely, the immolation of Christ. The historical saving event is described as "true" in relation to the "type." It would seem that he feels compelled here to use the most archaic of sacramental terminologies, while at the same time being unable to take advantage of its theological content. But in fact the word "true" is being used here not in the typological sense but in the ordinary sense: "Clearly, then, there is a sacrifice, without there being anything and without the sacrifice being the bishop's own; rather it is a memorial of that true immolation."[188]

Although Theodore clearly opts for sacramental realism, and this even in the immediate context of the sentence just cited, when he comes to the problem of the relation between saving historical event and sacrament, he has no other way than this of placing the question. As a result, he decides to think of the sacrament as the *type* and the historical event as the *truth*. But since he is unable take advantage of the theological import of the terminology, he ends up opposing *type* and *reality*:

"At the moment of giving the bread he did not say 'This is the type of my body,' but 'This is my body,' and in like manner the chalice: not 'This is the type of my blood,' but 'This is my blood,' for, now that these [the bread and wine] had received the grace and coming of the Holy Spirit, he wanted us to look no longer at their natural being but to take them as being the body and blood of our Lord."[189]

The necessary conclusion from all this is that Theodore's theology is incapable of explaining the relation between sacrament and event (be the latter historical or eschatological) so as to maintain the transcendence of the event while at the same time not denying sacramental realism. Theodore limits himself to affirming both requirements and is unable to give an account of the reciprocal intrinsic connection between them. The connection formerly guaranteed by biblical typology is no longer guaranteed in this way; this is clear from the effects just now formulated. Theodore uses typology, but he uses it as a tool that no longer has a place in his cultural horizon; he uses it while standing outside it, as it were; he uses it because it is the fashion.

Theodore uses typology, but the thinking it produces is not typological.

At this point, I must introduce a verbal clarification. The word "typology," which I have been using thus far, designates either a particular method of biblical interpretation or the liturgical and sacramental use of this method of reading the Scriptures. Properly speaking, when typology is used in interpreting the liturgy and the sacraments, it is called "mystagogy," but in order to avoid confusion, I have not used this word.

At the end of my discussion of Ambrose, I said that at times Ambrose postdates himself. I must now add that Theodore, who is from the same period, postdates Ambrose by far.

CHAPTER FOUR

John Chrysostom

Chrysostom was a close friend of Theodore. Like the latter, he was a native of Antioch; like him, too, he was a pupil of the pagan Sophist, Libanius, and subsequently of Diodore, who became bishop of Tarsus in Cilicia in 378.

When John Chrysostom was eighteen, Blessed Meletius, bishop of Antioch, was so taken by the young man's talents that he allowed him to be his constant companion. John was accepted for baptism, the bath of regeneration, and, after three years in the bishop's service, was promoted to the office of lector. This information comes to us from the life of Chrysostom that Palladius, bishop of Helenopolis, wrote before 415.[1]

Theodore and Chrysostom thus lived in the same city, Antioch, at the same period; they had the same kind of formation and shared the same enthusiasm for monasticism. Both became priests in Antioch and both preached to the candidates for baptism. Theodore was ordained a priest in 383. Chrysostom was ordained a deacon by Meletius in 381 and a priest by Flavian in 386. His ordination took place at the beginning of Lent, and he immediately began to preach.[2] Theodore, for his part, preached his mystagogical homilies during the period from 381 to 392, according to the opinion of his editor[3]; we must bear in mind, however, that it is questionable whether these homilies were preached at Antioch.[4]

Theodore later became bishop of Mopsuestia; Chrysostom was tricked and forced to become bishop of Constantinople. The relationship between these two great natives of Antioch did not, however, end when they became bishops, and Theodore was to show an unqualified solidarity with Chrysostom in the latter's dramatic exile.[5] Because of their common Antiochene origin and their continued fellowship, it is impossible to study Theodore without also taking into account the baptismal instructions of John Chrysostom.

Theodore's homilies are well constructed on the basis of typology; in addition, they are of great importance theologically because of the way in which eschatology is constantly related to the doctrine of sacramentality. The homilies of John Chrysostom, on the other hand, are more concerned with directly pastoral aspects of the sacrament and therefore allow greater scope for moral exhortation. What of typology? This, too, is constantly present in Chrysostom, even if it is not always in the foreground. In fact, the great Chrysostom often loses control of his discourse: under the influence of pastoral concern, he allows himself extensive digressions full of moral exhortation. Even here, however, we cannot say that he shortchanges typology. We must bear in mind that in the last analysis, the moral dimension is one aspect of typology, that is, one of the "four senses" that Scripture has when read spiritually.

It is clear, then, that Theodore and Chrysostom are closer than they might seem.

I. THE CATECHETICAL HOMILIES OF CHRYSOSTOM

A. The Choice of Texts
It is a simple matter to identify the mystagogical texts of such authors as Cyril of Jerusalem, Ambrose, Theodore of Mopsuestia, Maximus the Confessor, or Cabasilas. The matter is less simple when we turn to an author such as Chrysostom, as is clear because until quite recently, he was not recognized as having preached any series of mystagogical homilies,[6] although his writings do contain various homilies addressed to the candidates for baptism. Among the latter are two homilies, entitled "First Instruction" and "Second Instruction" by their editor, Montfaucon.[7] Four other homilies, the first of which has its counterpart in the edition of Fronton du Duc, were found and published by A. Papadopoulos-Kerameus; the second, third, and fourth had not been published previously.[8] Until 1955, however,

no complete series was known that embraced the whole of "Christian initiation."

On October 5, 1955, in the library of the monastery of Stavronikita on Mount Athos, Father Antoine Wenger found a codex containing homilies of Chrysostom (Stavronikita ms. 6). Eight of these had never been published and formed a complete series of baptismal instructions that we may describe as mystagogical. Father Wenger published them in 1957 and, in a second edition, in 1970.[9]

At Antioch, John Chrysostom had been appointed official preacher by Bishop Flavian, and he filled this office for twelve years, from 386 to 397.[10] We may, therefore, take it as certain that several times he developed the entire cycle of instructions that in part were an element in the preparation of catechumens for baptism and in part were addressed to the newly baptized in the week immediately following the sacrament, that is, the week after Easter. The discovery of the Stavronikita homilies shows what a complete cycle of mystagogical instructions was like. As a result, it is now possible to look for traces of other cycles in other texts of Chrysostom; this Father Wenger has done.

The existence of this series of homilies has shed new light on other, previously known texts,[11] such as Montfaucon's *First* and *Second Instruction* and the homilies published by A. Papadopoulos-Kerameus. Wenger's conclusions have been further confirmed by Paul Harkins[12]; to the latter's name, we can add those of A. Ceresa-Gastaldo[13] and D. Sartore.[14]

If we accept the subdivision proposed by Wenger, we can say that the catechetical homilies of Chrysostom belong to three different cycles of baptismal instructions. Here is how Wenger distinguishes the three series: (1) the first cycle, made up of the four homilies of the Papadopoulos-Kerameus series; (2) the second cycle, comprising Montfaucon's *Second Instruction* (the only surviving homily of this series); and (3) the third cycle, comprising the eight homilies of the Stavronikita series.[15] Since these are three parallel cycles, I must make a choice; for my purpose in analyzing the texts, I must choose the most complete series, the

Stavronikita, while keeping an eye at all times on the other two series.[16]

B. *The Date of the Texts*

On this important question, I am obliged to accept the carefully reasoned position of A. Wenger.

John Chrysostom began his preaching in 386. The eight Stavronikita homilies cannot date from that year because it was then that he preached the eight sermons on Genesis, and these display a style much different from that of the baptismal homilies.

The year 387 brought the homilies on the statues, with their heavy emphasis on the theme of oaths; this emphasis explains why Montfaucon assigned his *Homily* 1 to that same year. But Papadopolous-Kerameus later discovered three homilies (his homilies two, three, and four) that belong to the same series as Montfaucon's *Homily* 1. The four form a complete series, which cannot have been preached in 387. In fact, these four homilies are completely silent about (1) the terrible events of March, when the emperor threatened to take vengeance on the city for the insult offered to the imperial statues, and about (2) the happy return of Bishop Flavian with the emperor's pardon (at Easter, 387).

In 387, Chrysostom did preach a series of mystagogical homilies, all but one of which are lost, namely, *Homily* 21 on the statues, which was preached on Easter Sunday. This homily, the only survivor of the entire catechetical cycle of that year, is identical with Montfaucon's *Homily* 2.[17] This is a further reason for maintaining that the series of homilies published by Papadopoulos-Kerameus cannot have been delivered in 387. According to Wenger, this is even truer of the Stavronikita homilies.[18]

In 388, Chrysostom preached the customary cycle of instructions addressed to the candidates for baptism. This cycle comprises the first three homilies of Papadopoulos-Kerameus, followed by homilies 1–4 on the Acts of the Apostles[19] and by a fifth homily now lost.

Wenger, therefore, also excludes 388 as the year when the Stavronikita series was preached. But because of linguistic similarities with the thirty-two homilies on Genesis, which were preached in 388, he maintains that the Stavronikita series must have been preached not long after.[20] Perhaps in 390? Perhaps.[21]

All the catechetical homilies listed are mystagogical and belong to the period of Chrysostom's ministry in Antioch.

II. THE DISTINGUISHING TRAITS OF CHRYSOSTOM'S MYSTAGOGY

A. The Problem of the Moral Thematic
In his catechetical homilies, Chrysostom aims at preparing the catechumens for baptism in such a way that the sacrament will be fruitful. Therefore, when commenting on the baptismal liturgy and the various ritual elements in it, he lays heavy emphasis on the moral obligations flowing from them. This is to say that his mystagogy stresses an element not present like anything to the same extent in the mystagogy of the other Fathers of the Church: the continual emphasis on Christian moral behavior.

In Chrysostom's writings, Christian initiation is seen as closely connected with two things: a strictly orthodox faith and the control of one's own behavior. He makes an explicit, formal statement about this twofold connection: "Such is the strictness we wish you to show in regard to the dogmas of the Church, and we desire you to keep them fast fixed in your minds. It is also fitting that those who manifest such faith shine forth by their good conduct. Hence, I must also instruct in this matter those who are about to receive the royal gift."[22] This clearly enunciated outlook explains the emphasis on the moral consequences of baptism in Chrysostom's homilies.

A little reflection shows, of course, that Chrysostom's attitude is not a complete novelty, for every mystagogy allows some room for the problem of moral behavior. Even Theodore of Mopsuestia regards proper Christian behavior as playing an extremely important part in the attainment of the eternal blessings, to the point that he even develops a "theology of Christian living" in the true and proper sense of the term. In this view, it is by their lives that believers develop the "firstfruits" and "seeds" received in baptism, making them grow and come to maturity; it is as a result of this activity that believers are able to attain to the gift of the eternal blessings. But, perhaps, I ought to explain Theodore's thinking more fully.

In Theodore's view, the fruit of baptism, that is, what flows from the sacrament, cannot be defined simply as "the beginning of eternal blessings." For analogous reasons, life is not simply an interval between baptism and the eternal blessings. The fruit of baptism becomes part of life and takes up residence therein like the seed of a plant. This seed is assimilated and brought to maturity by Christian living, so that the invisible component of the baptismal rite is transformed into experiential life. To explain this situation, Theodore uses the example of the human seed that plays a part in procreation. Here is his fine description.

"It ought not surprise us that we receive a twofold birth and that we proceed from the one to the other, for even in our bodily development we have a twofold birth, one from a man and then another from a woman. First we are born, in a seminal state, from a man, without having the least resemblance to a human being; everyone knows, of course, that the seed has no resemblance to a human being. But when the seed has been conceived and molded in accordance with the laws God has established and imposed on nature, and when it has acquired a form and is born of a woman, then it acquires its likeness to human nature.

"In like manner we have a double [spiritual] birth. First of all, we are born in a seminal state in baptism; at this point we are not yet born into the immortal nature to which we expect to pass through the resurrection; in fact, we have not even acquired the likeness. But when, through faith and through hope of those (blessings) that are to come, we form and mold ourselves according to Christian ways of acting, and (when we have) remained steadfast until the time of the resurrection, then, in accordance with the divine decree, we who have been dust will acquire the second birth and take on that immortal and incorruptible nature, when 'Christ our Lord will transform our lowly bodies,' as

Blessed Paul says, 'and these will become like his glorious body' (Phil 3:21)."[23]

The same logical pattern supplies the framework within which Theodore discusses the Eucharist, for the Eucharist is essentially food, and food precisely for a Christian life conceived in the way just described. Here is a passage on the subject:

"For you, then, who have been begotten by grace and the coming of the Holy Spirit in baptism and have received this sanctification, it is fitting that there be a food which you receive through grace and the coming of the Holy Spirit and which is of like kind, so that it strengthens and develops the sanctification already given to you and leads you to the attainment of the awaited blessings."[24]

The thought here is completed in another passage: "The body and blood of our Lord and the grace of the Holy Spirit that is given to us thereby [that is, by "receiving the mysteries"] will win us help to do good works and will strengthen our (good) dispositions."[25]

Theodore here gives us a true and proper theology of Christian life in its relationship to both worship and eschatology. In his view, the connection between life and liturgy is not reducible to the question of whether or not we are worthy to approach the sacrament. His emphasis is rather on a theology of living: it is a life made fruitful by the fruits of the sacrament that will lead us to the attainment of the eschatological blessings. The sacrament is linked to the eschatological blessings, not directly and immediately (as "beginning" and "consummation"), but only through the mediation of the life we live.

There is a principle in Chrysostom's theology that must guide our interpretation of his thinking on morality: the principle that God saves human beings without any merit on their part. Chrysostom constantly repeats this principle as a premise of his discussion; next, he shows that God's mercy is manifested in saving human beings when they are still sinners[26]; only in third place does he stress the importance of behavior that is in accord with God's will and to which God then responds by granting still further graces. On these basic principles, Chrysostom builds an *a fortiori* argument: if God shows mercy when human beings are still sinners, much more does he show it when they respond positively to him.

The human response is thus very important. Chrysostom describes it as "contributing your fair share."[27] Human beings are not purely passive in receiving the work of redemption; they collaborate through their ascetical efforts, which are not reducible to a "doing nothing," but rather represent "their fair share." We can say that in Chrysostom, this formulation of the idea is almost a technical term[28] and recurs quite frequently.

In order to bring out more clearly the theological importance of the Christian's manner of life (and thus the similarity between Chrysostom and Theodore), I shall cite some passages in which Chrysostom expresses his theology of Christian living. Christians must take their "contribution" to the work that God accomplished in them in their baptism: "Our Master is kind; when He sees your gratitude for what He has already given, and that you are very careful to guard His great gifts, He bestows His grace upon you in abundance. Even if our contribution is small. He lavishes His great gifts upon us."[29]

The human response, however, consists not simply of gratitude, but also a certain behavior:

"Even though you had never done anything good, even though you had the burden of your sins lying heavy upon you, He imitated his own goodness and judged you worthy of these great gifts. For He not only delivered you from your sins and gave you justification by His grace, but He also showed you forth as holy and made you His sons by adoption. If He has taken the lead in giving you such gifts, if you are eager, after receiving so much, to contribute your fair share, if you will show care in guarding and managing the gifts that have already been given, how can He fail to judge you worthy again of still greater gifts?"[30]

Speaking of St. Paul as a witness who "contributed his fair share," Chrysostom tells us still more clearly in what this "contribution" consists: "Did you see how he reaped the benefit of God's liberality and then abundantly contributed his own share—I mean his zeal, his fervor, his faith, his courage, his patience, his lofty mind, and his undated will? This is why he deserved a larger measure of help from above."[31]

Despite some similarities between the two, it is not possible, in my opinion, to claim that Chrysostom is here proposing the doctrine of merit as understood and formulated in the West. I suggest rather that Chrysostom's thinking here is closer to Theodore's "theology of Christian living." The result is a very great emphasis on Christian living, and this precisely within the mystagogical approach and precisely because of its sacramental starting point, for, as we saw in the first of these passages from Chrysostom, his argument is based on his theology of the sacrament and its saving efficacy.

John Chrysostom and Theodore both were priests and preachers in the same city and at the same period. It is not surprising, therefore, that in their mystagogical instructions, both should emphasize the same theme: Christian living. What, then, is the difference between the two? Whereas Theodore highlights the importance of actual living by accentuating the relation between sacrament and eschatology, Chrysostom speaks directly, and with great fervor, of the several forms of moral behavior that call for censure or praise.

I think it can be said that the two men adopt the same perspective, but also that they approach it in two quite different ways.

It is very likely that Chrysostom's outlook is due to his having kept closer ties with a monastic formation that had been marked by rural simplicity. In justification of this interpretation, I call attention to the theme of "the angelic life," which Chrysostom sets before the faithful as a model for their behavior. In Theodore, the same theme is emphatically eschatological; in Chrysostom, however, "the angelic life" is the monastic life. Monks, he says, "imitate the angels' way of life"[32] inasmuch as, like the angels, "they devote [themselves] to hymns and prayers."[33] According to him, monks alone imitate the angels,[34] so that when the phrase "angelic life" occurs without further specification, we must think that he is referring to the monastic way.

The connection between asceticism and eschatology is quite clear here.[35] Conversely, the eschatological vision becomes the theme of monastic asceticism. At the same time, John Chrysostom has a program of Christian life that is inspired by the monastic ideal. He proposes this program to all, even the newly "enlightened," for in his view, this is the surest way of bringing Christians to heed the Lord. "If the soul is to live according to the Spirit it must be solidly established in temperance and in spiritual watchfulness," these being the essential conditions Chrysostom requires for any progress in virtue.[36]

We are far removed here from the eschatological theme expounded with such breadth and depth by Theodore. It is this difference in emphasis that chiefly differentiates the two writers, even though their ideas on the "theology of Christian living" are very similar.

In light of all these considerations, I think I can conclude that John Chrysostom's mystagogy calls for a very careful and nuanced judgment; it is certainly not to be described simplistically as "moralism." In his baptismal instructions, there is never any neglect of mystagogy in the proper and specific sense of the term, although it is admittedly handled in a quite particular way, namely, with a strong emphasis on moral behavior. This is not surprising, for this emphasis is one that Chrysostom found more congenial.

B. The Problem of the Eucharistic Thematic

It can be said in general that the several known authors of mystagogical homilies deal with baptism and, immediately afterwards, with the Eucharist.[37] Chrysostom's catechetical homilies, however, deal at length only with baptism and its immediate moral consequences; they do not directly tackle the Eucharist, which indeed is present only through allusions. We must, therefore, inquire into the reasons that led John Chrysostom thus to reduce the traditional place of the Eucharist in his instructions.

In order to find the explanation, I shall proceed by stages, as I bring together the various available factors and elements.

(a) Instructions on initiation and therefore on baptism and the Eucharist fall into two categories: (1) those delivered before the celebration of baptism, and (2) those delivered after the celebration of the sacraments of initiation. It is the homilies in the second category that are usually described as "mystagogical instructions."

Thus, Ambrose tells us that his mystagogical homilies, which were delivered after the listeners had received the sacraments, were preceded by a lengthy catechesis that had for its purpose to form the candidates so that their reception of baptism would be fruitful. The baptismal homilies of Cyril of Jerusalem were intended as a preparation for baptism, whereas those of Theodore of Mopsuestia were delivered in two stages: before baptism, the homilies on the Creed and the Our Father and the three on baptism; and after baptism the two on the Eucharist.

Chrysostom's catechetical homilies were likewise delivered in two stages: those dealing with baptism were delivered prior to baptism, during the period of preparation that began thirty days before Easter; and those dealing with the moral behavior of Christians were delivered during the week after Easter. The first homily in the Stavronikita series was delivered (it can be maintained) thirty days before Easter.[38] The second was delivered a few days before Easter, whereas the second in the Papadopoulos-Kerameus series was delivered on Holy Thursday. The third Stavronikita homily, which is the same as the fourth in the Papadopoulos-Kerameus series, is assigned to Easter morning.[39] The remaining five were delivered during Easter week,[40] the last of them on Easter Saturday.

(b) The practice of explaining the sacraments only after Christian initiation has been completed seems to stem from the discipline of secrecy (the *arcanum*)[41]; this is the case with John Chrysostom.[42] At the same time, however, according to Chrysostom, the discipline of secrecy also explicitly applies to the homilies delivered in preparation for baptism; for this reason, I do not think it quite accurate to make the discipline of secrecy the explanation of why the homilies explaining the sacraments were delivered only after these sacraments had been received. But, at the present time, we have no better explanations and, therefore, have no choice but to attribute the phenomenon to the discipline of secrecy.

Since the sacraments of initiation were celebrated at Easter and the mystagogical explanation was given only after this celebration, we can understand why the mystagogical explanation came during Easter week.

(c) The homilies that Chrysostom preached during Easter week deal predominantly with questions of morality. They exhort the newly "enlightened" to live as they were taught and as they in fact lived during the time of their preparation for baptism. They must continue to live as people who have been enlightened and to abstain from sin as though they were living in a new permanent Lent. Chrysostom can use this image because, in his view and that of other Fathers, the essential Lenten practice is the fast from sin. The fifth instruction has for its purpose precisely to inspire in the newly baptized a specific outlook, namely, that like Lent and Easter week, the rites and observances connected with baptism do not lose their meaning after a certain assigned period, but become a school of Christian living for the faithful.[43] In fact, the fruit of baptism in Christians should be that they reach the point of constantly doing God's will. The need of this kind of exhortation was not pressing during Lent, because the fast already suggested it. It is rather now that the problem of perseverance becomes urgent.[44]

It is possible at this point to draw a conclusion that is very important for properly assessing the emphasis on morality in the post-Easter instructions: Chrysostom bases the moral content of his preaching on the sacramental rites and observances of Christian initiation, his purpose being that the effect of these rites and observances should carry over into Christian life. His preaching thus has the same function as the liturgical observances of the postbaptismal period.

It can be said that what we have here is a properly sacramental conception of preaching, rather than a predominantly moral conception of Christian initiation. In fact, if we think of the Lenten fast as an *image* of a "fast from sin," we are taking a completely theological (and not a moralistic) approach to the liturgy of Christian initiation.[45]

Chrysostom is very conscious of the problem Christians face of persevering in the baptism they have received, so that they will remain "enlightened" for a lifetime and not just for a week. This is in fact a problem not only for those recently baptized, but for all the faithful, regardless of how long ago they were baptized. Consequently, Chrysostom's postbaptismal homilies are directed to all the faithful and not simply to the neophytes; "the postbaptismal instructions are not mystagogical instructions after the manner of Cyril and Ambrose, but are addressed to all the faithful."[46]

(d) We can take one further step in our attempt at a better understanding of Chrysostom's position.

According to Chrysostom, baptism takes sin away, gives the Holy Spirit, and makes us the body of Christ. This is a very rich theology of baptism, and he expounds it by lengthy developments of numerous motifs, including original sin.[47]

The theology of Christian initiation that Chrysostom represents allows plenty of room for the discussion of baptism. In baptism, believers receive the grace of rebirth and the gift of the Spirit, and are thereby already committed to God. All conditions have been met and they have now become worthy of approaching the royal banquet table, that is, the Eucharist. In Chrysostom's baptismal theology, the primary purpose of the Eucharist is to sustain and augment the strength needed for the struggle against the demon and his manifestations (his "pomps"). A further function is to show forth the magnificence of the baptismal calling.

The theme of the struggle against the demon has Christian initiation as its proper setting: the exorcisms and renunciation of Satan are heavily emphasized. Chrysostom regards the renunciation of Satan as extremely important[48] and he even seems to look upon it as sacramental in the strict sense.[49] In fact, the entire interpretation of baptism is based on an analogy with a struggle against an adversary; the adversary in this case is evidently the devil.

Since the Eucharist is part of Christian initiation, we shall not be surprised to find that it, too, is interpreted and described in terms of this special theology of initiation; that is, even the Eucharist is interpreted as a factor in the spiritual struggle against Satan. God has not only prepared the weapons that baptism provides for this conflict, "he has also prepared a food which is more powerful than any armor."[50] The explanation given in the passage here cited makes it very clear how Chrysostom looks at the Eucharist insofar as the Eucharist is part of Christian initiation. For here the Eucharist is not connected with the events of Christ's redemptive work, but is looked upon simply as something endowed with inherent power and, therefore, as useful to the person who receives it. The purpose of the Eucharist, as seen in this perspective, is to repulse the demon: "If the devil merely sees you returning from the Master's banquet, he flees faster than any wind, as if he had seen a lion breathing forth flames from his mouth."[51]

This description of the Eucharist is not simply one tossed off in passing, for Chrysostom expresses himself in similar terms elsewhere, thus showing that the perspective imposed by Christian initiation is constantly maintained and is part of his eucharistic theology as such. Thus, he says in another passage: "Let us come away from that table like fire-breathing lions of whom the devil is afraid."[52]

There is indeed a certain progression in Chrysostom's thinking. From the idea that the devil flees on seeing those who have received the body and blood of Christ, the homilist advances to the idea that the eucharistic blood in its physical reality has this effect on Satan: "If you show him a tongue stained with the precious blood, he will not be able to make a stand; if you show him your mouth all crimsoned and ruddy, cowardly beast that he is, he will run away."[53]

John Chrysostom approaches the theology of the Eucharist in this way, not because he advocates a superstitious use of the Eucharist, but because he takes his lead from the main themes of

Christian initiation. Since he takes initiation as his guide, he wants his entire explanation to be immediately reducible and applicable to Christian life, more specifically, to Christian life interpreted as a combat.

Given the thematic of Christian initiation as Chrysostom sees it, the Eucharist does not play a major role because it is simply the "food" for the life born in baptism.

Theodore, too, emphasizes the food aspect of the Eucharist. By doing so he is able to combine baptism and Eucharist in a single system that can be formulated in this way: the food by which the faithful are nourished must be consistent with their birth in baptism.[54] This kind of eucharistic theology was probably not one Theodore had developed for himself, but was rather characteristic of the Antiochene tradition. And, in fact, this very specialized theme is also to be found in Chrysostom: "Have you seen how Christ unites to Himself His bride? Have you seen with what food He nourishes us all? It is by the same food that we have been formed and are fed. Just as a woman nurtures her offspring with her own blood and milk, so also Christ continuously nourishes with His own blood those whom He has begotten."[55]

The mystagogical homilies of the other Fathers of the Church allow plenty of room for explanation of the gestures and texts that make up the eucharistic rite. Not so with Chrysostom. In his baptismal instructions, the Eucharist is described in terms of its effects and is seen as part of the life that originates in baptism rather than as part of the ritual of initiation as such. This peculiar approach is easily explained by the fact that the really important thing in Chrysostom's eyes is the direct connection between baptism and the moral life.

The eucharistic thematic, then, no less than the theme of moral behavior, belongs among the things that are explained to the faithful generally rather than among the specific points that the newly baptized need to have explained to them. See, for example, how Chrysostom ends his discussion of the Eucharist: "I speak both to you, the neophytes, and to you who have long since been instructed—even many years ago."[56]

In conclusion: references to the Eucharist in the baptismal instructions of Chrysostom are few and terse. The reason for this, in my opinion, is that Chrysostom chooses only themes that contribute to the main point of his theology of initiation, namely, that the fruit of baptism is the gift of justification and that this gift must find adequate expression in everyday life as a struggle against Satan. Because of this doctrinal approach, the homilist must turn directly to practice. He emphasizes the truth that baptism and its fruits are irreconcilable with certain forms of behavior, such as swearing, drunkenness, the shows in the hippodrome and stadiums, and the preference for amusements over liturgical gatherings.

According to the logic followed by Chrysostom, it is important that newly enlightened Christians live in a manner consistent with the rebirth they have received and "contribute their fair share." They will receive from the Eucharist all the strength they need to live in this way and to win out in their struggle against the demon. If this is the primary function of the Eucharist, then we must say that Chrysostom expresses himself with sufficient clarity on the subject and that after his explanation, the newly baptized need only put into practice the message they have received.

III. "MORALITY" AS A THEOLOGY OF INITIATION

We saw earlier that in his sacramental theology, Theodore of Mopsuestia lays great stress on eschatology, to the point even that eschatological realities become the very content of the sacrament. This emphasis raises no small problems in connection with sacramental realism, since this, by definition, remains unalterably eschatological and does not allow ritual anticipations. Here some further clarification is needed. If the realities to be achieved at the end of time include the resurrection of the body, immutability, and impassibility, then evidently there can be no ritual anticipation of these nor even a ritual approach to them.

Anyone maintaining this conception of the eschaton must necessarily regard the theology of Christian living, which I explained before, as extremely important. Furthermore, as I have already pointed out, Theodore also assigns the eschatological theme a moral function: we humans must become like the invisible powers, those heavenly powers that constantly glorify God.

John Chrysostom never loses sight of the importance of the gifts to be given at the end. Consequently, when he has to describe redemption, he presents it precisely as the gift of immortality: "He showed the devil how foolish were his attempts; He showed man the great care He manifested in his regard, for through death He gave man everlasting life."[57] The eschaton thus remains fully present in the form of a tension and as a model for living, but it is completely eliminated as the content of the sacraments.

At the same time, however, there must continue to be some connection between eschatology and sacrament since the life of believers springs from the sacraments and is ordered to the gifts of the eschaton. Chrysostom, therefore, retains a degree of connection between sacrament and eschatology, for the straining toward the ultimate blessings, which is proper to Christian life, originates directly in the content of initiation. The passage that I shall now cite is very clear on this point. After speaking out strongly against the excessive desire for elegance and external embellishments and after citing 1 Timothy 2:9 in support of his criticism, Chrysostom concludes: "Do deeds worthy of your profession he [the Apostle] says, and adorn yourself with good deeds. Let the good deeds you do imitate your profession; you profess godliness, so do what is pleasing to Him, that is, good deeds."[58]

According to Chrysostom, the imitation of Christ through Christian living has a very specific connection with baptism, for it involves an "imitation" of the profession of faith made in baptism. If we are to grasp the precise meaning of the term "imitation" in Chrysostom, we must turn to a quite special phrase that he uses with a precise technical meaning. When he speaks of God acting with mercy and kindness toward his creatures, he usually says that God "imitates His own goodness" when he so acts.[59] In other words, the interior, essential goodness of God is the basis and source of his action toward his creatures; his essential goodness is the basic model for all of his activities; in all his actions, he *reproduces* his essential goodness *ad extra.*

"Imitation" and "imitate" retain this same meaning when Chrysostom says that the behavior of the baptized should be an "imitation" of their profession of faith. The faithful must *reproduce* outwardly, in their behavior, the baptismal "godliness" that consists in their covenant with God; from this it follows that the good works done by Christians are an offshoot of their baptism. These good works include "yearning for the world to come" and "keeping our gaze ever straining upward, so that we are ever anxious for the things of heaven and desire the glory hereafter."[60]

Christians are able to act in this way only because in baptism they acquire the eyes of faith that allow them to see things that the eyes of the body cannot. It is very important to note that the theme of spiritual eyes also has an eschatological dimension, inasmuch as because of the great hope given to them, the newly baptized must henceforth keep their eyes fixed on heaven, in accordance with Paul's exhortation (Col 3:2). When Christians think of the things that are above, they "change their thoughts from earth to heaven, from visible things to those that are unseen" but that their spiritual eyes can see more clearly than the eyes of the body can see sensible things.[61]

Here we have the principle underlying the moral approach to the life of the baptized; the principle arises from the content of the sacrament and from faith. Among the fruits of baptism, Chrysostom includes one eschatological gift. Using a very effective literary device ("not only free, but also holy; not only holy . . ."), he names ten effects that he arranges in a progressive order. Human beings were formerly captives of sin, but now they are free, holy, just, sons and daughters, heirs, brothers and sisters of Christ, joint heirs, members, temples, and instruments of the Spirit.[62] In this bountiful list, the only eschatological effect is expressed in the word "heirs," which implies the kingdom of heaven, as is clear from parallel passages: "justification, sanctity, purity of soul, filial adoption, and the kingdom of heaven."[63]

122

The faithful must, therefore, be ever mindful of the ultimate things and always live in the eschatological dimension: their life is no longer earthly, but heavenly. Chrysostom draws all these conclusions in an instruction given during Easter week, as he comments on the life of the martyrs: "They abandoned all things upon earth and gazed with the eyes of faith on the King of heaven and the host of angels standing before Him; they pictured in their minds heaven and its ineffable blessings."[64] The attitude of the martyrs is offered to the faithful as a model, so that they may do likewise:

"When the soul gets an understanding of the ineffable goods of heaven, it is, as it were, loosed from the bonds of the flesh and lifted on high. Each day it pictures to itself the enjoyment of these goods and can take no thought for the things of earth. It sweeps past mundane affairs, as if they were dreams and shadows, and keeps the mind constantly straining toward heaven. With the eyes of faith, it considers that it all but sees the good things from on high and each moment it is alert to enjoy them."[65]

This shift in outlook is made possible by the interior activity of "picturing to oneself" or "setting before one's eyes," which Theodore describes at length. Chrysostom regards this as a means of obtaining the needed straining toward heaven. But the "picturing" is not simply an exercise of fantasy, for baptism has given the faithful a real enrollment in heaven. They are, therefore, picturing things that are real ("heaven") and translating the vision into historical behavior. that is, everyday experience: "It is possible for a man who is still in the embrace of his body to have nothing in common with the earth, but to set before his eyes all the joys of heaven and to contemplate them unceasingly."[66]

This eschatological theme is linked to the words of Paul: "Mind the things that are above"[67]; Chrysostom then further specifies the "above" in a christological sense: "where Christ is seated at the right hand of God."[68] "I wish you to mind," he says, "those things which can carry your thoughts to heaven, the things which withdraw you from the business of the world. *For your citizenship is in heaven.*"[69] Admission to heaven is not, as it might seem, an automatic result of the content of the sacrament; Christians must live their lives here below in order to attain to the heavenly gifts: "Hasten, he [Paul] says, to bring your whole mind to that country where you are enrolled as citizens, and resolve to do the things which can show that you deserve your citizenship in heaven."[70]

The ultimate basis for this radical eschatological tension, which should be characteristic of all the faithful, is to be found in Paul's theology of baptism, which he conceives as a death. Chrysostom writes:

"After he [Paul] said, *Mind the things that are above, not the things that are on earth*, he went on to add: *For you have died.*[71] . . . Your life is no longer seen, for it is hidden. Therefore, do not be active in the things of this life as if you were living, but be as if you had died and were corpses. For tell me this. Is it possible for one who has died as far as this life is concerned, to be active thereafter in the affairs of this life? . . . *For our old self*, he says,[72] *has been crucified and buried through baptism.*"[73]

This key passage has a close parallel in Ambrose[74]; we can think, therefore, that it was characteristic of mystagogy.

Although Chrysostom's eschatological teaching is different from that of his fellow great Antiochene (in whose view salvation *as such* was something essentially eschatological), we may nonetheless conclude that eschatology is not completely absent from his baptismal theology, inasmuch as Christian life has an eschatological character.

IV. THE ANGELS
An eschatological thematic includes the part played by heaven and the heavenly powers. In this area, Chrysostom is more open to the eschatological dimension, for the very first steps that candidates for Christian initiation take bring them into relation to heaven.

Christian initiation begins with the act of enrollment, and Chrysostom connects this first step with a military service: "Let me show them the power of the weapons they are about to re-

ceive."[75] The renunciation of Satan is interpreted as an enrollment in an army[76] and means admission to the city of God: "Let
all of you who have been esteemed worthy of being admitted to
citizenship . . . come forward!"[77] Enrollment in the catechu-
menate is an enrollment in a "heavenly book."[78] The interpretation of baptism as an enrollment in the books of the heavenly
city is one that recurs: "Do you, who are the new soldiers of
Christ, who have this day been inscribed on the citizen lists of
heaven. . . ."[79]

The baptismal rite is likewise explained by analogy with a struggle: just as athletes about to compete in the stadium are
anointed, so Christians are anointed with "the oil of gladness" in
the rite of initiation.[80] The analogy with competition in the stadium is followed by an analogy with armed combat. The meta-
phorical application of military terminology to spiritual weapons
comes from Paul in Ephesians 6:14–17. Chrysostom says that the
breastplate worn by the baptized is made not from metal but
from justice; the shield is made not of bronze but of faith; and
the sharp sword is the word of the Spirit.[81] This new combat in
the arena takes place under the eyes of the public: "Not only are
men watching the combats but the host of angels as well."[82]
"And whereas the angels are spectators, the Lord of angels presides over the contest as judge."[83]

From the evidence I have presented, we can conclude that according to Chrysostom, the heavenly world is present at the rite
of renunciation of Satan. We must even say that the angels take
part in the celebration: "The angels who are standing by and the
invisible powers rejoice at your conversion, receive the words
from your tongues, and carry them up to the common Master of
all things. There they are inscribed in the books of heaven."[84] It
follows that according to Chrysostom, there are moments in the
earthly liturgy at which the angels intervene and exercise a minis-
terial role that consists in acting as intermediaries between human beings and God. The part they play is very like that of the
angels (or angel) of sacrifice that is attested for the eucharistic
liturgy both in the Roman Canon[85] and in anaphoras of the
Alexandrine type.[86]

V. THE SYMBOLISM OF THE RITES

Like Theodore, Chrysostom states the purpose of his mystagogical homilies: he wants the catechumens to have a good knowledge of the reasons for each celebration and each individual rite; the baptized will then go their way armed with a surer understanding.[87] Consequently, the explanation of the various rites that is given in the mystagogical homilies plays a part in achieving the purposes of Christian initiation.

In speaking of baptism, Chrysostom uses the image of bride and bridegroom; he sees baptism as a marriage. This theme runs through his instructions and is based on 2 Corinthians 11:2[88] He makes a point regarding method and thus formally justifies his use of this kind of analogy: "The understanding must be led from things of the body to those which belong to the Spirit, to things which come closer to God."[89] Having said this, he begins his step-by-step explanation of baptism according to the analogy with marriage: the dowry contract consists of obedience and the agreement that will be made with the bridegroom (that is, the renunciation of Satan and the ranging of oneself on Christ's side); the nuptial gift of the bridegroom is Christ himself, who gave himself for the Church. After saying this, in order to give greater weight to his analogy, Chrysostom launches into a real celebration of the greatness of the gift of Christ, who shed his blood for his bride, the Church.

Within the image of marriage as applied to baptism, Chrysostom develops the doctrine of divine election: the bride is not beautiful and has not been chosen for her beauty or for the bloom of her body; for, in fact, she is deformed, ugly, and shamefully sordid.[90] At this point, Chrysostom inserts the theme of God's mercy as an explanation of justification. In his eyes, this is not simply an analogy; rather he sees baptism as a true and proper spiritual marriage:

"That is why, in my fear of the enemy's tricks, I am continually exhorting you to keep the marriage robe in its integrity, that with it you may enter forever into this spiritual marriage. And what takes place here is a spiritual marriage. Just as in marriage between man and woman the bridal feast is prolonged for seven days, see how we too extend for the same number of days your bridal feast, setting before you the table of the mysteries, filled with good things beyond number."[91]

Another image Chrysostom uses for the baptismal rites is that of a struggle. I have already spoken of this and need not repeat what I have said, but I may add one point concerning the interpretation of the days spent in preparation for baptism. Montfaucon's first homily was delivered thirty days before Easter; from this fact, Chrysostom derives an analogy with the training of athletes in preparation for their competitions, since this preparation also lasted thirty days. "So also for you, these thirty days are like the practice and bodily exercises in some wrestling school. Let us learn during these days how we may gain the advantage over that wicked demon."[92] This explanation, too, is in keeping with the method Chrysostom states at the beginning: to start with things perceptible to the senses in order to reach an understanding of things divine and spiritual.

During exorcisms, the catechumens were naked and unshod. The explanation Chrysostom gives for this practice is like that of Theodore,[93] namely, that the catechumenal rites signify a captivity: "The King has conquered in the battle and has taken captives. And captives go naked and unshod."[94] The symbolism of the exorcisms is heavily emphasized and seems to have been regarded as extremely important: "The show of bare feet and the outstretched hands"[95] are gestures pointing to a captivity; they signify the situation of human beings as slaves of the devil. Three gestures express this state of enslavement: "See here again the external attitude of captivity. The priests bring you in. . . . They bid you to pray, on bent knees, with your hands outstretched to heaven."[96]

In the second homily of the Papadopoulus-Karameus series,[97] the captivity theme also serves to interpret the period following upon baptism, for the baptized are now captives of Christ. The various secondary meanings of the captivity theme are unimportant; the important thing is that the rite always signifies a captivity of one or other kind. The condition of captivity from which human beings are delivered is followed by a new situation that is described as heavenly. The dress of the newly baptized is intended to be representative of this new life: "This captivity drives one forth from foreign soil and leads him to his homeland, the heavenly Jerusalem. . . . This one leads you to the citizens above, for St. Paul says: *You are citizens with the saints.*[98] This, then, is the reason why you appear naked and unshod."[99]

The action of kneeling also has a meaning of its own, and this meaning, too, is twofold: it can express enslavement to the devil, but it can also be regarded as a profession of faith in the lordship of Christ: "Sacred custom[100] bids you to remain on your knees, so as to acknowledge His absolute rule even by your posture, for to bend the knee is a mark to those who acknowledge their servitude. Hear what St. Paul says[101]: *To him every knee shall bend of those in heaven, on earth, and under the earth.*"[102]

The "signing" is also given an interpretation like that of Theodore.[103] Both homilists interpret the anointing in relation to the devil, who must flee at the mere sight of this sign (anointing in the form of a cross) on the foreheads of the newly baptized.[104]

The symbolism of stripping and donning new clothing is no longer greatly stressed; it is mentioned only in connection with passages in Paul: "We put off the old garment, which has been made filthy with the abundance of our sins; we put on the new one, which is free from every stain."[105] The symbolism here simply combines Colossians 3:10 and Galatians 3:27, which Chrysostom expressly cites.

The emergence from the baptismal pool, which symbolizes the resurrection,[106] does not seem to be regarded as very important, since it is mentioned only in passing and in a subordinate clause. Chrysostom's real interest finds expression at the end of the sentence: ". . . ask Him to be your ally, so that you may guard well the gifts that He has given you, and that you may not be conquered by the deceits of the wicked one."[107]

The really important thing in Chrysostom's eyes is the preservation of the garment received in baptism. Operative here are the christological theme and the theme of grace as image of Christ. The topic is always discussed in an interplay of allusions based on the fact that the baptized don resplendent garments that distinguish them from others. For Chrysostom, these baptismal garments become a sign of a relationship with Christ that must be maintained through moral behavior. We must now turn to this theme of "garments."

Chrysostom takes up this theme in the fourth Stavronikita homily, which A. Wenger thinks was delivered on Easter Monday or perhaps on Easter Sunday itself. The newly baptized put on the dress proper to them: a white garment that both Theodore and Chrysostom describe as "gleaming." Chrysostom turns immediately from the dress to that of which it is a sign: "Now the robe you wear and your gleaming garments attract the eyes of all; if you should will to do so, by keeping your royal robe shining even more brightly than it now does, by your godly conduct and your strict discipline, you will always be able to draw all who behold you to show the same zeal and praise for the Master."[108]

The royal robe signifies the fruit of baptism, namely, our relationship with Christ. There is a passage in which Chrysostom takes the baptismal garment as his starting point and then moves on to the christological theme as the decisive conclusion of his exhortation: "Especially you who have recently been judged worthy of divine initiation, who have put off the burden of your sins and put on the shining robe—and what do I mean by the shining robe?—do you, who have put on Christ Himself and have received the Master of all things to dwell within you, show forth a conduct worthy of Him who dwells within you."[109]

This movement from the baptismal garment theme to the christological theme is Pauline. Chrysostom loved Paul's writings and could not have been unaware of the direction shown him here by his "universal teacher." In fact, the fourth Stavronikita homily is a commentary on 2 Corinthians 5:17: "If, then, any man is in Christ, he is a new creature: the former things have passed away; behold all things are made new." Chrysostom works out the meaning of this text with the help of another: "All you who have been baptized into Christ have put on Christ."[110] Here is how he combines the two: "*All you who have been baptized into Christ have put on Christ.* So I exhort you to do your every deed and action just as if you had Christ, the Creator of all things and the Master of our nature, dwelling within you."[111]

Seen in this light, the theme of grace is the theme of Christ within us; the baptismal garment is a sign of this grace and therefore a sign of Christ as such: "How shall I say it? He has thrown Himself around us as a garment: *For all you who have been baptized into Christ have put on Christ.*"[112] Chrysostom thus takes the "putting on" of Galatians 3:27 in a most realistic sense: "putting on Christ" means "being in Christ," which in turn implies an ontological relationship.

There is only a hint of this point here, but it is sufficient, since Chrysostom elsewhere explains the ontological consequences of our incorporation into Christ. These are stated in his commentary on Galatians 3:27 (PG 61:656): "Since you have the Son of God in yourself, you have become like to Him and you have been brought into one relationship and into one form with Him." Chrysostom always draws the same conclusion regarding moral behavior: "If we have Christ within us, we must think and act in a way worthy of this quest."[113] From the indwelling of Christ in the baptized, Chrysostom concludes to the indwelling of the entire Trinity: "When I say Christ, I mean also the Father and the Holy Spirit. For this is what Christ Himself promised when He said[114]: *If anyone love me and will keep my commandments, the Father and I will come and make our abode with him.*"[115]

From all the data now in our hands, we can conclude that for Chrysostom, the symbolism of the baptismal rites is not a matter of simple allegory intended for the instruction and education of the catechumens. In his eyes, the symbolism speaks of realities and not simply of meanings, and is intended to give an experience of the mystical content present in every rite. Here is a unique passage that fully reveals this "sacramental" realism:

"For all you who have been baptized into Christ have put on Christ.[116] See how he has become your clothing. Do you wish to know how He has also become your food? *As I live through the Father,* Christ says, *so he who eats me, he also shall live because of me.*[117] And He also becomes your house: *He who eats my flesh abides in me and I in him.*[118] And He shows that He is our root and foundation

when He says: *I am the vine, you are the branches.*[119] To show that He is your brother, friend, and bridegroom, He says: *No longer do I call you servants, for you are my friends.*[120] Again, St. Paul says: *I betrothed you to one spouse, that I might present you a chaste virgin to Christ.*[121] And again: *that He should be the first-born among many brethren.*[122] Not only do we become His brothers but even His children, for He says: *Behold I and my children, whom God hath given to me.*[123] Not only do we become His children but His members and His Body.[124] As if the things already mentioned were not enough to prove the love and kindness which He shows towards us, He set down another thing, greater and more intimate than these, when He spoke of Himself as our Head.

"Since you know all these things, beloved, make answer to your Benefactor by the excellence of your conduct."[125]

In the perspective provided by typology, Christ is truly clothing, food, house, root, brother, friend, bridegroom, and head.

Since all these titles or descriptions can be given a realistic interpretation only in typology and in no other system, we can legitimately ask whether Chrysostom is truly using typology. If he is, we can interpret all the descriptions typologically; if he is not, we cannot.

If the answer is yes, then all the symbolism of the sacramental rites that Chrysostom describes will be truly realistic; otherwise, these symbolisms will all be simply beautiful images whose value will be purely literary: they will never enter into the reality of the "mystery."

VI. THE MYSTERY

John Chrysostom uses the term "mystery" almost exclusively of the Eucharist.[126] However, he does also use it to signify the baptismal rite or even a part of it: "Now let me speak to you of the mysteries themselves and of the contract which will be made between yourselves and the Master."[127] We must be careful to note that he is not speaking of what we today call simply the "sacrament." That is, "mystery" refers not only to the act of baptizing, but to all the ritual elements that make up the celebration.

The "contract which will be made" becomes a reality in the re-nunciation of Satan and the act of cleaving to Christ. This particu-lar rite, then, amounts to the making of a contract between the soul and Christ, and is described as a "mystery." This mystery has its own "efficacy" and, consequently, its own "sacramen-tality." The contract is entered into in "faith," a term and con-cept that has "reliance upon" or "the entrusting of oneself to" as one of its meanings: "A contract now exists between the person who entrusts himself or herself and the depository of this trust, and this contract is called 'faith.' "[128]

We have already met with an analogous situation in Ambrose. But we are far removed here from the position of Ambrose, who still recognizes the distinction between the historical saving act and its sacramental celebration. This distinction does not exist in the present passage. And yet, in typological contexts, we do find Chrysostom using the term "mystery" in speaking of events in the history of salvation. Consider, for example, how he explains the blood and water that flow from the side of Christ. The water and blood are not a "mystery" but rather a "symbol" of baptism and the mysteries. On the other hand, the coming forth of the blood and water is described as a "mystery": "Beloved, do not pass this mystery by without a thought. For I have still another mystical explanation to give."[129]

Another theological use of the term "mystery" occurs when Chrysostom speaks of the "mystical" (*mystikos*) meaning of cer-tain things. In his Italian translation of Chrysostom's baptismal homilies, A. Ceresa-Gastaldo customarily translates *mystikos* as "mysterious." Not always, however: in fact, in the passage just cited, he has "mystical [explanation]," as does A. Wenger. The emphatically theological context suggests the appropriateness of this translation.

In my opinion, a no less theological context suggests the same translation in two other passages in which Chrysostom is speak-ing of the time or season chosen for the liturgical celebration. He feels obliged to explain why the sacraments of initiation are cele-brated at Easter and why the renunciation of Satan is made on Friday at the ninth hour. In both cases, he answers that the choice of time has a *mystikos* meaning; in his ensuing explanation, he then connects this meaning with the "mystery" being celebrated. This kind of explanation is possible, of course, only because the liturgical season participates in the "mystery" character of the rite being celebrated.

Here is the first of the two passages:

"I was seeking to tell you why our fathers passed by all the other seasons of the year and ordained that your souls be initiated during this season, and I said that observance of the time was not a simple or random thing. For it is always the same grace and it is not hindered by the season, for the grace is from God. But the observance of the proper season does have some connection with the mystery of initiation."[130]

The reason, then, for choosing this particular season is that it is the season of the Lord's victory: "Now He has destroyed sin, now He has put down death and has subjected the devil, He has taken His captives."[131] Chrysostom concludes by connecting the remembrance of the past event with the salvific efficacy that it exerts today in the rites of initiation: "Our fathers ordained the celebration of this season first in order to remind you of the Master by the season of His victory. . . . This was not their only reason. Our fathers also ordained this celebration in order that you might also be the Master's partner throughout the season."[132]

Here is the second passage: "Tomorrow, on Friday at the ninth hour you must have certain questions asked of you and you must present your contracts to the Master. Nor do I make mention to you of that day and that hour without some purpose. A mystical lesson can be learned from them."[133] Here Chrysostom makes it clear that he regards even the determination of the day and hour for the sacraments as something "mystical," that is, belonging to the sacramental sphere.

He also tells us more specifically in what the sacramentality of the time for this liturgical action consists: "On Friday at the ninth hour the thief entered paradise; the darkness, which lasted from the sixth to the ninth hour, was dissolved; and the Light, perceived by both body and mind, was taken up as a sacrifice for the whole world. For at that hour Christ said[134]: *Father, into thy hands I commend my spirit."*[135] The "sacred" action that occurred at the ninth hour and that has now been explained is the salvation of the good thief.

But how, in all this, is the salvation of the faithful accomplished? They renounce Satan and profess their adherence to Christ: these are their "contracts" with the Master. And then: "When you are about to be led [into the church] at the ninth hour, do you also recall to mind the great number of your virtuous deeds and count those gifts which await you; you will no longer be on earth, but your soul will raise itself up and lay hold of heaven itself."[136]

As we saw earlier in connection with Stavronikita 2, 17, the rite of renunciation of Satan and adherence to Christ possesses a sacramentality of its own and is therefore a "mystery" in its own right. And, in fact, here is how Chrysostom ends his discussion: "The words which you utter here are registered in heaven, and the agreement you make by your tongue abides indelibly with the Master."[137]

All this makes very clear the mystical character of the time for the rites. A. Ceresa-Gastaldo's translation "mysterious" has its validity. For even if the translation "mystical" (in the sense of "participating in the reality of the mystery") is given precedence, it must absorb and retain the idea of "mysterious," since this is always latent in every usage of the term "mystery," whether it be applied to worship or to salvation-history.

From all that has been said here, we can conclude that John Chrysostom has the ability to think typologically, even if his preoccupation with moral behavior completely absorbs his attention. I shall, therefore, turn now to a more direct study of his typology.

VII. CHRYSOSTOM'S TYPOLOGY

I pointed out earlier that Chrysostom's mystagogy is distinguished from all others by its strong emphasis on morality. I have attempted to explain why this is so and have offered some explanations that seem to the point. I have noted in particular how Chrysostom's moral perspective is connected with the very theology of baptism, since he looks upon this as the beginning of a new life.

A further question must nonetheless be asked: Are Chrysostom's instructions mystagogical simply in that they accompany the course of Christian initiation, or do they also display the themes and methodology of the major patristic mystagogies? As we saw at the beginning of this book, mystagogy is simply typology applied to the sacraments. The question, therefore, becomes this: Does John Chrysostom use typology? My answer is that he does: in developing his theology of the sacrament, he has recourse to typology and uses the same method as is found in the mystagogies of the Fathers.

The development of mystagogical discourse can be described schematically as follows. First of all, the preacher asserts the value or power of the sacrament and reminds the faithful of it by brief allusions. He then has recourse to Scripture in order to explain why the sacrament possesses this value and power. In typology, recourse is had to the Old Testament because there the preacher finds *figures* of the sacramental event. A correct theology of the sacrament is developed by explaining the *saving power* of these figures. The reason is that the figures participated in the reality of the *truth (veritas)*, since they existed in relation to it and as participations in it, even though it was still in the future.

Once the Old Testament has explained the value and power of the Church's sacraments, typology passes on to the New Testament. It brings before the listener the events that show how Christ can be the agent and executor (or *truth*) of the salvation that was prefigured in the Old Testament and is now celebrated by the Church.—Such is mystagogical theology. It follows that what is called "liturgical theology" must necessarily be a biblical theology.

Chrysostom belongs to the Antiochene school and therefore does not seem much inclined to an allegorical interpretation of the Scriptures. And yet, he sees no problem about developing a typological interpretation of the Eucharist that uses among other things an allegorical interpretation of the Old Testament. Evidently, as I have said several times, typology is something that transcends the limitations of the various systematic approaches to the interpretation of the Scriptures.

Chrysostom introduces the theme with a rhetorical question: "Do you wish to know the power inherent in this blood?"[138] The question is meant to introduce the theology of the Eucharist that he wants to pass on to the baptized. Knowledge of the source and method of this theology is part of the contents of mystagogy. He, therefore, explicitly tells his listeners that he will have recourse to the Old Testament, which he will interpret by the typological method: "Let us go back to what prefigured it, to the ancient stories in Egypt."[139] And then: "Learn the power of the type, that you may learn the strength of the truth."[140] The mystagogical approach is very evident here: if one wishes to speak of a sacrament, one must speak of its Old Testament figures (types).

Baptism and its consequences for moral behavior are also discussed typologically. Those who have associated themselves with Christ by contract must not be unfaithful to their commitment; they must not sin. In addressing the baptized, Chrysostom applies the biblical images of the Exodus to them.[141] These newly enlightened Christians, he says, have truly come forth from Egypt and must not look back to the past with regret: "You came forth from Egypt. Never again seek Egypt nor the evils of Egypt. Never think of the mud and brickmaking. The things of the present life are mud and brickmaking, since gold itself, before it is converted into gold, is nothing more than earth."[142]

The type of the Eucharist comprises the events in Exodus 11:1–11 and 12:1–20. These are Passover texts that when read typologically show how the old Jewish Passover has its "truth" in the Eucharist of the Church.

Chrysostom begins his explanation by referring to the tenth plague that God was about to inflict on the Egyptians and immediately introducing the irrational lamb as a type of Christ:

"The plague sent by God was about to sweep down from above, and the destroying angel was assailing one house after another. What, then, did Moses do? *Sacrifice an unblemished lamb,* he said, *and smear your doors with its blood.*[143] What do you mean? Can the blood of an irrational animal save man who has reason? 'Yes,' he says. 'Not because it is blood, but because it prefigures the Master's blood.' "[144]

The thought is perfectly clear: the Old Testament realities have value through their relation to Christ, that is, by reason of their character as types; otherwise they are nothing. In this interpretational approach, an author can find it useful to point out the deficiencies of the Old Testament realities, for these make it all the more evident that their power does not come from themselves, but from their character as types, which connects them with Christ; their power resides not in themselves but elsewhere.

To clarify this idea, Chrysostom gives an example:

"Although statues of the emperor have neither life nor perception, they can save the men endowed with perception and life who flee to them for refuge, not because they are bronze, but because they are images of the emperor. So, too, that blood which lacked life and perception saved the men who had life, not because it was blood, but because it was a type of the Master's blood."[145]

In other words, the blood of the lamb is able to save, not by reason of what it "is," but by reason of that in which it "participates," that is, by reason of that of which it is a type, namely, the blood of Christ.

"On that day in Egypt, the destroying angel saw the blood smeared on the doors and did not dare to burst in. Today, will the devil not check himself all the more if he sees, not the blood of the type smeared on the doors, but the blood of the truth smeared on the mouths of the faithful, since these mouths have become doors of a temple which holds Christ? If the angel stood in awe when he saw the type, much more likely is it that the devil will flee when he sees the truth."[146]

In this passage Chrysostom argues on the basis of "type" and "truth" and asserts the full value of the type, a value that derives from the "truth." All this is said of Old Testament figures generally. When we turn to the doctrine of the sacraments, we find a very interesting phenomenon: the sacraments are the "truth" without qualification; in other words, there is no gap, no break to be observed between the sacraments and the events of which they are the sacraments. In Chrysostom's eyes, the sacraments are not simply types of the saving events in which they participate; they are identical with the events themselves.

After finishing what he has to say about Old Testament types, the homilist turns to what the New Testament tells us in John 19:33–34 about the power of the blood:

"Do you wish to learn from another source as well the strength of this blood? Look from where it first flowed and where it had its source! It flowed down from the cross, from the Master's side. St. John says that when Christ was dead but still on the cross, the soldier came and pierced His side with a lance, and straightway there came out water and blood. The one was a symbol of baptism, and the other of the mysteries."[147]

We must note here the deliberate inversion of the two words "water" and "blood." A. Wenger says the inversion probably represents a "different reading," even though Chrysostom "cites the text correctly elsewhere."[148] If this be the true explanation, I must at least add that Chrysostom's choice of this "different reading" is very opposite since the sequence "water and blood" is called for by the development of his argument.

His purpose is to show the significance of Christian initiation as the birth of the Church. His argument is as follows: the Church was born of the crucified Lord because from his crucified body flowed water and blood, that is, baptism and the Eucharist, which are the means by which believers become members of the Church. Since the sacraments are celebrated in this order—first baptism and then the Eucharist—the succession should be the same in the Bible. Otherwise the "connection of likeness" between the event narrated in the New Testament and the sacraments would be lacking and, therefore, the typology would be removed and Chrysostom's argument would become invalid. Listen to his explicit statement: "Therefore, he did not say: *There came out blood and water*, but first water came forth and then blood, since first comes baptism and then the mysteries. It was the soldier, then, who opened Christ's side and dug through the rampart of the holy temple, but I am the one who has found the treasure and gotten the wealth."[149]

One characteristic of the typological approach is that it allows for deriving several different meanings from the same passage. Thus, we find Chrysostom offering another interpretation of the water and blood that flowed from Christ's side. The water and blood are here connected with the sleep of Adam and the creation of the first woman. Here are the parallels: during the creation of woman, Adam was asleep; on the cross, Christ was sunk in the sleep of death. From the side of Adam, the first woman, Eve, was born; from the side of Christ, the Church was born. Eve was the bride of Adam; the Church is the bride of Christ.[150] Eve was formed from a rib; the Church was formed by the flowing forth of water and blood from Christ's side,[151] for these two elements represent, and in that order, the sacraments by which human beings become members of the Church.

Are these simply chance parallels and products of obvious analogies, or do they represent a truly typological outlook? Chrysostom himself gives the answer when he ends his discussion by saying: "And so Moses, too, in his account of the first man, has Adam say: *Bone of my bone and flesh of my flesh*,[152] hinting to us of the Master's side."[153] Here we have a superimposition of the first and second Adams: the experience of the first in the story of creation holds for the second at the moment of redemption. Therefore, the real meaning and nature of the events in which the first Adam was involved consists precisely in this, that they apply also to Christ; in other words, it consists in their typological character.

In these instructions that accompany baptism, Chrysostom is thus certainly practicing typology; not only does he use the typological method, but he even formally states that he is doing so and explains the theory of it. Furthermore, when the biblical text puts difficulties in the way of the typology, he even alters the text of the New Testament, as we saw in his reading of "water and blood" instead of "blood and water."

This willingness to change the text can itself be explained in the light of typology. Chrysostom never shows any excessive concern with the meaning of the text precisely as a received text. This being the case, it is possible for the interpretative method to force itself on the text being interpreted and sometimes even to superimpose itself. Not only is it possible for this to happen, in the case of Chrysostom, we have an example of its actually happening. The important thing for typology is that the typology be successful, as was abundantly clear in Ambrose. There can be no better proof of the extent to which Chrysostom was committed to typology.

After making clear the power and strength of Christ's blood by means of a typology based on the Old Testament, Chrysostom turns to the New Testament passage that we have just seen. Here, again, he explains his method. According to his explicit statement, this is another way of gaining an understanding of the Lord's blood, but it is not an alternative way; rather it must be compatible with the preceding, Old Testament typology. Here is how the homilist brings the two themes into harmony: "So it was with the lamb. The Jews sacrificed the victim, but I reaped the reward of salvation which came from their sacrifice."[154]

The two themes are here harmonized by means of typology; and, in fact, the realities (which are unified by a certain connection between them) call for one another, are superimposed on one another, and interchange even their most specifically proper traits. In the short text just cited, Chrysostom speaks of the victim of the Jewish sacrificial rite and the redemption that comes from the cross of Christ. "Lamb" applies to both; the two are therefore superimposed on each other and exchange their respective characteristics so as to become a single reality: the *type* is brought to fulfillment in its *truth*; it has ceased to exist in its own historical reality, but it continues to live on because it has been absorbed and transfigured in the splendor of the Truth.

140

In a mystagogical explanation of the Eucharist, the manna is an indispensable theme, and, in fact, Chrysostom deals with it at the end of a lengthy typological comparison of Jewish and Christian events in which he has emphasized the excellence of the latter. The manna is both compared with and opposed to the Eucharist:

"In those days Moses stretched forth his hands to heaven and brought down the bread of angels, manna.[155] This other Moses stretches forth His hands to heaven and brings down the food of eternal life. Moses struck the rock and made streams of water flow[156]; this other Moses touches the table, strikes the spiritual board, and makes the fountains of the Spirit gush forth."[157]

What we see in operation here is the principle according to which there is a superimposition and identification of the action of the priest at the altar and the work of Christ that fulfills the figure of Moses. Chrysostom thus applies a theological principle that, in his system of sacramental theology, brings him closest to the typological approach to sacramental doctrine.

All this shows how fully justified I am in concluding that in these passages, typology is being used accurately and in accordance with a deliberate plan. These catechetical homilies are, therefore, to be regarded as mystagogical in the fullest sense of this term, despite the strong emphasis on morality that pervades them.

Mystagogy is a way of doing theology. I must add, therefore, that since these homilies are indeed mystagogical, they must contain a true and proper sacramental theology, as do the homilies of the Fathers. This is what we shall now see.

VIII. THE EYES OF FAITH AND SACRAMENTALITY

The celebration of the mysteries consists of ritual actions that are composed of gestures and words and, therefore, are obviously sensible. Chrysostom's explanations start with the *visual elements* that are present in the liturgy; he even speaks of "what is seen," thus giving sight precedence over hearing. It may be that at the end of the fourth century, the visual element in the liturgy was regarded as more important than the auditory, for Theodore uses the same language; at the same time, however, the priority of sight over hearing is not as clear in Theodore as it is in Chrysostom.

As in Ambrose and Theodore, so in Chrysostom "what is seen" in the liturgy is contrasted with "what is not seen." Believers, therefore, are endowed with two kinds of eyes: bodily eyes and the eyes of faith. In fact, the thing that distinguishes Christians is precisely the fact that they also have the eyes of faith, which enable them to see those things that their bodily eyes are unable to see. In Chrysostom's view, this is the basic situation of the faithful: by the fact of being baptized, they are able to see beyond the data of the senses, and liturgical actions are only one area in which they exercise this kind of activity.

This way of looking at Christian life emerges when Chrysostom explains the title "the faithful." Who are "the faithful"? Chrysostom's answer is that they are those who are endowed with the eyes of faith. Here he is, enunciating the general principle and then immediately applying it to baptism:

"Why, then, are we called this ["the faithful"]? We faithful have believed in things which our bodily eyes cannot see. These things are great and frightening and go beyond our nature. . . . Only the teaching of faith understands them well. Therefore God has made for us two kinds of eyes: those of the flesh and those of faith. When you come to the sacred initiation, the eyes of the flesh see water; the eyes of faith behold the Spirit."[158]

In the celebration of the mysteries, the faithful start with what their bodily eyes see, but they go on to picture and make present to themselves God who is acting; they can even be said to see God acting. This is impossible without the eyes of faith. The passage from what is seen to what is unseen is effected by the interior activity of the baptized (guided by faith), which consists in "setting before themselves" or "picturing to themselves" the reality contained in the rite. In modern parlance, all this is called "active participation."

Faith is the essential and constitutive element in the entire process:

"What takes place here requires faith and the eyes of the soul, so that you pay heed not only to what is seen, but that you make the unseen visible from the seen. This is what the eyes of faith can do. The eyes of the body can see only those things which come under their perception, but the eyes of faith are quite the opposite. For they see nothing of visible things, but the invisible things they see as if they were lying before their eyes."[159]

This is a classical theme that is also to be found in Ambrose and Theodore. It is the theme that relates directly to the nature of the sacraments, for sacramentality consists in what is unseen, and faith alone can give access to it. As early as Stavronikita 1, 31, Chrysostom has said that faith gives us "different eyes" that are capable of seeing what eludes the senses.[160] The theme is a very rich one and can have two applications, which I shall now discuss: to the moral life of the faithful and to the doctrine of the sacraments.

A. The Eyes of Faith in the Moral Life of the Faithful
The theme of "the eyes of the spirit" transforms morality into eschatology. Because of the great hope that has been given to them, the newly enlightened must henceforth have their gaze fixed on heaven, in accordance with the exhortation of blessed Paul (Col 3:2). Contemplation of the things that are above entails a passage from the visible to the invisible, which, however, the eyes of the spirit see even more clearly than our bodily eyes see sensible things.[161] Here we have the start of a moral approach to the life of the baptized, an approach on the content of the sacrament and on a "fruitful" participation in it, which in turn rests on the contrast between visible and invisible and requires the faithful to "set" the invisible "before them" or "picture" it "to themselves."

B. The Eyes of Faith in the Liturgical Rites
In this application of it, the theme ultimately has its place in the theology of the sacraments and, more specifically, in the ontology of the sacraments. A passage already cited from the third homily in the Papadopoulos-Kerameus series can help us to get

a better grasp of the matter, since here the theme of "seeing" leads into the theme of the deeper "reality" of the sacraments: "Therefore, God has made for us two kinds of eyes: those of the flesh and those of faith. . . . Our bodily eyes see the priest as, from above, he lays his right hand on the head and touches [him who is being baptized]; our spiritual eyes see the great High Priest as He stretches forth His invisible hand to touch his head."[162] In other words, not what the eyes of the body see, but only what the eyes of faith see forms the real content of the sacrament. We must conclude that in speaking thus, Chrysostom takes us into the theology of the "image" and consequently into the theology of "imitation."

But this short passage calls for further reflection. It is necessary, in fact, to read this entire section of the homily in order to acquire a more accurate grasp of this theology that is so perfectly attuned to the liturgy and yet, unfortunately, so remote from us.

The liturgical theology that Chrysostom represents is sufficiently clear and lies open before us: every liturgical act is an *image* of saving realities. In the world of typology, the action that is the *image* really participates in the reality of which it is the *image*. Such is the idea of *sacramentality* that is native to this archaic sacramental theology. It must be noted that for Chrysostom, all the elements in a celebration have a *sacramentality* of their own, since each is an *image* of a particular saving reality:

"When you come to the sacred initiation, the eyes of the flesh see water; the eyes of faith behold the Spirit. Those eyes see the body being baptized; these see the old man being buried. The eyes of the flesh see the flesh being washed; the eyes of the spirit see the soul being cleansed. The eyes of the body see the body emerging from the water; the eyes of faith see the new man[163] come forth brightly shining from that purification. Our bodily eyes see the priest as, from above, he lays his right hand on the head and touches [him who is being baptized]; our spiritual eyes see the great High Priest as He stretches forth His invisible hand to touch his head. For at that moment, the one who baptizes is not a man but the only-begotten Son of God."[164]

Let me interrupt my reading of the homily to pose a problem. I said before that the theology of the *image* is connected with the theology of *imitation*, since the *image* is an image because it *imitates*. If we ask why it is that in the baptismal liturgy, the (visible) actions described by Chrysostom have an invisible correlative or referent, his answer is quite clear and to the point: because our baptism is an *imitation* of the Lord's baptism in the Jordan. Listen as he continues his discourse and explains *sacramentality* in terms of the theology of *imitation*:

"And what happened in the case of our Master's body also happens in the case of your own. Although John appeared to be holding His body by the head, it was the divine Word which led His body down into the streams of the Jordan and baptized Him. The Master's body was baptized by the Word and by the voice of His Father from heaven which said: *This is my beloved Son*,[165] and by the manifestation of the Holy Spirit which descended upon Him. This also happens in the case of your body. The baptism is given in the name of the Father and of the son and of the Holy Spirit. Therefore, John the Baptist told us, for our instruction, that man does not baptize us, but God: *There comes after me one who is mightier than I, and I am not worthy to loose the strap of His sandal. He will baptize you with the Holy Spirit and with fire.*[166]

"For this reason, when the priest is baptizing he does not say, 'I baptize so-and-so,' but, 'So-and-so is baptized in the name of the Father and of the Son and of the Holy Spirit.' In this way he shows that it is not he who baptizes but those whose names have been invoked, the Father, the Son, and the Holy Spirit.

"Therefore my sermon today is called 'faith.' "[167]

There can be no doubt about the sacramental realism of this theology of *image* and *imitation*, for in this passage, Chrysostom offers us a true and proper ontology of baptism,[168] as is clear from his categorical conclusion: "Our spiritual eyes see the great High Priest as He stretches forth His invisible hand to touch his head. For, at that moment, the one who baptizes is not a man but the only-begotten Son of God."[169] Another instruction provides the same teaching, although in a slightly different form that combines the several factors at work:

"What is this I am saying and why did I say to pay no heed to visible things, but to have the eyes of the spirit? I say it in order that when you see the bath of water and the hand of the priest touching your head, you may not think that this is merely water, nor that only the hand of the bishop lies upon your head. For it is not a man who does what is done, but it is the grace of the Spirit which sanctifies the nature of the water and touches your head together with the hand of the priest."[170]

There is a slight difference between the two passages just cited: what was attributed in the first to Christ is attributed in the second to the Holy Spirit. But this causes no difficulty in the view of the markedly Trinitarian evolution of Chrysostom's theology: "When I say Christ, I mean also the Father and the Holy Spirit. For this is what Christ Himself promised us when He said[171]: *If anyone love me and will keep my commandments, the Father and I will come and make our abode with him.*"[172]

A *sacrament* is an *action of Christ*: this theological formulation brings together in a profound way the three classical points to be retained in every sacramental theology: sacramental efficacy, the presence of Christ, and the presence of Christ's saving actions.

Sacramental efficacy is ensured because the "sacrament" is an *action of Christ* and not simply of a human being. This emerges quite clearly from Chrysostom's explanation of the sacramental formula he used, which, as everyone knows, is passive in structure. Here is his commentary on the formula:

"When the priest says: 'So-and-so is baptized in the name of the Father, and of the Son, and of the Holy Spirit,' he puts your head down into the water three times and three times he lifts it up again, preparing you by this mystic rite to receive the descent of the Spirit. For it is not only the priest who touches the head, but also the right hand of Christ, and this is shown by the very words of the one baptizing. He does not say: 'I baptize so-and-so,' but, 'So-and-so is baptized.' "[173]

146

The sacraments derive their efficacy and content from the fact that they are *actions of Christ* in the most literal sense of the phrase. In fact, as seen in typology, the concrete, visible minister is an *image* of Christ; consequently, it is not the minister, but Christ who acts. We can say that in this approach based on *imitation*, the *sacraments* are essentially and always christocentric.

C. *Traces of Regression*

The passage that I have just cited contains a further interesting point. It displays a movement that must be described as a regression rather than a development. Concretely: the doctrine of the "image" and "imitation" is in process of being transformed along Trinitarian lines.

The period of history in which Chrysostom lived was one in which the great crisis of the christological and Trinitarian disputes was barely over. The crisis had ended with the victory of the orthodoxy represented by the great Fathers of the fourth century. Trinitarian formulas made a decisive entrance into liturgical texts, even where there was no need of them. For proof of this statement, we need only think of the eucharistic anaphoras into which the Trinitarian formulas were introduced (in the form of the *Postsanctus* prayer) as an embolism for the *Sanctus*, thus giving the latter an interpretation of which it is not susceptible.[174] The very structure of the anaphora lends itself to a Trinitarian reading, even though this is historically unfounded.[175]

In the homily of Chrysostom, which I was citing a moment ago, we see him introducing a Trinitarian modification of the doctrine of sacramental efficacy and thus of the entire doctrine of "imitation." In the period in which he lived, such a modification was perfectly logical, given the intense commitment of the Church to the defense of Trinitarian orthodoxy.

At the same time, however, by making this alteration, Chrysostom shows that he no longer grasps the doctrine of the *image* and *imitation*, since by its nature this can be applied only to the action of Christ.

Here is how Chrysostom modifies the doctrine of sacramental efficacy: it is not only the high priest (= Christ) in heaven who extends his hand and acts in the sacrament, but the entire Trinity: "The one fulfilling all things is the Father and the Son and the Holy Spirit, the undivided Trinity. It is faith in this Trinity which gives the grace of remission from sin; it is this confession which gives to us the gift of filial adoption."[176] This evolution in a Trinitarian direction is undeniable, even if it is located within a broader perspective, that is, within the theology of Chrysostom, who says: "When I say Christ, I mean also the Father and the Holy Spirit. For this is what Christ Himself promised us when He said[177]: *If anyone love me and will keep my commandments, the Father and I will come and make our abode with him.*"[178]

John Chrysostom is a determined proponent of the teaching in question, but two new factors have also played a part in the evolution I have been describing: (a) the evolution of liturgical interpretation along Trinitarian lines; and (b) the connecting of sacramental efficacy, not so much with the saving actions of Christ (of which the rite is the sacrament) as with the sacramental rites considered in themselves as having a power of their own. Think, for example, of what Chrysostom says about Satan fleeing at the mere sight of the mouths of the faithful reddened with the blood from the eucharistic chalice as they return from participating in the mysteries. The doctrine of *imitation* has nothing to do with this way of interpreting the power of the Lord's Supper.

On the one hand, Chrysostom is a faithful heir to the traditional doctrine that the sacraments are actions of Christ. On the other, he is already open to new perspectives, such as, for example, the evolution along Trinitarian lines. One point emerges clearly: the doctrine of the *image* and *imitation*, which is at the basis of sacramental theology and therefore of mystagogy, is gradually abandoned as two other doctrines become increasingly important: the doctrine of the Trinity and the doctrine of the efficacy of the sacraments, which are henceforth looked at more in themselves than in the light of the saving historical events in which they participate. The doctrine of the *image* does not, however, disappear; we find it being broadly used, but in a spiritual sense (as basis for a true elevation of the soul) rather than in a sacramental sense.[179]

Sacramental teaching thereby ceases to be typological and instead adopts new procedures and new perspectives that seem to offer a superior guarantee of the ontological value of the sacraments. We must recognize that in this respect, John Chrysostom, too, already postdates himself.

CHAPTER FIVE

Cyril of Jerusalem

It is difficult to determine whether the five mystagogical catecheses attributed to Cyril of Jerusalem were in fact his or were delivered by his successor, John of Jerusalem. A. Piédagnel discusses the problem with the aid of extensive documentation in his critical edition of these homilies.[1] The problem is not an unimportant one, since the decision regarding the author will play a part in deciding the period to which the texts are to be dated. Cyril became bishop of Jerusalem in about 350 and died in 387, and John succeeded him in 387 and died in 417. A. Piédagnel takes very seriously the hypothesis that John is the true author of this mystagogy, but, in the end, he prefers to assign it to Cyril; for this reason, his critical edition of the text bears the name of Cyril, not of John.

Because I choose to use Piédagnel's critical edition, I, too, shall speak of Cyril and not of John, although I am convinced that John is more probably the author. My reasons for thinking so are two: (a) the commentary on the baptismal anointings in Cyril's prebaptismal catecheses does not seem sufficiently consistent with what is said of these anointings in the mystagogical catecheses; and (b) the structure of the anaphora that is supposed in the fourth and fifth mystagogical catecheses is still evolving[2] and is quite close to the structure of the likewise evolving anaphora that is described in the catecheses of Theodore of Mopsuestia[3]; the latter, however, displays a slightly more advanced stage of development in comparison with the Jerusalem anaphora.[4]

If, as seems to be the case, the catecheses of Theodore are to be dated after 392, it follows that the mystagogical catecheses of "Cyril" should be dated to a period not far removed from 392.

150

This makes the authorship of John more probable than that of Cyril, although the latter cannot be completely excluded.

A. The Structure of the Anaphora

In his article on the mystagogical catecheses of Cyril, E. J. Cutrone says that it is possible to infer from these texts the structure of the Jerusalem anaphora in use at the time. The structure Cutrone comes up with is this: dialogue, prayer for creation, *Sanctus*, epiclesis, and intercessions.[5]

To this, J. M. Sanchez Caro replies that it is at least risky to take this succession literally and assume that it represents the complete structure of the Jerusalem anaphora. He has difficulty with the direct passage from *Sanctus* to epiclesis and with the absence of what he calls the "central block," especially since this is the only instance of such a structure that is known to us.[6]

In my own study of the structure of the anaphora in the catecheses of Theodore, I point out that the structure set forth by E. J. Cutrone is the same as that in the Ritual on which Theodore is commenting[7]; the relevant part of the Ritual is cited at the beginning of the sixteenth homily (the second on the Mass).[8] Therefore, Cyril does not represent the only instance of Cutrone's structure, and Cutrone's hypothesis deserves greater consideration. This identity of structure has escaped the commentators because their primary concern has been to study Theodore's commentary, which in fact displays an anaphora with a richer structure and more parts. The eucharistic celebration that took place in Theodore's church had moved far beyond the structure of the Ritual that Theodore cites as the basis for the liturgy of his church.

Theodore's commentary shows that there has already been a radical evolution, not only in the structure of the anaphora, but in eucharistic theology as well. It contains, for example, the doctrine of the Eucharist as the offering of the body and blood of Christ and the doctrine of consecration by means of the pneumatological epiclesis; neither is to be found in the Ritual he cites. For Theodore, the Ritual is the "law of the Church." How can he say this while at the same time effecting such radical changes in the structure and theology of the anaphora?

He himself gives us the answer: he justifies the changes by appealing to the "law of the priesthood," which evidently refers to the duty of adapting tradition to the needs of the present time. In his homilies, this "law of the priesthood" is invoked whenever he is explaining something that is part of the actual eucharistic celebration, but is not to be found in the Ritual quoted at the beginning of the homily.[9] I cannot cite all the evidence here (it is readily available in the article mentioned); I did, however, feel obliged to mention these few points as the basis for my full acceptance of E. J. Cutrone's description of the anaphoric structure to be found in Cyril's catecheses.

B. Cyril's Mystagogy

The Eucharist attested by Cyril and the Ritual attested by Theodore are very similar, not only in the structure of the anaphora, but in many of the contents of the anaphora. At the same time, however, in both Cyril and Theodore, some aspects of the anaphora and of eucharistic theology show an evolution when compared to the Ritual. By way of example, I can cite the epiclesis, which has undergone a development even in Cyril. In the Ritual, the epiclesis looks only to the sanctification of the communicants; in Cyril and in Theodore's commentary, it has already become an act whereby the holy gifts are sanctified. But we should not think that because both authors have the same Ritual before them, that they have, therefore, developed along the same lines. There are in fact differences which A. Piédagnel points out clearly in his edition of Cyril's catecheses.

One of the most obvious differences between Theodore's commentary and that of Cyril is to be seen in their respective mystagogical methods. In this area, Theodore is heavily dependent on the Ritual, whose allegorizing interpretation of the liturgy he accepts without reserve. In the fifteenth homily, for example, he comments on the entrance of the deacons who carry the prosphora and place it on the altar[10]; it is here that he develops his commentary on the Eucharist as an "image" of the passion of Christ. Sacramentality thus becomes dramatization; due to this dramatizing interpretation, which is effected by the interior activity of "picturing to oneself" or "setting before one's eyes," sacramentality moves from the realm of what is invisible and an object of faith to the realm of what is visible and an object of contemplation. Every time the Ritual provides an interpretation of this kind, Theodore accepts it in his commentary.

Cyril, for his part, never accepts this particular mystagogical method, which consists in interpreting a sacrament as a visible representation of the Lord's death and resurrection. This attitude prevents him from interpreting the prothesis as the entrance of the prosphora; it is possibly the reason why the fourth homily[11] is limited, for practical purposes, to the single theme of sacramental realism.

In Theodore, too, this last theme appears chiefly in the first of the two homilies devoted to the Eucharist; in Theodore, too, it is discussed mainly in light of the words of Jesus at the Last Supper.[12] His formal discussion of sacramental realism reaches its climax in section 10 with the contrast between "reality" and "type."[13]

Historians ask why Cyril discusses the words of the Last Supper in the first and not the second of his homilies on the Mass.[14] But if we inquire where Theodore most fully deals with the words of institution as proof of sacramental realism, the answer must be that he does so in the first of his two homilies on the Mass. We should not be surprised, therefore, to find Cyril citing the account of institution and discussing sacramental realism in his first catechesis on the Mass and not in the second. He was following the traditional subdivision of themes, which was based in turn on the sequence of themes in the Ritual on which both he and Theodore depended.[15]

For the rest, Cyril, in his mystagogy, follows the classical rules for using citations from the Old and New Testaments.

In his second catechesis on the Mass, Cyril moves step by step through the anaphora whose structure I described earlier (following Cutrone). In this homily, he again refuses to use the method we have already seen in Theodore, that is, he refuses to interpret the liturgy as a dramatization of its sacramental contents. This particular form of typology having been rejected, Cyril's interpretation emerges as restrained, focused on fundamentals, and concerned only with the meaning to be assigned to each section of the anaphora. Having said what is strictly necessary in order properly to understand the theological significance of each part of the anaphora, Cyril quickly moves on to the next without getting bogged down in further discussions.

Since the interpretative method connected with dramatization had the angelic liturgy as its object,[16] the latter too has no place in Cyril, with the one exception of the commentary on the *Sanctus*. Even here, however, he says simply that the seraphim gave us this doxology and that when we recite it, we enter into communion with the heavenly hosts and are thereby sanctified. It can be said, therefore, that the theology of the angelic liturgy and its sanctifying role is fully present in Cyril's catecheses, even though he does not follow the typological method that interprets the earthly liturgy as a *typos* of the angelic liturgy.

Cyril is well acquainted with the method of typological commentary that interprets the liturgy as an *imitation* of the saving work performed by Christ, as we shall see shortly when we turn to his instructions on baptism. In his interpretation of the eucharistic liturgy, however, the *image* has become a representation rather than an analogy based on the internal contents of the Eucharist. This may be the reason why Cyril departs from this method, that is, why after applying it to baptism, he carefully avoids it in his catecheses on the Eucharist.

II. BAPTISM AND IMITATION

Cyril's concept of *imitation* is grounded in the idea of *identity*. E. J. Cutrone rightly emphasizes this point: "Cyril regards the rite as the place where the individual achieves identification with Christ[17] in the central moment of his salvific activity. Imitation does not consist in a reactualization of the historical events of Christ's life."[18] Cyril's view could not be more clearly explained.

In Cyril, imitation (*mimēsis*) is a very carefully defined sacramental concept, the content of which can be understood only through a study of his vocabulary, since he is very careful to use an appropriate terminology. When he speaks of *mimēsis*, he is not referring to the external, ritual, visible aspect of the celebration, but to its sacramentality, that is, its internal and invisible dimension. Let us look at some passages, taking first the ritual and then the sacramental aspects of the celebration.

A. Symbol

According to Cyril, rites belong to the order of symbol, although not in the modern sense of this world. It is the external, ritual, visible aspect of the liturgy that is described by the word "symbol." Thus, when the candidates renounce Satan, they turn to the West, since the West is the place of darkness; they look to the West "symbolically"[19] because of the connection between darkness and Satan. When the rite of renunciation is complete, the candidates turn to "the East, the region of light," in order to make their profession of Trinitarian faith. This action too is called "symbolic,"[20] and is not thought of as endowed with sacramentality.[21] In fact, this "orientation," or turning to the East, signifies only the greatness and importance of the East due to the fact that God had placed paradise there.

The same conception of symbol recurs in connection with the oil for anointing: "Just as after the invocation (*epiklēsis*) of the Holy Spirit the bread of the Eucharist is no longer simple bread but the body of Christ, so too by reason of the invocation this holy perfume is no longer a pure and simple or, one might say, ordinary perfume but a gift of Christ." Therefore, since it is sacramental, "this perfume is used for a symbolic anointing of your forehead and other senses. The body is anointed with this visible perfume, but the soul is sanctified by the Holy and life-giving Spirit."[22]

Anointing with the oil of exorcism has removed the candidates from the wild olive tree and united them to the true olive tree with all its richness. The oil that has been exorcized is a symbol of the abundance of Christ, the true olive tree in which the candidates now participate.[23] "Symbol," therefore, is to be understood not in a sacramental sense, but simply as indicative of meaning and explanatory power, despite the fact that the anointing and the oil do as such have sacramental value and efficacy.[24]

The symbolic and didactic character of the rites also emerges in *Homily* 5 (which is devoted to the explanation of the anaphora), when Cyril says that the washing of the hands is a "symbol" of our need of purification, since the hands are symbolic of our activities.[25]

The last two texts I shall consider are especially important. The first has to do with the rite of the triple immersion of the candidates in the water: this triple immersion is a "symbol" of Christ's three days in the tomb.[26] The second has to do with the relation between New Testament and the Old. Here Cyril establishes that the anointings in the Old Testament are symbols of the baptismal anointing[27]; he does not, however, confuse the levels and he carefully avoids the conception of typology that we saw in Ambrose, who applied the sacramentality of baptism to the Old Testament events and read these into the baptismal rites. Cyril does not take that approach; as we shall see a little later in his typology, he is careful to keep the two Testaments and the liturgical celebration suitably distinct and separate.

A study of the cited passages allows the conclusion that the term "symbol" points to the purely representative function of the rites and does not imply any sacramental efficacy. The rites have a representative and didactic capacity that can shed light on the contents of the celebration; this capacity does not, however, play a constitutive part in the sacramentality of the rites, but stands alongside it in a purely accessory and nonconstitutive role.

B. Imitation
Parallel with their symbolism, the rites have a dimension of sacramentality, which finds expression in the concept of "imitation." After saying that the triple immersion in baptism is a symbol of Christ's three days in the tomb, Cyril continues: "so you in your first immersion imitated Christ's first day in the earth where he was immersed in darkness."[28]

At this point, everything suggests a nonsacramental use of the term "imitate," including the fact that the statement is in close continuity with the preceding use of the word "symbol." The sacramental significance of the term does, however, emerge clearly in the immediately following comment: "In one and the same moment you died and were born: this saving water was your tomb and your mother. . . . One and the same moment produced these two events, and your [new] birth coincided with your death."[29] There can be no doubt about the sacramental value of this "imitation." We can say, therefore, that insofar as the immersions and emergences are three, they are symbolic; insofar as they are actions that imitate what happened to Christ, they are endowed with sacramentality.

A similar point can be made in connection with nudity during the rite of baptism: just as Christ "by his nakedness on the cross stripped the principalities and powers," so the candidates stripped themselves and caused the image (eikōn) to slough off the old self. In both cases, there are questions not of meanings, but of actions, events that are vehicles of salvation. And so we find the word "imitate" used to describe the relation between the nakedness of the candidates for baptism and the nakedness of Christ on the cross.[30] The fruit of "imitating" is a "likeness" or "image" (mimēma). Because the candidates have imitated Christ, they have regained the original justice of the first human being: "you were naked in the sight of all but you did not blush. Truly you possessed the image (mimēma) of the first human being, Adam, who was naked in paradise and did not blush."[31]

It is clear from these passages that Cyril assigns a sacramental efficacy and value to the actions signified by the words "imitation" and "imitate."

Cyril's thought can be further clarified with the help of other passages of the same homily, in which he contrasts "image" and "truth":

"We are not really dead, we have not really been buried, we have not really been crucified and raised to life again, but while the imitation (mimēsis) is only an image (eikōn), the salvation is real. Christ was really crucified, really buried, and truly raised to life again, and all this grace has been given to us in order that, participating in his sufferings by imitating them, we may really obtain salvation."[32]

This passage does not, of course, cast doubt on the ontological value of the sacrament. It does, however, distinguish carefully between the historical phase of salvation, which is characterized by the words "really" (*ontōs*) and "truly" (*alēthōs, en alētheia*), and the sacramental phase, which is conveyed by the paired terms "imitation" and "image." The object of the imitation is the passion of Christ, the point being that by imitating it, one truly participates in it: "participating in his sufferings by imitating them."

The paragraph that follows immediately repeats this last idea with equal clarity. Our baptism (it is stated) cannot be said to bring only the forgiveness of sins, as did the baptism of John, or to be a means only of filial adoption, and not a participation in the passion of Christ. Cyril forcefully asserts that, on the contrary, Christian baptism is "a participation, through imitation, in the real sufferings of Christ."[33] This view of Cyril is based on Romans 6:3–4, which he cites here. In the next paragraph, the citation is completed with the addition of verse 5. This verse, which contains the term *homoiōma* (likeness), seems to be the basis for his teaching on "image–imitation."

For the moment, I need only conclude that the sacramentality of the liturgical rites is described by the two words "image" and "imitation," which are understood in an ontological sense and not in the sense of a ritual representation, that is, a kind of dramatization. The element of ritual representation has to do rather with the symbolic value of the rites.

C. Likeness

In Cyril's commentary, the Pauline word "likeness" has the same sacramental significance as "image"and "imitation."[34] Here is how Cyril explains Romans 6:5:

"He does not say, 'If we have been planted together by death,' but 'by the likeness of death.' In Christ's case there was a real death, his soul being separated from his body; his burial was likewise a real burial, his body being wrapped in a clean linen cloth; in his case all this truly happened. In our case, on the other hand, there is a likeness of death and suffering; but when it comes to salvation there is not a likeness but the reality itself."[35]

Homoiōma (likeness) is here contrasted with "truth" exactly as *eikōn* (image) is contrasted with "truth" in *Homily* 2, 5; we can, therefore, conclude that the two words are equivalent.

"Likeness" occurs not only in the passage just cited, which is a commentary on Romans 6:5 and therefore displays the influence of Pauline language, but also in another passage in which one would expect the more usual *eikōn* as indication of sacramentality: "As Christ was truly baptized and buried and raised up, so you have been deemed worthy of being crucified, buried, and raised up with him in a likeness (*en homoiōmati*) through baptism."[36] Cyril, therefore, has made his own the Pauline theology of baptism as a likeness of Christ's death.

Baptism is a death. Lest, however, it be confused and identified with bodily death, a specification is added: baptism is certainly a death but death in a different mode, namely, death in likeness. The death of Christ was a death in the usual sense; ours is a death in likeness, because it is not a bodily but a baptismal death. Both are real but in different ways; because of this realism, it can be said that the salvation received is not a likeness but the reality.

This particular form of sacramental realism (*eikōn–homoiōma–mimēsis*) is further explained by the concomitant use of *koinōnia* to describe the relation between the rite and the passion of Christ. The word *koinōnia* here is taken directly from the passage on the Eucharist in 1 Corinthians 10:16–17. In these verses, Paul does not say, strictly speaking, that the cup is the blood of Christ and the bread his body; he says rather that the eucharistic cup is a communion in the blood of Christ and the eucharistic bread a communion in his body.[37] The word *koinōnia* points to sacramentality and defines the nature of the eucharistic cup and bread.

The Pauline words *homoiōma* and *koinōnia* do not recur verbatim in the texts of Cyril, but, because of their influence on the formulas he uses to express sacramental realism, they are to be regarded as the direct foundation of Cyril's sacramental teaching, which is neatly expressed in the words "imitation in an image" (*en eikoni hē mimēsis*).[38]

D. Antitypos

The word *antitypos*[39] is not an alternative to the three already discussed; in fact, the baptismal use of *antitypos* can be connected directly with *homoiōma*. Cyril mentions those who claim that as the baptism of John brought only the forgiveness of sins, so Christian baptism can bring only the forgiveness of sins, along with adoption as children. In response, he asserts that baptism is also an "*antitypos* of the sufferings of Christ."[40] A little later, when ending his discussion of this theme, he speaks of baptism as a "*homoiōma* of the death and sufferings of Christ"[41] and says that it includes a "*koinōnia*, by an imitation, in the real sufferings of Christ."[42]

When Christians receive "the sacrament" (*to antitypon*) of the Holy Spirit, they become images (*eikones*) of Christ,[43] for the anointing with chrism that follows the baptismal bath is "the *antitypon* with which Christ was anointed. This is the Holy Spirit."[44] Here we see clearly the sacramental significance of *antitypos*, which ensures the identity between the descent of the Spirit on Christ and the sacramental descent of the Spirit on Christians. In a later homily, Cyril will use the same sacramental terminology to bring out more clearly the difference that exists between the "sacrament" and that of which it is the sacrament: "When you eat, it is not bread and wine that you eat but the *antitypon* of the body and blood of Christ."[45]

It is the carefully determined meaning that Cyril gives to this word that makes it possible for him to underscore both the identity of the liturgical rite with the foundational events and the difference between the two, since the two are never on the same plane. In Cyril's terminology, *typos* has the same meaning as *antitypos*.[46] This accounts for his peculiar sacramental use of *typos* and *antitypos* that do not form a pair, with one referring to the event and the other to the sacrament of the event. No, the two are now treated as synonyms and no longer represent the application of typology to the theology of the sacraments. But this shift was not due to any ignorance of biblical typology on Cyril's part; in fact, his other two uses of the word *typos* are located in that area.

III. CYRIL'S TYPOLOGY

In Cyril, as in the other Fathers I have been discussing, we find the same characteristic elements of typology and mystagogy. He sets up a typological relation between the Old Testament and the New and then applies this relationship to the explanation of liturgical rites. It must be acknowledged, however, that he does so with great restraint and that he does not absolutize typology. In fact, typology is only one component of his theological method; it is one fact among many that must be taken into account, and not the essential constituent of his mystagogical method.

Cyril deals with typology in a very orderly way at well-defined points in his homilies; he limits this type of argument to a specific moment in his total treatment of a given subject. Thus, it comes at the beginning of his commentary on baptism,[47] at the end of his discussion of anointing,[48] and at the end of the first homily on the Eucharist.[49]

The rite of renunciation of Satan, which is described at the beginning of the first homily on baptism, is explained by means of Old Testament typology. Cyril cites the events of the Exodus: the wickedness of the pharaoh, the sending of Moses by God in order to rescue the Hebrew people from enslavement to the Egyptians, the blood of the lamb smeared on the homes of the Hebrews, and the crossing of the Red Sea.

Before I go any further, I must call attention to the difference between Cyril's mystagogical typology and that of other commentators, such as Ambrose. In the latter's view, the events of the Old Testament receive their meaning, interpretation, and raison d'etre from the events of the New Testament. The events of the one Testament are not only connected with those of the other, but even belong to them at the ontological level. Typology seems to remove all distinction between the New and Old Testaments, so that every event of the New Testament belongs also to the

161

Old, whereas every event of the Old Testament acquires its true meaning only in the New. Thus, baptism is already a fact in the Old Testament, and Melchizedek is an author of the sacraments.

Not so in Cyril: here there is a clear distinction made between the two testaments, and it is no longer the case that the saving events of the New Testament belong also to the Old. The Old Testament contains not the events, but their *typos*: "This you must understand: that this type is contained in the ancient story."[50]

The Old Testament events are related, one by one, to their New Testament correlatives in a real and proper learning process: "Pass with me now from things ancient to things new, from the type to the truth. There Moses was sent by God to Egypt; here Christ is sent from the Father's bosom into the world. . . ."[51] Cyril's thought is very clearly stated: there is question not of seeing the one reality present in the other, but of passing from one reality to another. If this is to be done, there must be a correspondence between the events of the two Testaments; this correspondence is ensured by a likeness between them,[52] in accordance with the method usual in typology.

I think it can be said, in conclusion, that in Cyril's view, the passage from the one Testament to the other is based on the correspondence that exists between the two and not on any reciprocal immanence. The difference between the two Testaments is important because it has to do with the ontological structure of their relationship. I must now ask whether Cyril's further uses of typology confirms or undermines this conclusion.

One might regard as probative his citation of Ecclesiastes 3:2, which he introduces with the statement that "what Solomon says of another subject can doubtless be adapted to you."[53] But the citation seems too limited to a particular occasion; it is, in addition, belied by another, equally occasional, that says exactly the opposite: "It is you that God had in mind when he said: 'Do not touch my anointed ones' (Ps 104:14)."[54]

The question must be asked whether *typos* is used in biblical typology in the same way as it is in sacramental realism, where it is equivalent to *antitypos,* or whether, on the contrary, *typos* in biblical typology is to be regarded as effectively stripped of onto-logical value, as is the case with the word "symbol," as we saw earlier.

Cyril's typological commentary on the anointing gives us the an-swer, because it treats "type" and "symbol" as exact parallels. He begins his discussion of scriptural prefigurations by saying: "You must realize that the symbol of this anointing is to be found in the ancient scriptures." Then, after telling his audience how Moses communicated the divine command to his brother and how he bathed him in water and anointed him, Cyril con-cludes that Aaron was called "christos" (anointed) "in virtue of this obviously typical anointing." He then goes on to the case of Solomon, who was likewise anointed. He ends by applying what he has been saying to Christians: "But these things happened to them in a type (*typikōs*); to you, however, they happen not in a type (*typikōs*) but in truth (*alethōs*)."[55]

This opposition of *typos* and "truth" is not yet conclusive proof, however, since a similar opposition holds between *homoiōma* and "truth," even though, as we have seen, Cyril uses *homoiōma* as the equivalent of *antitypos.*

Conclusive proof is to be found in what immediately follows in Cyril's text, when he tells his audience the difference between anointing "in type" and anointing "in truth": "To you, however, they happen not in a type (*typikōs*) but in truth (*alethōs*), because he who was anointed with the Holy Spirit is truly the source of your salvation. He is truly the firstfruits, and you are the dough; if the firstfruits are holy, then holiness will certainly permeate the entire lump." The relation "firstfruits–mass of dough" (*aparchē—phurama*) is what guarantees the "truth" (i.e., reality) of salvation, but the operation of this relation is restricted to "you" in contrast with what happened "in type" in the Old Testament.

It is legitimate, therefore, to conclude that the word *typos,* as used in biblical typology, belongs to the same semantic field as *symbolon* and not to the semantic field of *typos, homoiōma, eikōn,* and *mimēsis,* which is the sacramental field.

The Old Testament passages that Cyril cites at the end of his first instruction on the Eucharist[56] add nothing to what we have seen thus far. It is clear, there too, that according to Cyril, the Old Testament does indeed speak of the liturgy of Christian initiation, but only in a symbolic way.[57] A final confirmation of this interpretation can be seen in Cyril's interpretation of the Lavabo, which symbolizes the need of purification because the hands are the symbol of human activity. This symbolic meaning, which is expressly stated as such, is supported by a biblical citation that plays the usual typological role: "Have you not heard blessed David unveiling this same mystery (*mystagogountos*) and saying: 'I will wash my hands among the innocent and I will circle your altar, O Lord' (Ps 25:6)? Therefore, to wash one's hands is to be not guilty of sins."[58]

IV. CONCLUSION

We may conclude that Cyril's biblical typology can serve to explain the meaning of the rites, but not to ensure the connection between saving event and liturgical rite. The reason is that his biblical typology operates on the level of symbolism and that he does not use this hermeneutical method to support sacramental realism. He does forcefully maintain sacramental realism, but he backs it up, so to speak, with the theory of "image" and "imitation" of the saving actions of Christ.

This method is applied to baptism and anointing but, oddly enough, it does not seem to be applied to the Eucharist. The omission is not easy to explain, especially since the Last Supper is Cyril's point of reference. The reason is possibly his concern to prevent the ontological category of "image"–"imitation" from being interpreted in the purely external terms of allegorical representation, as if the image and imitation were a matter simply of dramatization. This concern is fully justified by the fact that the Ritual underlying the liturgy that Cyril celebrated had already moved in that direction and that other authors, such as Theodore of Mopsuestia, had faithfully taken their lead from it.

CHAPTER SIX

Final Reflections

I. MYSTAGOGY AS THEOLOGY

The mystagogical homilies I have now finished studying are regarded as among the most important witnesses to the liturgy of the late fourth century. They were delivered in the context of Christian initiation and as such make up a literary genre with special characteristics that differentiate them from other mystagogies, although, of course, they share certain fundamental traits with all of these.

These homilies are fairly homogeneous among themselves, all of them having been delivered within a rather circumscribed period and geographical area. Despite this major advantage for the student, it proves difficult to formulate a general theory that would account for all the aspects that have emerged from analysis of these texts. As a matter of fact, we know very little about these great mystagogies of the late fourth century; we have the texts but almost nothing else that would help us situate them in a detailed way.

Were we to attempt, under these conditions, to construct at all costs a general theory of mystagogy, we might well end up taking positions that are historically erroneous because vitiated by anachronism. In fact, from all the material discussed in the preceding chapters, it becomes very clear that the mystagogical method of each author differs from that of the others, despite the fact that all these men share a common purpose: to give the baptized the understanding and motivation that will enable them to live the life in Christ that has been bestowed in them in the liturgical celebration. To this end, the Fathers develop a theology of this liturgy wherein the new life of the neophytes has its origin.

As I made clear in the general remarks at the beginning of this study, the liturgical theology I have been studying always uses typology and indeed does so necessarily. And, in fact, each of the four authors uses typology as the proper method for developing a theology of the liturgy. At the same time, however, each of the four differs from the others in his use of typology; it should come as no surprise, therefore, that this difference makes itself felt in their mystagogical method and leads to the radical differences we have been seeing.

The different ways of using typology and, therefore, the different mystagogical methods do not correspond to the school to which the author belongs (Alexandrian school, Antiochene school) or to the direct influence of the method used by Philo of Alexandria. On the contrary, we have seen Theodore developing a profoundly allegorical mystagogy, even though he belongs to the Antiochene school; his method is due rather to his source, that is, the Ritual that regulated the liturgical celebrations of his Church. At the same time, however, we have seen that Cyril of Jerusalem, whose liturgy is a development of the same Ritual, rejects the method of allegorical interpretation of the liturgy, at least for the Eucharist.

From these facts, it is clear that when it came to mystagogy, there was a wide range of choices and that each author could develop his mystagogy along definitely personal lines. This is true in particular of John Chrysostom, who makes morality the keystone of all his mystagogical homilies; these do not on this account become any less mystagogical than the homilies of the other authors.

It is possible that in these choices, not only the pastoral needs to which the preacher had to respond, but also his personal taste played a part. Thus, Ambrose's use of liturgical typology is very different from Cyril's. For Ambrose, the two Testaments are, as it were, superimposed on one another, thus giving rise to a unique liturgical perspective that explains sacramental realism and sacramental efficacy, while at the same time maintaining a degree of distinction between event and sacrament. In Cyril's approach, on the other hand, the two Testaments remain fully distinct, and the sacraments are in no way confused with the saving realities of which they are the sacraments; at the same time, however, Cyril comes down decidedly on the side of efficacy and realism. Theodore, too, maintains a strong realism, perhaps even an exaggerated realism, and yet his theory on the relation between eschatology and sacrament successfully preserves a difference or, better, a distance between the sacraments and the saving historical events that are the objects of the sacraments.

In Ambrose's view, biblical typology directly conveys the contents of the sacraments, whereas for Cyril, it only provides an external confirmation of sacramental theology, the latter being established by nontypological means.

In light of all this, only one claim can be made: mystagogy, or typology applied to the liturgy, is a way of constructing a theology of the sacraments. Given the mystagogical texts that we have, we must acknowledge that in the actual construction of this theology, many other factors play a part and explain the profound differences that exist among the several authors.

II. IMITATION AND TYPOLOGY

If mystagogy is the method used in constructing a theology of the sacraments, we will not be surprised to find that there are as many mystagogies as there are sacramental theologies or that there is more than one mystagogical method at work in the same text.

An example: in Ambrose, biblical typology serves to establish an ontological connection between two events, namely, the liturgical celebration and the event narrated in the Scriptures. It matters not whether the Scriptures are those of the Old Testament or the New. For, in fact, the Christian sacraments are older than those of the Jews, and Melchizedek is an author of the sacraments. This procedure ensures the historico-salvific realism and efficacy of the sacraments, but it also opens the way to a subsequent development that is already present in some passages of Ambrose himself and that he fully shares: the complete identification of the rite with the historical saving event.

Typology lends itself very well to this development. The theory of "imitation" and "likeness," on the other hand, does not lend itself as well and is therefore regressive, to the point of falling into complete disuse and being replaced by the doctrine of "presence" pure and simple.

This replacement is not an eccentric development but rather is perfectly consistent, inasmuch as the "imitation" and "likeness" apply not to the realm of the external and visible, but to the ontological structure of the liturgy. The problem with them is that they overemphasize otherness and difference and are therefore no longer compatible with a theology that is concerned more with the immanence of the event in relation to the rite than with the transcendence of the event over the rite.

The choice, of course, is not between immanence and transcendence, since, as Theodore teaches without using the vocabulary, immanence is possible only because of transcendence. The doctrine of "imitation" and "likeness" has a specific and strong ontological connotation that definitely implies "presence." As soon as otherness is seen as opposed to identity, the concept of "presence" prevails and then becomes the sole category of sacramental realism. The event is transformed into the liturgical rite; the body and blood of Christ are transformed into the bread and wine and are, therefore, "within" the bread and wine just as the Holy Spirit is "within" the water of baptism and the oil of anointing.

III. A CULTURAL AND PHILOSOPHICAL PROBLEM?
This evolution gives one the impression that the problem belongs less to the history of the liturgy and its interpretations than to the history of culture and philosophy.

In the homiles I have been considering, the discussion of sacramental realism starts with the observation that what is seen in the sacrament differs from what is believed about it (*aliud videtur, aliud intelligitur*). In order to move from appearances, which are the object of the senses, to true reality, which is the object of faith, some account must be given of the relationship between these two levels. The doctrine of sacramentality is intended to do precisely that; it is an answer to the question of the connection between two levels of *being* that correspond to two levels of *knowledge*, namely, seeing and believing.

If we turn to Cyril, we find that the entire technical vocabulary that he uses with great care in this context is already present in Plato's *Phaedo*.[1] The problem with which Plato is dealing is not, of course, sacramentality or the connection between what is seen and what is believed, but the relation between the one and the many and therefore the connection between the sensible and the intelligible.

"As a matter of fact, in his writings, Plato adopts various perspectives in this matter; he says that between the sensible and the intelligible there is a relation (a) of *mimēsis* or imitation, or (b) of *methexis* or participation,[2] or (c) of *koinōnia* or association, or (d) of *parousia* or presence."[3] And again: "The sensible is a *mimēsis* of the intelligible because it imitates it, though without ever attaining equality with it. . . . To the extent that the sensible achieves its own essence, it *participates*, that is, shares in the intelligible (and, in particular, through this 'sharing' in the Idea the sensible reality is and is knowable)."[4]

The distinction between two levels of reality, the intelligible and the sensible, is truly the master thread running through all of Platonic thought.[5] We should, therefore, not be surprised to find that when the Fathers of the Church were faced with an analogous problem in connection with the ontological value of the sacraments, they made use of concepts already developed by Plato and Platonism.

The development of the theory of the "supracelestial" (*hyperouranion*) helps Plato to explain the variety of sensible things with the aid of a superior and unifying principle (the Idea). The Idea provides an ontological explanation[6] of the sensible things that depend on it. In like manner, the historical saving event provides an ontological explanation of the sacrament that participates in it. We should bear in mind that the Middle Platonists "codified the interpretation of the Ideas as being thoughts of the divine mind"[7]; they also adopted the view that the Ideas "as such are the eternal paradigm and rule of all things."[8]

If the Platonism that the Fathers used sometimes casts doubt on the adequacy of their theoretical approach when it comes to ensuring sacramental realism, we ought to recall that the first function of the Idea and the Supracelestial is ontological, that is, the Idea exercises a function in the ontological structuring of the beings that participate in it.

At this point, a further step has to be taken. H. Krämer and K. Gaiser of the Tübingen School and G. Reale of the Catholic University of Milan have begun a new era in the interpretation of Plato with their retrieval and utilization of the Protology contained in the "unwritten teachings." G. Reale has this to say when speaking of the "unwritten teachings": "Only in the light of these is it possible to give the ontology of the Ideas (and therefore the entire thought of Plato) its unity and complete meaning."[9] In fact, "the reality which derives from the Principles is conceived by Plato not as existing on the horizontal plane but as forming a vertical structure, with a series of successive levels, each subordinate to those above it, and all depending in a similar manner on the two supreme Principles."[10]

If we adopt this perspective, it is completely logical to think of the sacrament as analogous, and not identical, with the historical saving event that is its ontological foundation and measure.[11]

A problem to which I constantly called attention as I analyzed the mystagogical homilies is that of the full identity or simple analogy between the sacrament and the object of which it is the sacrament. Here is how the problem is seen in Plato's ontology: "According to the predominance of the one or the other Principle, a thing can be 'equal' or 'unequal,' but insofar as it is a *particular being* it participates in both Principles. . . . Moreover, the same difference in the degree of the commingling of the two Principles is also at the basis of the relation between the intelligible and sensible worlds."[12] And again: "Plato therefore accepts the axiom that the foundation of ultimate principle can only be that which is *similar* in essence to the principiated and not that which is equal in essence to it, and consequently that there must be a difference in dimension between principle and principiated."[13]

In light of this new interpretation of Plato that is based on the Protology, Aristotle too undergoes a reappraisal, for he now appears as the continuator, albeit a critical one, of the Platonic system rather than as the author of a completely alternative system. One of the more important criticisms that Aristotle levels against Plato concerns precisely the Supracelestial; Aristotle suggested instead that the Ideas be understood "as forms-in-matter. This view of Aristotle had great success."[14]

If I am correct, in many passages of the patristic homilies that I have studied, the same itinerary is to be seen: (a) the starting point is the assertion that participation, imitation, likeness, and type explain the relation of identity between events and sacraments,[15] but then (b) the authors change course and end with a doctrine of events that become sacraments. The object of the sacrament becomes identical with the sacrament in the sense that it is immanentized and is henceforth within the sacrament. In this kind of development, we can see something like the problem Aristotle felt in face of the Platonic Ideas; he produced "a strong theoretical criticism" of them "which argued for the necessity of immanentizing them; he therefore reformulated the Ideas as forms-in-matter."[16] Be it noted: Ambrose himself is the author of the sacramental concept of "transfiguration," which is the remote ancestor of the medieval development of the theme of "transsubstantiation."

IV. A FINAL QUESTION
But were the Fathers conscious of all this? Certainly not. We, however, must indeed be conscious of it, for otherwise we will not properly understand the ontological thrust underlying patristic thought in this area. In fact, this thrust emerges with clarity only when we turn to the Platonic thought in the background and use it as a hermeneutical principle. If we are conscious of all this, we will also understand why the Fathers, who did not have full mastery of the ontology of the "second voyage" and the "unwritten teachings," finally abandoned typology as a

doctrine of the sacraments, because they felt the need of a greater sacramental realism.

This development depended less on the Fathers themselves than on the wider history of Platonic and Aristotelian thought. In fact, the meaning of the "second voyage" was forgotten as early as Speusippus, Plato's first successor as head of the Academy; in Speusippus' thinking, the great Platonic discovery of the suprasensible was already radically compromised and had almost entirely lost its deeper meaning.[17] Speusippus was succeeded by Xenocrates, who continued the movement of the Academy away from the metaphysical approach of its founder,[18] to the point where it must be acknowledged that Aristotle was Plato's true heir.[19] But even Aristotle had no better fate, inasmuch as the fruitful period of the Peripatetic School did not last much beyond the death of its founder.[20] Not until Philo and, subsequently, Middle Platonism was there a full recovery of the concept of the incorporeal and with it a return to the authentic spirit of Platonism.[21] Philo "reversed the perspective shared by all the Hellenistic schools and refused to allow the corporeal any ontological autonomy, that is, any ability to account for itself."[22] G. Reale concludes that in this way, the metaphysical advances made by Plato were fully retrieved.

Against this background, we must ask ourselves whether the Fathers whom we have been studying could have bridged the temporal and cultural distance separating them from Plato. Could they have reached back beyond the successive interpretations and schools and recovered the benefits of the Platonic "second voyage"? Could they have become aware of the "unwritten teachings" so as to have a good grasp of the ontological significance of Platonic thought? The answer is evidently that they could not.

The Fathers were men of their times and shared the culture and philosophical horizons of their age; they were not primarily professional philosophers. Theirs was a general kind of Platonism, unorganized and unsystematic, that allowed them only to derive from the works of the great master what was useful for their theological and pastoral needs. The fact is that they were pastors whose interests were not primarily systematic or speculative, as is very clear from their mystagogical homilies.

In conclusion, I can say that when we read passages of mystagogical thought that have some touch of Platonic phraseology, we must be aware that Platonic thought has a precise ontological dimension that was not fully taken over into the typology of the Fathers.[23]

On the one hand, then, we must grant that the Fathers were conscious of some ontological implications when they applied typology. Among the many examples we have seen in this study, I can cite the prothesis as described by Theodore: the prothesis seems to possess a sacramentality of its own insofar as it is a type of the death of Christ.

On the other hand, we must also grant that the Fathers were not fully conscious of this ontological dimension. For the fact is that they frequently treat "imitation" as the basis not of the innermost structure of the reality with which they are dealing[24] but of the ritual action insofar as this is externally visible and perceptible. The ritual action thus becomes an external representation, a kind of staging, of the death and resurrection of Christ. Even Ambrose, who has a precisely defined ontological concept of "likeness" (in the context of the Eucharist), ceases to appeal to this genre of typological categories when he is obliged to give a more cogent explanation of sacramental realism in the Eucharist.

The Fathers I have been studying show that they have difficulties in using biblical typology, so much so that they even abandon it precisely at the point where it must serve as vehicle for the ontological dimension of sacramentality. In the typological perspective, the "event" remains too much separated from the celebration that ought to contain it: the event remains "transcendent" in relation to the rite. The kind of question being asked and the kind of situation being faced are more in tune with the typical approach of Platonism than with that of Middle Platonism.[25]

This imperfect awareness of the ontological value of the categories being used had two consequences, even in the patristic period and even in the very authors I have studied. On the one hand, sacramental realism (required by faith) ceased to find its best expression in the categories of typology and began to be discussed in everyday language. The latter placed full emphasis on a true and proper sacramental "physicism" that ended in assertions of a "new" death and "new" resurrection of Christ in the liturgical action. This situation I would describe as "naive realism" or even "exaggerated realism."

On the other hand, the ancient mystagogical conception of things continued to influence the interpretation of the sacraments, both by its vocabulary and by its specific theology and specific method (biblical typology). But, since the ontological perspective proper to typology had been lost, this entire hermeneutical method came to be regarded as inadequate for expressing sacramental realism. As a result, it came to have a purely formal, symbolic, and external representational value of the allegorical type; it was suited now for developing the role of didactic sign that could bring out some of the content of the liturgy.

V. CONCLUSION

In offering these reflections of Platonism, I am not suggesting that they explain all the doctrines and problems that have emerged from the analysis of the mystagogical homilies. Were I to suggest this, I myself would be succumbing to the dangerous temptation of trying to produce a general theory of mystagogy. These reflections are offered, then, purely with a view of methodology, that is, to keep us mindful of some factors in the culture of the patristic age that could not but influence the Fathers of the late fourth century, all of them men in the public eye, all of them important figures and leaders of thought.

174

Abbreviations

CCL	Corpus Christianorum, Series Latina
CSEL	Corpus Scriptorum Ecclesiasticorum Latinorum
EL	*Ephemerides Liturgicae*
Greg	*Gregorianum*
OCP	*Orientalia Christiana Periodica*
PG	Patrologia Graeca, ed. J.-P. Migne
RivLit	*Rivista Liturgica*
RSR	*Recherches de science religieuse*
SC	Sources chrétiennes
ST	Studi e Testi
TDNT	*Theological Dictionary of the New Testament*, ed. G. Bromiley

Select Bibliography

SOURCES

Botte, B., (ed.), *Ambroise de Milan. Des sacrements. Des mystères. Explication du symbole*, SC 25bis (Paris, 1961).

Cerbelaud, D., (ed.), *Cyrillonas. L'agneau véritable. Hymnes, cantiques, homélies* (Chevetogne, 1984).

Ceresa-Gastaldo, A., (ed.), *Giovanni Cristostomo. Le catechesi battesimali* (Rome, 1982).

Chrysostom, John, *Catecheses* I and II (ed. Montfaucon), in PG 49:223–232, 231–240.

———, *Homilia de proditionae Judae*, in PG 49:373–382.

Férotin, M., (ed.). *Le Liber Mozarabicus Sacramentorum et les manuscrits mozarabes*, Monumenta Ecclesiae sacra 6 (Paris, 1912).

Funk, F. X., (ed.), *Didascalia et Constitutiones Apostolorum* (Paderborn, 1905).

Hänggi, A., and Pahl, I., (eds.), *Prex Eucharistica. Textus e variis liturgiis antiquioribus selecti*, Spicilegium Friburgense 12 (Fribourg, 1968).

Hanssens, I. M., (ed.), *Amalarii episcopi opera liturgica omnia II. Liber officialis*, ST 139 (Vatican City, 1948).

Harkins, P. W., (trans.), *St. John Chrysostom. Baptismal Instructions*, Ancient Christian Writers 31 (New York, 1963).

Hussey, J. M., and McNulty, P. A., (trans.), *Nicholas Cabasilas. A Commentary on the Divine Liturgy* (London, 1960).

Metzger. B. M., *A Textual Commentary on the Greek New Testament* (London and New York, 1971).

Metzger, M., (ed.)., *Les Constitutions apostoliques* (Livres I-II; III and VI; VII-VIII), SC 320, 329, 336 (Paris, 1985, 1986, 1987).

176

Mingana, A., (trans.), *Commentary of Theodore of Mopsuestia on the Lord's Prayer and on the Sacraments of Baptism and the Eucharist*, Woodbrooke Studies 6 (Cambridge, 1933).

Papadopoulos-Kerameus, A., (ed.), *Varia Graeca Sacra* (in Russian) (St. Petersburg, 1909).

Perler, O., (ed.), *Méliton de Sardes. Sur la Pâque*, SC 123 (Paris, 1966).

Piédagnel, A., (ed.), *Cyrille de Jérusalem. Catéchèses mystagiques*, SC 126 (Paris, 1966).

Salaville, S., Bornert, R., Gouillard, J., and Périchon, P., (eds.), *Nicolas Cabasilas. Explication de la Divine Liturgie*, SC 4bis (Paris, 1967).

Tonneau, R., and Devreesse, R., (ed.), *Les homélies catéchétiques de Théodore Mopsueste*, ST 145 (Vatican City, 1949).

Wenger, A., (ed.), *Jean Chrysostome. Huit catéchèses baptismales inédites*, SC 50bis (Paris, 1970).

DICTIONARIES

Bornkamm, G., *Mystērion*, in *TDNT* 7.

Lampe, G. W. H., (ed.), *A Patristic Greek Lexicon* (Oxford, 1961).

Simonetti, M., "Teodoro di Mopsuestia," in A. Di Berardino (ed.), *Dizionario patristico e di antichità cristiane* (Casale Monferrato, 1984), 3382–3386.

Stephanus, H., *Thesaurus graecae linguae* (Graz, 1954), 1244.

BOOKS

Bornert, R., *Les commentaires byzantins de la divine liturgie du VIIe au XVe siècle*, Archives de l'Orient Chrétien 9 (Paris, 1966).

Bouëssé, H., *Théologie et sacerdoce* (Chambéry, 1938).

de la Taille, M., *Mysterium fidei. De augustissimo corporis et sanguinis Christi sacrificio et sacramento Elucidationes L in tres libros distinctae* (Paris, 1931).

de Montclos, J., *Lanfranc et Bérenger. La controverse eucharistique du XIe siècle* (Louvain, 1971).

Devreesse, R., *Essai sur Théodore de Mopsueste*, ST 141 (Vatican City, 1948).

Eliade, M., *Birth and Rebirth. Rites and Symbols of Initiation*, trans. W. R. Trask (New York, 1958).

Finn, T., *The Liturgy of Baptism in the Baptismal Instructions of St. John Chrysostom* (Washington, D.C., 1967).

Fittkau, G., *Der Begriff des Mysteriums bei Johannes Chrysostomus*, Theophaneia 9 (Bonn, 1953).

Francesconi, G., *Storia e simbolo* (Brescia, 1981).

Jugie, M., *Theologia dogmatica christianorum orientalium ab ecclesia catholica dissidentium* III (Paris, 1930), 318.

Kramer, H., *Platone e i fondamenti della metafisica. Saggio sulla teoria dei principi e sulle dottrine non scritte di Platone con una raccolta dei documenti fondamentali in edizione bilingue e bibliografia*, trans. from the German with an introduction by Giovanni Reale (Milan, 1987).

Laurance, J. D., *"Priest" as Type of Christ. The Leader of the Eucharist in Salvation History according to Cyprian of Carthage* (New York, 1984).

Ligier, L., *La confirmation* (Paris, 1973).

Luneau, A., *L'histoire du salut chez les Pères de l'Eglise. La doctrine des âges du monde* (Paris, 1964).

Quasten, J., *Patrology*, 3 vols. (Westminster, MD, 1950, 1953, 1960).

Reale, G., *Per una nuova interpretatione di Platone* (Milan, 1987).

————, *Storia della filosofia antica 2. Platone e Aristotele; 3. I sistemi dell'età ellenistica; 4. Le scuole dell'età imperiale* (Milan, 1987).

Reine, F. J., *The Eucharistic Doctrine and Liturgy of the Mystagogical Catecheses of Theodore of Mopsuestia* (Washington, D.C., 1942).

Rentinck, P., *La cura pastorale in Antiochia nel IV secolo* (Rome, 1970).

Riley, H. M., *Christian Initiation. A Comparative Study of the Interpretation of the Baptismal Liturgy in the Mystagogical Writings of Cyril of Jerusalem, John Chrysostom, Theodore of Mopsuestia, and Ambrose of Milan* (Washington, D.C., 1974).

Sanchez Caro, J. M., *Eucaristia y Historia de la Salvaciòn* (Madrid, 1983).

van de Paverd, F., *Zur Geschichte der Messliturgie in Antiocheia und Konstantinopel gegen Ende des vierten Jahrhunderts. Analyse der Quellen bei Johannes Chrysostomos*, Orientalia Christiana Analecta 187 (Rome, 1970).

ARTICLES

Bori, P.-C., "Attualità di un detto antico: 'La sacra scrittura cresce con chi la legge,' " *Intersezioni* 6 (1986): 15–49.

Botte, B., "L'onction postbaptismale dans l'ancien patriarcat d'Antioche," in *Miscellanea liturgica in onore di S. E. il Card. G. Lercaro* (Rome), 2(1967): 795–888.

Brock, S. P., "The Transition to a Post-baptismal Anointing in the Antiochene Rite," in B. D. Spinks (ed.), *The Sacrifice of Praise. Studies on the Themes of Thanksgiving and Redemption in the Central Prayers of the Eucharistic and Baptismal Liturgies. In Honour of A. H. Couratin* (Rome, 1981), 215–225.

Camelot, T., "Note sur la théologie baptismale des Catéchèses attribuées à S. Cyrille de Jérusalem." in *Festschrift J. Quasten* (Münster, 1970), 724–729.

Ceresa-Gastaldo, A., "Teoria e prassi nella catechesi battesimale di S. Giovanni Crisostomo," in S. Felici (ed.), *Catechesi battesimale e riconciliazione nei Padri del IV secolo* (Rome, 1984).

Cutrone, E. J., "Cyril's Mystagogical Catecheses and the Evolution of the Jerusalem Anaphora," *OCP* 44 (1978): 53–64.

Daniélou, J., "Figure et événement chez Méliton de Sardes," in *Neotestamentica et patristica (Festgabe O. Cullmann)* (Leiden, 1962), 282–292.

———, "Traversée de la Mer Rouge et baptême aux premiers siècles," *RSR* 33 (1946): 402–430.

Dekkers, E., "Limites sociales et linguistiques de la pastorale liturgique de s. Jean Chrysostom," *Augustinianum* 20 (1980); 119–129.

de Lubac, H., " 'Typologie' et 'allégorisme,' " *RSR* 34 (1947): 180–226.

Di Stefano, T., "La libertà radicale dell'immagine in S. Gregorio di Nissa," *Divus Thomas* (Piac.) 4 (1972): 431–454.

Federici, T., "La mistagogia della chiesa. Ricerca spirituale," in E. Ancilli, *Mistagogia e direzione spirituale* (Milan, 1985), 162–245.

Guardini, R., "La prédication mystagogiue," *La Maison-Dieu* 158 (1984): 137–147.

Gy, P.-M., "La notion chrétienne d'initiation. Jalons pour une enquête," *La Maison-Dieu* 132 (1977): 33–54.

Jourjon, M., "Quatre conseils pour un bon usage des Pères en sacramentaire," *La Maison-Dieu* 119 (1974): 74–84.

Kretschmar, G., "Nouvelles recherches sur l'initiation chrétienne," *La Maison-Dieu* 132 (1977): 7–32.

Laurance, J.-D., "Le présidente de l'Eucharistie selon Cyprien de Carthage: un nouvel examen," *La Maison-Dieu* 154 (1983): 151–165.

Léon-Dufour, X., "Corps du Christ et eucharistie selon Saint Paul," in *Le corps et le corps du Christ dans la Première Epître aux Corintiens* (Congrès de l'ACFEB, Tarbes, 1981; Paris, 1983), 225–255.

Ligier, L., "L'anaphore de la *Tradition apostolique* dans le *Testamentum Domini*," in B. D. Spinks (ed.), *The Sacrifice of Praise* . . . (Rome, 1981), 91–106.

Lietzmann, H., "Die Liturgie des Theodor von Mopsuestia," *Sitzungsberichte der preussischen Akademie der Wissenschaften* (Berlin, 1933), 915–936.

Longeat, J.-P., "Les rites du baptême dans les homélies catéchétiques de Théodore de Mopsueste," *Questions liturgiques* 66 (1985): 193–202.

Petit, I., "Sur les catéchèses postbaptismals de S. Ambroise," *Revue bénédictine* 68 (1958): 256–264.

Renoux, A., "Les catéchèses mystagogiques dans l'organization hiérosolimitaine du IVᵉ et Vᵉ siècle," *Le Muséon* 78 (1965): 355–359.

Sartore, D., "Il mistero del battesimo nelle catechesi di S. Giovanni Crisostomo," *Lateranum* 50 (1984): 358–395.

————, "La mistagogia, modello e sorgente di spiritualita cristiana," *RivLit* 73 (1986): 508–521.

Vaccari, A., "La teoria esegetica antiochena," *Biblica* 15 (1934): 94–101.

Vanni, U., "*Homoiōma* in Paolo," *Greg* 58 (1977): 321–345, 431–470.

Wenger, A., "La tradition des oeuvres de saint Jean Chrysostome. I. Catéchèses inconnues et homélies peu connues," *Revue des études byzantines* 14 (1956): 5–48.

Notes

1. Baptism includes several anointings, one of which in the West became an independent rite, separate from baptism: the rite of confirmation.

2. I have in mind here two anaphoras, one archaic and very simple, and the other evolving from the first; see my article, "La struttura dell'anafora nelle Catechesi di Teodoro di Mopsuestia," *EL* 102 (in press).

3. E. J. Cutrone, "Cyril's Mystagogical Catecheses and the Evolution of the Jerusalem Anaphora," *OCP* 44 (1978): 52–64.

4. End of the fourth century. See P.-P. Joannou (ed.), *Discipline générale antique (II-IX s.)* (Fonti per la redazione del Codice di Diritto Caronico, fasc. IX, 4 vols.; Grottaferrata [Rome], 1962– 1964), 127. L. Ligier, *La confirmation* (Paris, 1978),134, gives excellent arguments for dating the Council of Laodicea before the First Canonical Letter of Basil to Amphilochius.

5. This is how Ligier (n. 4) translates the page (131).

6. Joannou (n.4) 149.

7. *Ibid.*, 150.

8. See also Canon 47.

9. G. Francesconi, *Storia e simbolo* (Brescia, 1981).

10. The same words are used both for the sacraments and for the relation between the two Testaments (see L. F. Pizzolato, *La dottrina esegetica di Sant'Ambrogio* [Milan, 1978], 68–87), but the meaning and the way in which the same words are used differ in the two applications.

11. See note 2.

12. In his teaching on exegesis, Theodore is profoundly "Antiochene," that is, he does not indulge in allegorical interpretation. On the other

hand, he makes extensive use of allegory in interpreting the liturgy; in fact, it is difficult to find anywhere else so marked an allegorical approach as in Theodore. This is another fact that bids us to avoid confusing the exegetical and sacramental vocabularies of these authors, even when the words are materially the same.

CHAPTER ONE

1. H. Stephanus, *Thesaurus graecae linguae* (Graz, 1954), col. 1244; G. Bornkamm, "Mysterion," *TDNT* 7:645–716; T. Federici, "La mistagogia della chiesa. Ricerca spirituale," in E. Ancilli, *Mistagogia e direzione spiritual* (Milan, 1985), 165–169 and esp. 194–196; E. Mazza, "La portata teologica del termine 'mistero,'" *RivLit* 74 (1987): 321–338.

2. Federici (n. 1), 165ff.

3. R. Bornert, *Les commentaires byzantins de la divine liturgie du VII\(^e\) au XV\(^e\) siécle*, Archives de l'Orient chrétien 9 (Paris, 1966), 29.

4. For a complete list of references to the works of the Fathers cited here and for a more complete inventory of the meanings of the word, see Bornert (n. 3), 29, note 1; and G. W. H. Lampe (ed.), *A Patristic Greek Lexicon* (Oxford, 1961), s.v.

5. S. Salaville, R. Bornert, J. Gouillard, and P. Périchon (eds.), *Nicolas Cabasilas. Explication de la divine liturgie*, SC 4bis (Paris, 1967), 20.

6. *Ibid.*, chap. 34 (212–218); see also the mediation of Christ and the sanctification of the dead (chaps. 44–45 [252–258]).

7. *Ibid.*, 44.

8. Chaps. 29–30 (178–198).

9. Chap. 32 (202–206).

10. M. de la Taille, *Mysterium fidei. De augustissimo corporis et sanguinis Christi sacrificio atque sacramento Elucidationes L in tres libro distinctae* (Paris, 1931), 101–104, 109–110, 36–39; see also 83, 195, 303–317, and 676.

11. H. Boüessé, *Théologie et sacerdoce* (Chambéry, 1938), 145–146, 125–126.

12. M. Jugie, *Theologia dogmatica christianorum orientalium ab ecclesia catholica dissidentium* III (Paris, 1930), 318.

13. Gouillard (n. 5), 26.

14. On this point, Cabasilas depends on the source as Ambrose, namely, John Chrysostom, *De proditione Judae homilia* 1, 6 (PG 49:380).

15. Ambrose, *De sacramentis* IV, 15 (Botte 110): "Which words of Christ? The words by which all things were made. The Lord commanded and the heavens were made; the Lord commanded and the earth was made, the Lord commanded and all creatures were brought into being. You see, then, how effective the words of Christ are. If then the words of Christ are so powerful that things which were not began to be, how much more effective must they be in changing what already exists into something else! The heavens were not, the sea was not, the land was not, but listen to what David says: 'He spoke and they were made; he commanded and they were created.' "

Again, in *De sacramentis* IV, 23 (Botte 114): "Before the words of Christ the cup is full of wine and water; when the words of Christ have exerted their power, the water and wine become the blood that redeemed the people. See, then, the ways in which the words of Christ are powerful to change all things. The Lord Jesus himself then tells us that we receive his body and blood. Shall we doubt his trustworthiness and testimony?"

Cabasilas (n. 5), chapter 29 (180–190): "The blessed Chrysostom, they [the Latins] say, bears witness that these words [the 'words of consecration'] consecrate the offerings, when he says that just as the words of the Creator, 'Be fruitful and multiply,' spoken on a single occasion by God, continue to take effect, so the words once spoken by the Savior are also operative for ever. . . . We too believe that the Lord's words are what accomplishes the mystery, but they do so by means of the priest and his intervention and prayer. These words do not have their effect everywhere and in no matter what circumstances; rather many conditions are required, and if these are lacking the words do not produce their effect. . . . The Creator's word has its effect not because it is spoken by a human being in each action, but because it was spoken by God once and for all."

16. *De sacramentis* V, 5 (Botte 122) (*antitypon*).

17. *Ibid.* V, 6 (Botte 122).

18. See *ibid.*, I, 15 (Botte 63): "You saw the water, but not all water heals; only that water heals which has the grace of Christ."

19. *Ibid.*

20. *De sacramentis* I, 16 (Botte 68). The point about the institution of the rite of baptism must have been traditional, since Ambrose uses the same expression elsewhere: "Naaman the Syrian went down into the Jordan and was cleansed of his leprosy. Christ was baptized in the Jordan when he instituted the rite of the saving bath" (*De interpellatione Iob et Dauid* 4, 14).

21. Ambrose expressly poses the problem of the correspondence between the two actions when he asks why Christ first went down into the Jordan and then the Spirit came upon it, whereas in the rite and practice of baptism, the water is first consecrated by the descent of the Spirit upon it and only then does the baptizand go down into the font (see *De sacramentis* I, 18 [Botte 70]).

22. In dealing with the baptism of Jesus as model and rite of institution for Christian baptism, Ambrose takes a Trinitarian approach. The presence of the Trinity at the baptism of Jesus (Mt 3:16–17) is the model and guarantee of the same presence in the rite of Christian baptism; the presence is won by the prayer that consecrates the water.

23. M. Simonetti, *Profilo storico dell'esegesi patristica* (Rome, 1981), 9.

24. *Ibid.*

25. See *ibid.*, 10–11.

26. *Ibid.*, 15.

27. *Ibid.*, 17.

28. The Red Sea, the manna, the water from the rock, Abraham, Melchizedek, and the sacrifices in the temple are all "figures" of New Testament realities.

29. Both pre-Christian Judaism and Greek culture were very familiar with allegorical interpretation, whereas typology, understood in the sense which I shall explain, is specifically Christian. See H. de Lubac, " 'Typologie' et 'Allégorisme,' "*RSR* 34 (1947): 183.

30. See Bornert (n. 3), 82.

31. J. Daniélou, "Le symbolisme des rites baptismaux," *Dieu-Vivant* 1 (1945): 17.

32. A. Méhat (ed.), *Origène. Homélies sur les Nombres*, SC 29 (Paris), 110–113.

33. Bornert (n. 3), 63.

34. Simonetti (n. 23), 18.

35. *Ibid.*, 35.

36. That is, in the Old Testament.

37. O. Perler (ed.), *Méliton de Sardes. Sur la Pâque*, SC 123 (Paris, 1966), 78.

38. J. Daniélou, "Figure et événement chez Méliton de Sardes," in *Neotestamentica et patristica (Festgabe O. Cullmann)* (Leiden, 1962), 288.

39. Bornert (n. 3), 44–45.

40. Even in interpreting Paul, it is in fact not possible to apply in practice this distinction between allegory and typology.

41. J. Daniélou, "Traversée de la Mer Rouge et baptême aux premiers siécles," *RSR* 33 (1946): 416.

42. For example, Ambrose in his *De sacramentis* and *De mysteriis* or, according to H. de Lubac, Augustine in his *Contra Faustum manichaeum* (see de Lubac [n. 29], 185).

43. R. Tonneau and R. Devreesse (eds. and trans.), *Les homélies catéchétiques de Théodore de Mopsueste*, ST 145 (Vatican City, 1959).

44. Bornert (n. 3), 80.

45. The principle is already vaguely present in John Chrysostom. This historicizing interpretation of the liturgical rites was to become part of the Syrian mystagogical tradition (Bornert, 82).

46. See J. M. Hanssens (ed.), *Amalarii episcopi opera liturgica omnia* II. *Liber officialis*, ST 139 (Vatican City, 1948).

CHAPTER TWO

1. B. Botte (ed.), *Ambroise de Milan. Des sacrements. Des mystères. Explication du symbole*, SC 25bis (Paris, 1961). (References to these works of Ambrose will be followed in parentheses by the page number in Botte's edition.)

2. G. Francesconi, *Storia e simbolo* (Brescia, 1981).

3. See *ibid.*, 37: "Events form as it were the framework of the plan. The *mysteria historiae* carry the divine mystery."

4. See A. Luneau, *L'histoire du salut chez les Pères de l'Eglise. La doctrine des âges du monde* (Paris, 1964), 252.

5. *Ibid.*, 260.

6. *Ibid.*, 261.

7. Francesconi (n. 2), 220.

8. *Ibid.*, 35.

9. Credit belongs to Francesconi for elucidating the specific meaning of each of these terms.

10. The application of this vocabulary to the eschatological aspect is too complex for me to go into it here.

11. Francesconi (n. 2) 329. See 284: "One of the most widespread convictions shown in many texts is that before the coming of Christ the Old Testament concealed the plan (the *mysterium*) of God, which now comes to light through the Christian reading of the Old Testament by the Church. This conviction finds expression, of course, in the application of the typological method to the Old Testament."

12. *Ibid.*, 60.

13. *Ibid.*, 256.

14. *Ibid.*, 248.

15. *Ibid.*, 256.

16. See *ibid.*, 264: "A *figura* thus acquires a prophetic role; it is always related to a *veritas* and calls upon the reader to look beyond the signs to this promised truth. This is a basic idea in Ambrosian catechesis, which has for its purpose to show how the ancient prefigurations have their fulfillment in Christ (and in Christian realities)."

17. *Ibid.*, 261.

18. *Ibid.*, 256.

19. In the *Hexaemeron* of Ambrose, "*umbra* is almost never used in the perspective of the history of salvation, whereas this is practically the only way the term is used in the other writings. . . . A 'shadow,' is self-evident common experience shows, is connected with an object that casts it" (*ibid.*, 201).

20. *Ibid.*, 204.

21. *Ibid.*, 205.

22. *Ibid.*, 167.

23. *Ibid.*, 169.

24. *Ibid.*, 178.

25. *Ibid.*, 188.

26. *Ibid.*, 118. See also: "Christ is therefore an image, and not a shadow, of God; and not an empty image but the truth" (*De excessu fratris* II, 109; CSEL 73:312).

27. *Imago* for Ambrose means identity with God, whereas likeness is expressed by the phrase *ad imaginem* (see Francesconi 112).

28. T. Di Stefano, "La libertà radicale dell'immagine secondo S. Gregorio di Nissa," *Divus Thomas* (Piacenza) 4 (1972): 436.

29. See Francesconi (n. 2), 131: "To walk in Christ the image means to follow the gospel, to be conformed to the 'image which is Christ.' Baptismal rebirth makes this following and conformity possible. To walk in Christ the image means to bear witness to him, to have the 'likeness of Christ' in oneself, to live 'in his likeness,' for he is the 'origin of those who are in his likeness.' It means to preserve the likeness 'which Christ has painted in you by his works.' In short, the phrase sums up the sacramentality of Christian existence. . . . So real is this likeness in human beings that it sets them in motion toward God in a continual movement of transformation and conformation to him."

30. See *ibid.*, 264: "In this context the representational function of images is fundamental; in images the original model of them is present; they are filled with the power of God, and the Spirit works through them. When we are dealing with the sacraments in the strict sense an image becomes itself a mystery, sending us back to that to which it refers. The image par excellence of God will be Christ, and the image par excellence of Christ in the Church will be the Eucharist."

31. "Flight from evils is a likeness of God, and by the virtues is the image of God acquired" (*De bono mortis* 17; CSEL 32/1:719). Francesconi remarks: "In Ambrose *similitudo* is interchangeable with *imago*; both are gifts given at creation and both are really lost by sin and restored by the saving action of Christ" (148).

32. "What is meant by 'into the death'? The meaning is that just as Christ died you also must taste death; and that as Christ died to sin and lives to God you also, through the sacrament of baptism, must die to the old sinful attractions and be raised up by the grace of Christ. There is then a death, not a real bodily death but a symbolic death. For when you sink beneath the water you receive the likeness of death and burial; you receive the sacrament of Christ's cross" (*De sacramentis* II, 23 [86–88]).

33. "But perhaps you will object: 'I do not see the appearance of death.' But the likeness is there. For as you have received the likeness of death, so you drink the likeness of the precious blood" (*De sacramentis* IV, 20 [112]).

34. Text in F. X. Funk (ed.), *Didascalia et Constitutiones Apostolorum* (Paderborn, 1905), 2:174. See E. Mazza, "L'anafora di Serapione: una ipotesi di interpretazione," *EL* 95 (1981): 510–528.

35. See Francesconi (n. 2), 150–151: "The connection between *similitudo* and *imitatio* is important. . . . Ambrose says that the human being is blessed 'who walks in the likeness of God through faith' (Ps 38:23; CSEL 64:201), thus indicating that faith is the dynamic energy that makes human beings like God. . . . 'Do not say to a block of wood "you

are my father," do not become like a block of wood' (*In Luc.* 7, 214; CCL 14:289)."

36. Francesconi 155.

37. "He alone is the image of God who said: 'I and the Father are one' (Jn 10:30), thus possessing the likeness of the Father. There is then a oneness of divinity and plenitude when he says 'Let us make. . . . ' How can there be any inequality. And when he says 'our likeness,' where is there any unlikeness?" (*Exam.* 6, 41; CSEL 32/1:232–232). And again: "Why does he not possess the image and likeness?" (*De fide* 1, 48; CSEL 78:21).

38. See U. Vanni, "*Omoioma* Paolo," *Greg* 58 (1977): 321–345, 431–470.

39. "You saw what can be seen by your bodily eyes and human glances; you did not see what is being effected but only what is visible. What is unseen is much greater than what is seen, 'for things seen are temporal, things unseen are eternal' (2 Cor 4:18)" (*Explanatio symboli* 1, 10 [66]).

40. "But perhaps you will object: 'I do not *see* the appearance of blood.' But the likeness is there. . . . *You have learned*, therefore, that what you receive is the body of Christ" (*De sacramentis* IV, 20 [112]).

41. Francesconi (n. 2), 228.

42. *Ibid.*, 237.

43. *Ibid.*, 75.

44. *Ibid.*, 79–80.

45. *Ibid.*, 74.

46. *De mysteriis* 2 (156).

47. *Ibid.*, note 2.

48. *De sacramentis* IV, 20 (112).

49. R. Bornert, *Les commentaires byzantins de la divine liturgie du VIIe au XVe siècle*, Archives de l'Orient chrétien 9 (Paris, 1966), 64.

50. *Ibid.*, 90.

51. *Ibid.*, 68.

52. *Ambigua* 2, 19 (PG 91:1233); in fact, "this contains 'reasons' (*logoi*) capable of being taught" (Bornert 90). See *Ambigua* 2, 10 (PG 91:1120, 1128).

53. "Open your ears, then, and breathe in the fragrance of eternal life that is poured over you in the gift of the sacraments. That was our

meaning when in celebrating the mystery of the opening we said: 'Eph-phatha, that is, be opened,' in order that all who would come to grace would know what they were being asked and would remember what they should reply" (*De mysteriis* 3 [156]).

54. "This is the mystery Christ celebrated in the gospel when, as we read, he healed the deaf-mute" (*De mysteriis* 4 [156]).

55. From these two points, we can conclude that the *Ephphatha* has a properly sacramental quality; it is analogous to the washing of the feet in the baptismal rite practiced by Ambrose.

56. *De mysteriis* 9 (160).

57. *Ibid.*, 10 (160).

58. *De sacramentis* III, 5 (94).

59. "But the one is a gesture of humility, the other a sanctifying action"' (*De sacramentis* III, 5 [94]).

60. *Ibid.*

61. "See the fullness of justice, see humility, see grace, see sanctifica-tion. 'If I do not wash your feet,' he says, 'you have no part in me' " (*De sacramentis* III, 4 [94]).

62. *De mysteriis* 31 (172).

63. "Peter was clean, but he had to have his feet washed, for he had the sin which comes from succession to the first man, when the serpent caused him to stumble and led him into error. Therefore his feet are washed to removed inherited sins. For our personal sins are washed away by baptism" (*De mysteriis* 32 [172]).

64. The *mysterium* of this rite consists in the humble service by which Jesus redeems the world: "At the same time recognize that the mystery consists in the very service of humility. . . . For when the author of salvation himself redeemed us through obedience . . . " (*De mysteriis* 33 [118]). Therefore, *mysterium* points to the deeper content, namely, redemption.

65. Jn 13:9–10; *De mysteriis* 31.

66. *De sacramentis* II, 13 (80).

67. "The water, then, is bitter, but when it has received the cross of Christ, when it has received the heavenly sacrament, it begins to be sweet and pleasant" (*ibid.*).

68. "Marah was a bitter spring; Moses threw a piece of wood into it, and it became sweet. For water without mention of the Lord's cross is

of no use for future salvation; but when it has been consecrated by the saving mystery of the cross, it becomes fit for use as spiritual bath and cup of salvation. Just as Moses, that is, the prophet, threw a piece of wood into that spring, so the priest casts into this one the mention of the Lord's cross, and the water becomes sweet for grace" (*De mysteriis* 14 [162]).

69. "It is for this reason that you were told earlier not to believe only in what you were seeing" (*De mysteriis* 19 [164]). And, further on: "Believe therefore that the water is not empty of power" (*De mysteriis* 21 [1661]).

70. "Lest perhaps you say: Is this that great mystery 'which eye has not seen nor ear heard and which has not entered the human mind' (2 Cor 2:9)" (*De mysteriis* 19 [164]).

71. "Learn from this that water does not cleanse apart from the Spirit" (*De mysteriis* 19 [164]).

72. In the *De sacramentis*, the young servant girl who sends Naaman to Israel is interpreted as a figure of the Church ("she had the appearance of the Church and was its figure"), whereas the captivity of the people is understood as captivity by the devil (II, 8 [78]). This captivity evidently could not be called a figure.

73. *De mysteriis* 20 (166).

74. "Again, without water there is no mystery of rebirth, for 'unless a person is born again of water and the Spirit, he cannot enter the kingdom of God.' Catechumens believe in the cross of the Lord Jesus with which they are signed, but if they are not baptized in the name of the Father and of the Son and of the Holy Spirit, they cannot receive the forgiveness of sins nor draw the gift of spiritual grace" (*ibid.* 20 [166]).

75. *Ibid.*, 27 (170).

76. *Ibid.*, 53 (186).

77. *Mysterium* is parallel to *exemplum* and has the same meaning: "Let us use his examples and by means of the mystery of the incarnation establish the truth of the mystery" (*ibid.*, 53 [186]).

78. *De sacramentis* IV, 17 (110).

79. In fact, we saw Ambrose appealing to the incarnation (which he calls *exemplum* and *mysterium*) as a parallel to justify attributing to the eucharistic consecration the mysterious and miraculous character of the virginal conception. Earlier, he had used a series of biblical examples to show that the transformation of the eucharistic bread belongs in the category of miracle: Moses and the serpent; the Red Sea; the turning

back of the Jordan; the water from the rock; the bitter water of Marah; Elisha and the axe (*De mysteriis* 51 [184]).

80. Francesconi (n. 2), 329.

81. It is in the sense that the doctrinal datum is identical with the hermeneutical method.

82. *De sacramentis* IV, 2 (102).

83. *Ibid.*, I, 15 (68).

84. *Ibid.*

85. *Ibid.*, I, 16 (68).

86. "Naaman the Syrian went down into the Jordan and was cleansed of his leprosy. Christ was baptized in the Jordan when he instituted the salutary rite of baptism" (*De interpellatione Iob et Dauid* 4, 14).

87. The presence of the Trinity in the baptismal rite is likewise inferred from the story of the baptism of Jesus (Mt 3:16–17) and is the fruit of the prayer that consecrates the water.

88. See *De sacramentis* I, 18 (70).

89. Jn 5:4. In all of these references to the Bible, except for the story of Naaman, which is told in a free manner, exact citation of the Scriptures is the norm.

90. *De sacramentis* II, 4 (74).

91. *Ibid.* (76).

92. From the literary point of view, the procedure here is the same as when, further on, Ambrose speaks of the body and blood of Christ as the true reality of the eucharistic bread and wine (*De sacramentis* IV, 20 [112]).

93. *Ibid.*, II, 13 (80).

94. *Ibid.*, II, 9 (78).

95. I deliberately leave aside the eschatological aspect, which would require a more complex treatment.

96. At the same time, the *veritas* always requires *figurae* if it is to be understood.

97. *De sacramentis* IV, 6 (104).

98. If we today wish to speak of the invisible content of baptism, we address ourselves directly to the baptismal rite; Ambrose, however, begins by speaking of the "mysteries" of the Jews: "We marvel at the

mysteries of the Jews that were given to our fathers. These mysteries are excellent first of all by reason of the antiquity of their sacraments and secondly by reason of their holiness. Here is my promise: the sacraments of Christians are even more divine and older than those of the Jews" (De sacramentis I, 11 [66]). We must keep two points in mind: the Jewish mysteries are the figures we have been considering up to this point; the greater importances ("more divine," "older") is connected with the concept of "truth."

99. De sacramentis IV, 10 (106).

100. Ibid., IV, 11 (106–108).

101. Ibid., IV, 12 (108).

102. Ibid., IV, 13 (108).

103. Ibid., V, 1 (120).

104. De mysteriis 46 (102).

105. Ibid.

106. Let us recall once again that for Ambrose, the realism of the figura means a true and proper presence of the veritas in it or, more accurately, a kind of identification of the two realities.

107. De sacramentis V, 12 (124).

108. Those who do not have experience of the Eucharist cannot understand such a psalm, which, therefore, remains obscure to them: "How often have you heard the twenty-second Psalm and failed to understand it? See how well it applies to the heavenly sacraments: 'The Lords feeds me, and I shall want for nothing; he has set me in a place of pasture. He had led me to refreshing water and brought me back to life. He has led me on the path of justice for his name's sake. For although I should walk in the shadow of death, I will fear no evil, because you are with me. Your scepter and your staff have strengthened me' (Ps 22:1–5). The scepter stands for sovereign power, the staff for suffering; that is, for the eternal divinity of Christ and for his bodily passion: the former created, the latter redeemed. 'You have prepared a table before me in the sight of those who afflict me. You have anointed my head with oil, and your intoxicating cup, how marvelous it is!' " (De sacramentis V, 13 [124–126]).

109. Francesconi (n. 2), 319.

110. "The figures of the sacraments possess historical concreteness: they signal specific moments in a history which, precisely because of these meaningful events, is perceived as a history of salvation" (Francesconi 311).

1. R. Tonneau and R. Devreesse, *Les homélies catéchétiques de Théodore de Mopsueste*, ST 145 (Vatican City, 1949), XVI. (References to the Homilies will be followed by the page number, in parentheses, in Tonneau-Devreesse.)

2. A first difference is the anointing at the end of baptism: this is absent from Chrysostom and present in Theodore as a signation or anointing. Another considerable difference is in the structure of the anaphora, as I have shown in my article, "La struttura dell'anafora nelle Catechesi di Teodoro di Mopsuestia," soon to appear in *EL*.

3. The Mingana manuscript is in the Selly Oak Colleges' Library, Birmingham, England.

4. The first ten homilies are strongly doctrinal; they deal with the Creed and go deeply into the dogmatic problems raised by developments in christology. The Council of Constantinople (381) is cited several times in *Homily* 10.

5. Tonneau-Devreesse 281.

6. *Ibid.*

7. For documentation, see *ibid.*, XV, as well as R. Devreesse, *Essai sur Théodore de Mopsueste*, ST 141 (Vatican City, 1948).

8. A. Mingana, *Commentary of Theodore of Mopsuestia on the Lord's Prayer and on the Sacraments of Baptism and the Eucharist*, Woodbroke Studies 6 (Cambridge, 1933), X.

9. This would explain the differences in vocabulary that we find.

10. I have not forgotten to make a comparison with the homilies on the Creed, when this proves needful.

11. D. Cerbelaud, *Cyrillonas. L'agneu véritable. Hymnes, cantiques, homélies* (Chevetogne, 1984), 31.

12. The translation in Tonneau and Devreesse is very carefully done, and the choices made follow the logic of the text. It is to be regretted, however, that the editor does not take into account the strict pattern followed by the Syriac translator. In trying to interpret the text, the modern translator translates *typcs* now as figure, now as sign, now as image, and so on; *mystērion* as mystery or sacrament; *'ata* as sign or figure, and so on. In the passages of Theodore that I quote, I attempt to convey as far as possible the rigorous uniformity that marks the Syriac translation (according to the photographs of the manuscript).

13. *Hom.* 14, 12 (429).

14. See, e.g., *De mysteriis* I, 1 (Botte 156).

15. Type, figure, sign, truth, and so on.

16. *Hom.* 15, 18 (493).

17. *Hom.* 15, 14 (483–484).

18. Thus Tonneau-Devreesse XXV.

19. *Ibid.*

20. We must not overlook the fact that in the first series, on the Creed, the doctrinal aspect is always accompanied by the existential; once the difference in subject matter is taken into account, it can be said that whereas the existential aspect is not especially emphasized in the first series, it is no less present than in the second.

21. See Tonneau-Devreesse XXV: "Faith is here no longer required and looked upon simply as the mind's acceptance of a revealed doctrine; rather it is considered chiefly in its action, whereby it draws to itself the visible world and what is invisible, and unites these with each other. . . . Faith calls upon the soul to form and develop the outlook of hope that is impressed upon it by contemplation of its future state."

22. The answer will be complete only at the end of this discussion of Theodore, when we have seen the various theological questions he raises.

23. *Hom.* 11, 1 (283).

24. Mt 28:19.

25. *Hom.* 11, 1 (283).

26. *Ibid.*

27. *Hom.* 11, 3 (287).

28. *Ibid.*

29. This term can be explained as meaning "to imitate the kind of life we expect to lead in heaven" (*Hom.* 11, 12 [303]).

30. *Hom.* 11, 13 (307).

31. *Hom.* 15, 1 (465).

32. *Hom.* 13, 1 (369).

33. *Ibid.*

34. *Hom.* 12, 10 (337–339).

35. *Hom.* 12, 2 (325).

36. At the beginning of each homily, the text of the *Ordo* (*Taxis*, Rite or Ritual), or ecclesiastical regulations, is given, which describes and regulates the liturgical celebration. After citing the relevant section, Theodore launches into a detailed commentary on the liturgy therein described.

37. *Hom.* 12, 1 (325).

38. A. Vaccari, "La theoria esegetica antiochena," *Biblica* 15 (1934): 94–101.

39. M. Simonetti, *Profilo storico dell'esegesi patristica* (Rome, 1981), 65–66.

40. Typology and allegory are very closely related, and the problem of vocabulary is often an echo of the underlying theological problem. In my opinion, it is necessary to accept the distinction that Cardinal Henri de Lubac has established between *allegoria verbi* and *allegoria facti*, while not denying the importance of the clear distinction that Cardinal Jean Daniélou has drawn between typology and allegory; see, e.g., J. Daniélou, "Figure et événement chez Méliton de Sardes," in *Neotestamentica et patristica (Festgabe O. Cullmann)* (Leiden, 1962), 282–292. For a comparison of de Lubac and Daniélou, see H. de Lubac, *Esegesi medievale. I quattro sensi della Scrittura* (Rome, 1972), Part II, p. 1210. I prefer to adopt de Lubac's viewpoint here as better suited for gaining an understanding of Theodore's vocabulary.

41. *Hom.* 16, 38 (595).

42. We would expect, however, that the opposite would be true in Theodore. For in his theological scheme, the earthly liturgy participates in the heavenly liturgy that is narrated in the Old Testament episode; in the present passage, on the other hand, the Old Testament event participates in the "truth" of the New Testament as embodied in the liturgical action.

43. *Hom.* 16, 27 (577).

44. *Ibid.* The next passage cited is from the same place.

45. *Hom.* 13, 19 (401).

46. *Hom.* 13, 17 (395).

47. *Hom.* 14, 26 (455–457).

48. *Hom.* 13, 17 (397).

49. *Hom.* 15 (Ritual) (463).

50. *Hom.* 13, 2 (371).

51. *Hom.* 14, 18 (441).

52. *Hom.* 15, 1 (465).

53. *Hom.* 15, 1 (469).

54. *Ibid.*

55. *Hom.* 15, 8 (473).

56. *Ibid.*

57. *Ibid.*

58. *Ibid.*

59. *Hom.* 15, 9 (473).

60. The problem of penance is discussed in connection with the theme of communion.

61. *Hom.* 15, 26 (505).

62. *Hom.* 15, 29 (511).

63. *Hom.* 15 (Ritual) (463).

64. *Hom.* 15, 17 (507).

65. *Ibid.*

66. *Ibid.*

67. *Hom.* 15, 25 (503).

68. *Ibid.*

69. *Hom.* 15, 9 (473–475).

70. In the passage just cited, Theodore shows he has inherited an archaic terminology that he is no longer in a position to use, namely, type and antitype. When he says that Jesus makes his own body and blood a type of bread and wine in the Eucharist, the statement is also implicitly being made that the bread and wine are the antitype of the body and blood. This takes us into a sacramental theology that uses two terms for its expression. But Theodore's theology is not of that kind; his is a sacramental theology that is in a position to express sacramentality by a single term. As a result, what he says here is somewhat recondite and obscure; if we introduce the term "antitype," everything becomes clearer, and the meaning of his argument is greatly improved.

71. *Ibid.*

72. The fruit of redemption is an eschatological gift and belongs in the world to come: " 'This is my blood which is shed for you for the remission of sins.' This is what he means: that by his death he will give the world to come in which the remission of all sins will take place. He

orders us to participate in the mystery and thus commemorate, in a type, his passion whereby we shall obtain possession of the blessings that will come, including the remission of sins" (*Hom.* 15, 7 [473]). Christ's death wins the world to come and all the eschatological blessings it contains, beginning with the remission of sins. The eschatological blessings are the totality of the salvation brought by Christ; the list of these blessings can therefore begin with any gift whatsoever, without there being any real difference. Once can speak indifferently of immortality or the remission of sins.

73. *Hom.* 15, 9 (475).

74. In Theodore's interpretation, Paul is saying in Rom 6:3–5 that "the resurrection has been proven by the death of Christ" (*Hom.* 15, 6 [471]).

75. "Just as by the death of Christ our Lord we receive the birth of baptism, so too there is a food in type which we receive by means of his death. Blessed Paul bears witness to this when he says: 'Every time you eat this bread and drink this cup, you will commemorate the death of our Lord, until he comes' (1 Cor 11:26). He shows that to take the oblation and participate in the mysteries is to commemorate the death of our Lord, which wins for us resurrection and the enjoyment of immortality; for it is fitting that we who through the death of our Lord the Christ have received a sacramental birth should also receive through that same death the food of the sacrament of immortality. We ought to be nourished from the same source from which we were born, in keeping with the practice of all animals at their birth, for they are naturally fed by those who brought them forth" (*Hom.* 15, 6 [471]).

76. *Hom.* 16, 9 (547).

77. *Ibid.* (549).

78. This phrase signifies liturgical rules that derive their authority not from "law of the Church," that is, the Ritual, but from liturgical custom that has developed on the basis of the Ritual and depends on the role of the bishop.

79. *Hom.* 15, 29 (511).

80. *Hom.* 16, 15 (557).

81. "Our Lord, then, in giving the two (body and blood) says: 'This indeed is my body which is broken for you for the remission of sins' and 'This is my blood which has been shed for you for the remission of sins' (1 Cor 11:24). In the first set of words he reveals the passion, but in the second the violence and extent of the passion, in which a great deal of blood was shed" (*Hom.* 16, 16 [557]).

82. *Ibid.* (557–559).

83. *Hom.* 16, 17 (559).

84. *Ibid.*

85. This is the familiar theme of the meals taken with the risen Christ.

86. See also *Hom.* 16, 18 (561).

87. *Hom.* 16, 17 (559).

88. This phrase refers to the eucharistic prayer or anaphora.

89. See above on the relation between baptism and the Eucharist, understood as birth and food.

90. Theodore, unlike the Ritual, regards the body and blood of Christ as the object of the oblation.

91. At times—and this is a sign of an especially archaic text—the epiclesis is simply a petition that grace or the divine blessing would descend (or that the Father would send it). A few scattered texts ask for the descent of the Word.

92. It is possible that this idea was inspired by the Ritual of his Church.

93. *Hom.* 16 (Ritual) (533).

94. *Hom.* 16, 12 (553).

95. *Ibid.*

96. *Hom.* 16, 11 (551).

97. " 'And he was acknowledged as Son of God in power and the Holy Spirit, through the resurrection of Jesus Christ our Lord from the dead' (Rom 1:4); and, on the other hand, 'if the Spirit of him who raised Jesus Christ from the dead dwells in you, he who raised Christ from the dead will also give life to your dead bodies because of his Spirit who dwells in you' (Rom 8:11). Thus says our Lord as well: 'It is the Spirit who gives life; the body is useless' (Jn 6:63)" (*Hom.* 16, 11 [553]).

Faults committed through frailty, that is, without thinking of them, or through weakness and indeliberately, should not keep us from communion: "Communion in the holy mysteries will undoubtedly give us the remission of such faults, for our Lord himself said clearly: 'This is my body, which has been broken for you for the remission of sins' and 'This is my blood which has been shed for you for the remission of sins' (Mt 26:26–28); and, he says 'I have come to call not the just but sinners to repentance' (Mt 9:13)" (*Hom.* 16, 35 [589–591]).

99. For Isaiah, the heavenly vision of the seraphim singing the triple "Holy" is a revelation of the economy with all that it contains. Just as Theodore had expressly cited the Lord's words about the bread and

wine for the remission of sins, so now he expressly cites the words of the angel: "Behold, this has touched your lips; let your guilt pass away and your sins be forgiven" (Is 6:7). The conclusion Theodore draws is categorical: just as we are certain that the seraphim purified the prophet, so we should be certain that "by communion in the holy mysteries our debts are completely covered, provided that we repent and that we suffer and feel compunction in our hearts because of our sins" (*Hom.* 16, 36 [593]).

100. Not "identical," since Christ is utterly unrepeatable.

101. J. D. Laurance, *"Priest" as Type of Christ. The Leader of the Eucharist in Salvation History according to Cyprian of Carthage* (New York, 1984); *idem*, "Le président de l'Eucharistie selon Cyprien de Carthage: un nouvel examen," *La Maison-Dieu* 154 (1983): 151–165.

102. Keep in mind, however, that the two terminologies are not equivalent.

103. See Rom 6:3–6.

104. See the Anaphora of Serapion, in A. Hänggi and I. Pahl (eds.), *Prex Eucharistica. Textus e variis liturgiis antiquioribus selecti*, Spicilegium Friburgense 12 (Fribourg, Switzerland, 1968), 130.

105. *Hom.* 12, 20 (355). The basis for this interpretation of redemption as comprising victory over the devil, death and ascension, is found in Jn 12:31–32, which Theodore cites a moment later.

106. *Hom.* 12, 18 (351).

107. *Hom.* 12, 16 (347).

108. The renunciation of Satan is interpreted along the same line: "This is in fact what is meant by this 'I renounce': I will no longer choose or accept association with him" (*Hom.* 13, 6 [377]). In Theodore's soteriological perspective, the renunciation of Satan as agent of every evil fits nicely into its context, since redemption consists in "the manifestation of an immense and wonderful grace . . . which gained for us a marvelous share in the blessings . . . and granted us not only the removal of evils but also hope of the ineffable blessings which he set before us" (*ibid.*).

109. *Hom.* 12, 26 (363).

110. *Ibid.* (365).

111. *Hom.* 14, 5 (411–413).

112. *Hom.* 13, 19 (401).

113. *Hom.* 13, 15 (393).

114. *Hom.* 15, 10 (475).

115. *Ibid.*

116. *Hom.* 16, 3 (539).

117. *Ibid.*

118. Christ was the first to become immortal and incorruptible through resurrection; since that is now his situation, Theodore concludes that it will "therefore" be ours as well (*Hom.* 14, 25 [455]).

119. *Hom.* 12, 21 (357).

120. *Hom.* 14, 3 (407).

121. *Hom* 12, 15 (393).

122. *Ibid.*

123. *Hom.* 14, 1 (405).

124. *Hom.* 16, 30 (583).

125. *Hom.* 12, 5 (331).

126. *Hom.* 16, 6 (543).

127. *Hom.* 16, 7 (545).

128. *Ibid.*

129. *Hom.* 16, 36 (591). (The passages in the next two paragraphs are from the same place.)

130. "The food of the sacred mystery likewise had to be something similar" (*ibid.* [593]).

131. Theodore expressly refers to the Spirit: "What is presented is ordinary bread and wine, but through the coming of the Holy Spirit it is changed into body and blood; thus it is changed so as to have the power of a spiritual and immortal food" (*ibid.*). This direct reference to the Spirit is not found in the transformation of the burning coals; nonetheless Theodore states: "That is why (Isaiah) sees in the vision of the burning coals a sign and revelation of what was to take place" (*ibid.*). The explanation is perhaps to be found in the immediately following sentence, which says that the Spirit descended in the form of fire on the assembled disciples; through them the grace of the Holy Spirit "has united itself" to all human beings.

132. "Now the seraphim took the burning coal, not with his hand but with tongs. This vision shows that even those spirits fear to approach the mysteries without some intermediary" (*Hom.* 16, 38 [595]).

133. That is, filled with sorrow for sin, as Isaiah was.

134. *Hom.* 16, 37 (593–595).

135. *Hom.* 16, 36 (593).

136. See *Hom.* 16, 8 (547).

137. "The unmarried man is occupied with the affairs of the Lord, how he may please his Lord; while the married man is occupied with worldly affairs, how he may please his wife" (1 Cor 7:32–33).

138. It follows from this that the relation to the eschatological blessings can be formed either directly by an ascetical life or through participation in the mysteries.

139. *Hom.* 16, 32 (587).

140. *Hom.* 16, 33 (587).

141. *Ibid.*

142. *Hom.* 14, 22 (449).

143. *Hom.* 14, 23 (451).

144. *Hom.* 14, 24 (451)

145. *Hom.* 15, 7 (471). It is clear that in this passage, "mystery" means the liturgical celebration.

146. It is in the sense that the ritual *imitation* really contains the *archetype*.

147. *Hom.* 16, 10 (551).

148. *Hom.* 16, 18 (561).

149. Tonneau and Devreesse translate this phrase as "shares himself."

150. *Hom.* 16, 18 (561).

151. *Hom.* 15, 15 (485).

152. *Hom.* 16, 25 (575).

153. *Hom.* 15, 6 (413).

154. *Ibid.* (415).

155. *Hom.* 14, 9 (419–421).

156. "In a second figure he places the two, the bread and wine, before us; they are his body and his blood, in which we eat the food of immortality" (*Hom.* 16, 25 [575]).

157. *Hom.* 16, 36 (593).

158. *Hom.* 16, 24 (569).

159. *Hom.* 16, 12 (553). (The passage cited in the next paragraph of the text is from the same source.) The theme is already included in the epiclesis, which is a "petition and supplication to God that the coming of the Holy Spirit may take place and that grace may come from above on the bread and wine that have been presented, so that they may be seen to be truly the body and blood of our Lord, which are the memorial of immortality" (*Hom.* 16, 12 [553]). From this summary of the words of the epiclesis, we can infer that the liturgical text to which the Ritual refers was much more sober and restrained than Theodore's own theology; but we must not forget that the Ritual has in mind anaphora formulas earlier than the one in use at that moment. Proof of this is the discrepancy between the structure of the anaphora described in the Ritual and the structure of the anaphora on which the homily is actually commenting. See E. Mazza, "La struttura dell'anafora nelle Catechesi di Teodoro di Mopsuestia," *EL* (in press).

160. *Hom.* 16, 27 (577).

161. In explanation of this term, I would say that Theodore is at the opposite end of the spectrum from, for example, Paschase Radbert, who said that in eucharistic communion human beings are physically fed by the body of Christ or, more accurately, by his flesh.

162. *Hom.* 16, 26 (577).

163. *Ibid.* (575).

164. *Hom.* 15, 20 (495–497).

165. *Ibid.* (497).

166. It is really not correct to use this modern term here, since it does not fully correspond to Theodore's way of thinking; it does, however, express the concept with sufficient clarity and without any great danger of ambiguity.

167. *Hom.* 12, 2 (325).

168. Theodore manages well enough with the theological heritage he has received, while at the same time developing good interpretations of his own; he shows, however, that he is not able to produce a really well-grounded "Antiochene" synthesis. But, perhaps, he was not even thinking of attempting such a synthesis.

169. By "natural being," I do not mean here the innermost reality of a thing, but simply what "naturally" belongs to it as a creature.

Notes for Pages 88 to 92

170. *Hom.* 15, 10 (475).

171. See the text of the profession of faith drawn up by the Council of Rome in 1059; it is given and analyzed in J. de Montclos, *Lanfranc et Bérenger. La controverse eucharistique du XIe siécle* (Louvain, 1971), 171ff.

172. There is no need of citing further texts on this point; the reader need only refer to one or other of the many texts already cited in preceding sections.

173. *Hom.* 14, 2 (405–407).

174. *Ibid.*

175. *Hom.* 14, 6 (415).

176. Theodore gives clear expression to this conviction in the many passages in which he speaks of the Holy Spirit as effecting the resurrection of Jesus. But this is only one of many instances.

177. *Hom.* 14, 8 (415–417).

178. *Hom.* 16, 12 (553).

179. The sacraments are not homogeneous with the stages in the history of salvation, so that one might call them the "beginning" of salvation and eschatology its "completion" (as one can indeed say that the life and death of Christ are the "beginning" of salvation and his second coming its "completion"). The sacraments are memorials, commemorations, and ways of access to the salvation accomplished in history; they are not stages in salvation.

180. *Hom.* 14, 5 (413).

181. *Hom.* 14, 22 (449). (The citations in this paragraph are from this source.)

182. *Hom.* 12 (Ritual) (461).

183. "Clearly, then, there is a sacrifice, without there being anything new and without it being his own sacrifice which the bishop carries out; rather it is a memorial of that true immolation" (*Hom.* 14, 15 [485]).

184. *Hom.* 15, 15 (485).

185. *Hom.* 15 (Ritual) (461).

186. Another unacceptable solution is provided by those who, when dealing with the eschatological value of the sacraments, reduce eschatology to the sacraments, in the sense that, according to them, the gifts of the end-time are really present by anticipation in the sacrament. As a result, the Eucharist would be a memorial not only of the past, but of

the second coming of Christ. The proponents of this view rely heavily on the anamnesis in the Anaphora of James and other anaphoras. Not only does this solution not solve the problem of the nature of sacramental realism, in the final analysis, it also does away with the importance of eschatology, since we already have a real sacramental anticipation of it. The solution represents a reckless application of Charles Dodd's views on eschatology. It should be kept in mind that Dodd's views were themselves inspired by the anaphoras of the Eastern Churches.

187. I am here using the term in its broadest acceptance, without distinguishing between *allegoria litterae* and *allegoria facti*.

188. *Hom.* 15, 15 (485).

189. *Hom.* 15, 10 (475).

CHAPTER FOUR

1. See J. Quasten, *Patrology* 3 (Westminster, MD, 1963), 414–425.

2. A. Wenger (ed.), *Jean Chrysostome. Huit catéchèses baptismales inédites*, SC 50bis (Paris, 1970), 63. (Henceforth: Wenger, with page reference.)

3. R. Tonneau and R. Devreesse, *Les homélies catéchétiques de Théodore de Mopsueste*, ST 145 (Vatican City, 1949), XVI. (Henceforth: Tonneau-Devreesse, with page reference.)

4. B. Botte, "L'onction postbaptismale dans l'ancien Patriarchat d'Antioche," in the collective work, *Miscellanea liturgica in onore di S. E. il Cardinale G. Lercaro* II (Rome, 1967), 806.

5. R. Devreesse, *Essai sur Théodore de Mopsueste*, ST 141 (Vatican City, 1948).

6. The several series of homilies are called "mystagogical" on the basis of both their content and their function: they are explanations of the sacraments of baptism and the Eucharist for the spiritual profit of the hearers, who were customarily the candidates for baptism and the newly baptized.

7. PG 49:223–232, 231–240. The first instruction comes from a single manuscript, perhaps Coislin 245, which Fronton du Duc discovered; English translation in Harkins (see n. 12, below), 131–146. The second instruction is identical with *Homily* 22 on the statues; English translation in Harkins, 173–192. (These two homilies will be cited as Montfaucon I and II.)

8. A. Papadopoulos-Kerameus, *Varia Graeca Sacra* (a collection of previously unpublished Greek theological texts dating from the fourth to the fifteenth centuries) (St. Petersburg, 1909). (Henceforth: PK, with homily

and/or page reference.) English translation of the four in Harkins, pp. 131–146, 147–160, 161–172, and 56–65, respectively.

9. Wenger (n. 2, above). English translation of the Stavronikita series in Harkins, pp. 23–130. (Henceforth the instructions published by Wenger will be referred to as Stav., with reference to homily and subjection.)

10. Quasten (n. 1), 425.

11. See A. Wenger, "La tradition des oeuvres de saint Jean Chrysostome. I. Catéchèses inconnues et homélies peu connues," *Revue des Etudes Byzantines* 14 (1956): 5–48.

12. P. F. Harkins, *St. John Chrysostom: Baptismal Instructions*, Ancient Christian Writers 31 (Westminster, MD, 1963).

13. A. Ceresa-Gastaldo, *Giovanni Crisostomo. Le catechesi battesimali* (Rome, 1982); *idem*, "Teoria e prassi nelle catechesi battesimali di S. Giovanni Crisostomo," in S. Felici (ed.), *Catechesi battesimale e riconciliazione nei Padri del IV secolo* (Rome, 1984).

14. D. Sartore, "Il mistero del battesimo nelle catechesi di S. Giovanni Crisostomo," *Lateranum* 50 (1984): 360. Sartore's carefully compiled bibliography lists some further works: T. Finn, *The Liturgy of Baptism in the Baptismal Instructions of St. John Chrysostom* (Washington, D.C., 1967); P. Rentinck, *La cura pastorale in Antiochia nel IV secolo* (Rome, 1970); and H. M. Riley, *Christian Initiation. A Comparative Study of the Interpretation of the Baptismal Liturgy in the Mystagogical Writings of Cyril of Jerusalem, John Chrysostom, Theodore of Mopsuestia and Ambrose of Milan* (Washington, D.C., 1974).

15. See Wenger's introduction.

16. On the basis of the studies of Harkins and Finn, Ceresa-Gastaldo and Sartore organize the several series into a single scheme, while taking logical and chronological succession into account (see Sartore [n.14] 360).

17. PG 49:231–240.

18. Wenger 64.

19. PG 51:65–112.

20. Wenger 65.

21. *Ibid.*, 63.

22. Stav. 1, 25 (Wenger 121; Harkins 32).

23. *Hom.* 14, 28 (Tonneau-Devreesse 459–461).

24. *Hom.* 16, 23 (Tonneau-Devreesse 567).

25. *Hom.* 16, 34 (Tonneau-Devreesse 589).

26. One example from among many: Stav. 1, 3. The theme of God's mercy "is evidently one of the guiding themes of these homilies" (Wenger 110, note 2).

27. "Ta par'heautou eispherein."

28. For example, Stav. 1, 19: "Therefore, do you contribute your fair share, and make a strong confession of faith in Him, not only with your lips but also with your understanding," followed by the citation of Rom 10:10 (Wenger 118; Harkins 30).

29. Stav. 4, 6 (Wenger 185; Harkins 58).

30. Stav. 4, 11 (Wenger 188; Harkins 70).

31. Stav. 4, 10 (Wenger 188; Harkins 70).

32. Stav. 8, 4–5 (Wenger 249–250; Harkins 121).

33. Stav. 8, 5 (*ibid.*).

34. It must be pointed out that in tackling the theme of imitation of the angelic powers, Theodore likewise asserts that it is the unmarried who should strive for this imitation; only in a second stage does he suggest, on the basis of a rather intricate and roundabout argument, that the married too should strive for this imitation as far as possible. The basis for urging this heaven-centeredness is the "sacramental food" (*Hom.* 16, 32–33; Tonneau-Devreesse 585–587).

35. Stav. 8, 6 (Wenger 250; Harkins 121).

36. Wenger 198, note 1.

37. At the end of their eucharistic theology, the Fathers often offer reflections on repentance; these, in turn, provide a starting point for consideration either of the Eucharist as bringing forgiveness of sins or of ecclesiastical penance.

38. This is the date proposed by Wenger (38) because of the likeness between this homily and the first in the Papadopoulos-Kerameus series.

39. *Ibid.*, 40.

40. That is, within a period of seven days, as for the celebration of a marriage.

41. In my opinion, this view needs to be much more nuanced, at least as applied to authors such as Ambrose, whose motivation seems to be pastoral and based on psychological considerations.

42. Wenger 71. See also: Chrysostom, *First Instruction* (Montfaucon, in PG 49:223); *Second Instruction* (Montfaucon, in PG 49:234). Wenger (73, note 2) cites other passages of Chrysostom.

43. Stav. 5, 1–3 (Wenger 200–202; Harkins 80–81).

44. Stav. 5, 15 (Wenger 208; Harkins 86).

45. The Western liturgy is likewise familiar with the idea of fasting as a figure; it speaks, for example, of the "ieiuniorum magnifica sacramenta"; see M. Férotin (ed.), *Le Liber Mozarabicus Sacramentorum et les manscrits mozarabes* (Paris, 1912), 420.

46. Sartore (n. 14), 363.

47. I refer the reader, in passing, to Wenger's concern and critical reaction when he finds Chrysostom's thinking on original sin not to be in complete accord with the teaching of the Roman Church (154, note 1).

48. For example, Stav. 2, 20 (Wenger 145; Harkins 51).

49. In their commentaries, the Fathers often single out ritual actions that, though parts of a larger rite, are endowed with a sacramentality of their own. We saw a comparable case in Ambrose, for whom the washing of the feet brings remission of the sin of the first parents, that is, original sin.

50. Stav. 3, 12 (Wenger 158; Harkins 60).

51. *Ibid.*

52. *Homiliae in Joannem* 46 (PG 59:260), translated in Harkins 235, note 26.

53. Stav. 3, 12 (Wenger 158; Harkins 60).

54. We need only look at the transition from the third homily on baptism to the first on the Eucharist: *Hom.* 15, 4 (Tonneau-Devreesse 467). Theodore constantly tries to integrate the theme of food with the other themes of the eucharistic liturgy, though it must be acknowledged that the integration is not always easy or fully successful, as is very clear for the relation between "food" and "anamnesis" and between "food" and "sacrifice"; see, as one example from among many, *Hom.* 15, 6 (Tonneau-Devreesse 471).

55. Stav. 3, 19 (Wenger 162; Harkins 62).

56. Stav. 3, 20 (Wenger 162; Harkins 62).

57. Stav. 2, 7 (Wenger 137; Harkins 45–46).

58. Stav. 1, 36 (Wenger 126; Harkins 37).

59. Stav. 1, 17 (Wenger 117 [see his note 4]; Harkins 29).

60. Stav. 1, 36 (Wenger 127; Harkins 37).

61. Stav. 2, 28 (Wenger 149; Harkins 53–54).

62. Stav. 3, 5 (Wenger 153; Harkins 57).

63. Montfaucon II, 6 (PG 49:232; Harkins 175).

64. Stav. 7, 18 (Wenger 238; Harkins 111).

65. Stav. 7, 15 (Wenger 236; Harkins 109–110).

66. Stav. 7, 11 (Wenger 234; Harkins 108).

67. Col 3:1.

68. Col 3:2.

69. Stav 7, 12 (Wenger 234–235; Harkins 108).

70. *Ibid.*

71. Col 3:3.

72. Rom 6:6.

73. Stav. 7, 21–22 (Wenger 239–240; Harkins 112–113).

74. Ambrose, *De sacramentis* II, 17 (Botte 82–84).

75. Stav. 2, 1 (Wenger 130; Harkins 43).

76. See Stav. 1, 20: "It is fitting, therefore, that those who have enlisted in this special army of the spirit believe. . . . [the profession of faith follows]" (Wenger 118; Harkins 31). The description of baptism as a marriage becomes secondary to its description as a military combat.

77. Stav. 1, 18 (Wenger 118; Harkins 30).

78. Stav. 2, 9 (Wenger 138; Harkins 46).

79. Stav. 4, 6 (Wenger 185; Harkins 68).

80. Stav. 3, 9 (Wenger 156; Harkins 58).

81. Stav. 3, 11 (Wenger 158; Harkins 59–60).

82. Stav. 3, 8 (Wenger 155; Harkins 58).

83. *Ibid.*

84. Stav. 2, 20 (Wenger 145; Harkins 51).

85. Text in A. Hänggi and I. Pahl (eds.), *Prex eucharistica. Textus e variis liturgiis antiquioribus selecti*, Spicilegium Friburgense 12 (Fribourg, 1968), 435.

86. For example, the Anaphora of St. Mark (Hängii-Pahl 108) and comparable texts.

87. Stav. 2, 12 (Wenger 139; Harkins 47–48).

88. Stav. 1, 3 (Wenger 111; Harkins 23–24).

89. Stav. 1, 16 (Wenger 116; Harkins 29).

90. Stav. 1, 3 (Wenger 110; Harkins 23–24).

91. Stav. 6, 24 (Wenger 227; Harkins 102–103).

92. Montfaucon I, 29 (PG 49:228; Harkins 140–141).

93. We may assume that this way of interpreting the exorcisms was traditional in Antioch.

94. PK II, 6 (= 14) (PK 160; Harkins 154).

95. Stav. 2, 14 (Wenger 141; Harkins 48).

96. Stav. 2, 18 (Wenger 143; Harkins 50).

97. PK II, 6 (=14) (PK 161; Harkins 154).

98. Eph 2:19.

99. PK II, 6 (= 15) (PL 161; Harkins 154).

100. The reference is to the liturgical regulations (today we would call them "rubrics") governing the celebration of baptism. Theodore provided a real commentary on the Ritual; Chrysostom simply records its existence.

101. Phil 2:10.

102. PK III, 4 (= 22) (PK 171; Harkins 167).

103. The reference is the prebaptismal anointing; for the problem of the relation between this anointing and the postbaptismal anointing in the Church of Antrioch, see B. Botte (n. 2), II, 795–888; for a broader picture, see S. P. Brock, "The Transition to a Post-baptismal Anointing in the Antiochene Rite," in B. D. Spinks (ed.), *The Sacrifice of Praise. Studies on the Themes of Thanksgiving and Redemption in the Central Prayers of the Eucharistic and Baptismal Liturgies. In Honour of A. H. Couratin* (Rome, 1981), 215–222; L. Ligier, *La confirmation* (Paris, 1973).

104. Stav. 2, 22–23 (Wenger 143; Harkins 51–52).

105. Stav. 2, 11 (Wenger 139; Harkins 47).

106. Stav. 2, 29 (Wenger 149; Harkins 54).

107. *Ibid.*

108. Stav. 4, 18 (Wenger 192; Harkins 73).

109. Stav. 5, 18 (Wenger 209; Harkins 87–88).

110. Gal. 3:27.

111. Stav. 4, 4 (Wenger 184; Harkins 67).

112. PK III, 2 (= 7) (PK 168; Harkins 162–163).

113. Wenger 184–185, note 2.

114. Jn 14:23.

115. Stav. 4, 4 (Wenger 184; Harkins 67).

116. Gal. 3:27.

117. Jn 6:57.

118. Jn 6:56.

119. Jn 15:5.

120. Jn 15:14–15.

121. 2 Cor 11:2.

122. Rom 8:29.

123. Is 8:18.

124. 1 Cor 12:27.

125. Montfaucon II, 2 (= 13–15) (PG 49:233; Harkins 176–177).

126. For example: from the side of Jesus on the cross, blood and water flow forth, which in typology are the Eucharist and baptism; Chrysostom speaks of them as "a symbol of baptism and the mysteries" (Stav. 3, 17 [Wenger 161; Harkins 621]).

127. Stav. 2, 17 (Wenger 143; Harkins 49–50).

128. Wenger 143, note 1.

129. Stav. 3, 17 (Wenger 161; Harkins 62).

130. PK II, 3 (= 5) (PK 156; Harkins 150).

131. *Ibid.*

132. PK II, 3 (= 7) (*ibid.*).

133. PK III, 4 (= 19) (PK 171; Harkins 166).

134. Lk 23:46.

135. PK III, 4 (= 18) (PK 171; Harkins 166).

136. PK III, 4 (= 20) (PK 171; Harkins 166–167).

137. Stav. 2, 17 (Wenger 143; Harkins 50).

138. Stav. 3, 13 (Wenger 158; Harkins 60).

139. *Ibid.*

140. *Ibid.*

141. See Ex 1:13–14.

142. Stav. 3, 23 (Wenger 164; Harkins 64).

143. Ex 12:21–25.

144. Stav. 3, 13–14 (Wenger 159; Harkins 60).

145. Stav. 3, 14 (Wenger 159; Harkins 60–61).

146. Stav. 3, 15 (Wenger 159; Harkins 61).

147. Stav. 3, 16 (Wenger 160; Harkins 61).

148. Wenger 160, note 1.

149. Stav. 3, 16 (Wenger 160; Harkins 61).

150. Stav. 3, 17 (Wenger 161; Harkins 62).

151. Stav. 3, 18 (Wenger 161; Harkins 62).

152. Gn 2:23.

153. Stav. 3, 18 (Wenger 161; Harkins 62).

154. Stav. 3, 16 (Wenger 161; Harkins 61).

155. See Ex 16:9ff.

156. See Ex 17:1ff.

157. Stav. 3, 26 (Wenger 166; Harkins 65).

158. PK III, 3 (= 11–12) (PK 169; Harkins 164).

159. Stav. 2, 9 (Wenger 138; Harkins 46).

160. Stav. 1, 31 (Wenger 124; Harkins 35).

161. Stav. 2, 28 (Wenger 149; Harkins 53–54).

162. PK III, 3 (= 11–12) (PK 169; Harkins 164).

163. Eph 4:24.

164. PK III, 3 (= 11–12) (PK 169; Harkins 164).

165. Mt 3:17.

166. Jn 1:27; Lk 3:16.

167. PK III, 3 (= 13–15) (PK 169–170; Harkins 164–165).

168. The arguments used show that this statement holds not only for baptism, but for all the sacraments.

169. PK III, 3 (= 12) (PK 170; Harkins 164).

170. Stav. 2, 10 (Wenger 138; Harkins 46–47).

171. Jn 14:23.

172. Stav. 4, 4 (Wenger 184; Harkins 167).

173. Stav. 2, 26 (Wenger 147–148; Harkins 52–53).

174. For example, the Anaphora of John Chrysostom and the Greek Anaphora of James the Brother of the Lord; see Hänggi-Pahl (n. 85) 224 and 246.

175. See L. Ligier's penetrating analysis of the anaphora in the *Testamentum Domini*: "L'anaphore de la *Tradition apostolique* dans le *Testamentum Domini*," in Spinks (n. 103), 91–106.

176. Stav. 2, 26 (Wenger 148; Harkins 53).

177. Jn 14:23.

178. Stav. 4, 4 (Wenger 184; Harkins 67).

179. This application of the doctrine is quite evident in, for example, Chrysostom's treatise *On the Priesthood*.

CHAPTER FIVE

1. A. Piédagnel (ed.). *Cyrille de Jérusalem. Catéchèses mystagogiques*, SC 126 (Paris, 1966), 18–40, 75–78. (Cyril's catecheses will be cited as *Hom.* 1, 1, etc., with the page number in Piédagnel's edition in parentheses.)

2. See Cutrone's excellent remarks in explanation of the relation between the fourth and fifth catecheses: E. J. Cutrone, "Cyril's Mystagogical Catecheses and the Evolution of the Jerusalem Anaphora," *OCP* 44 (1978): 52–64.

3. R. Tonneau and R. Devreesse, *Les homélies catéchétiques de Théodore de Mopsueste*, ST 145 (Vatican City, 1949).

4. The problem is discussed in an article now in press: E. Mazza, "La struttura dell'anafora nelle Catechesi di Teodoro di Mopsuestia," to appear in *Ephemerides liturgicae*.

5. Cutrone (n. 2), 59, note 30.

6. J. M. Sanchez Caro, *Eucaristia y Historia de la Salvaciòn* (Madrid, 1983), 199, note 11.

7. The two models also have in common the omission of the doxology that concludes the anaphora.

8. Tonneau-Devreesse (n. 3), 531–535.

9. The text of the Ritual that is to be commented on is given at the beginning of the three homilies on baptism and the two on the Eucharist; Theodore himself describes it as "Text of the book" (321, 367, 401, 461, 531).

10. Theodore, *Hom.* 15, 25ff. (Tonneau-Devreesse 502ff.).

11. This fact may also explain the different length of the fourth catechesis, which is notably shorter than the others.

12. Theodore, *Hom.*, 15, 3–15 (Tonneau-Devreesse 467–487). This approach helps bring out the point that the bread and wine are a real and efficacious food. In his second homily on the Mass, just before the commentary on the fraction, Theodore once cites the words of the Last Supper according to the version in 1 Cor 11:24, in order to make the point that Christ shed a great deal of blood in his passion. In the first homily, he cites the account of institution at least twice: once according to the version in Mt 26:26 (the eschatological words in Mt 26:29 are also cited), and once in a version that combines Mt. 26:26–28 and 1 Cor 11:24–25.

13. Theodore, *Hom.*, 15, 9 (Tonneau-Devreesse 475).

14. Cutrone (n. 2).

15. Right at the beginning of the Ritual, the special character of this sacramental food is brought out: that which feeds us is a kind of sacrifice, but not the personal sacrifice of the pontiff. The commentary and the exposition of this theme lead into a discussion of the sacramental food.

16. In this perspective, the *typos* not only gives access to the sacrament, but is a real representational image, a kind of dramatization.

17. "Identification" in the sense of becoming one with Christ.

18. Cutrone (n. 2) 54.

19. *Hom.* 1, 4 (88).

20. *Hom.* 1, 9 (98).

21. In another passage, "symbols" might well be translated as "rites": "When, in the following mystagogical homilies, we enter into the Holy

of Holies, we shall know the symbols of what is accomplished there" (*Hom.* 1, 11 [1021]). Similarly in *Hom.* 2, 1 (104).

22. *Hom.* 3, 3 (124).

23. *Hom.* 2, 3 (108).

24. See *ibid.*: "The exorcized oil, through the invocation of God and the prayer, receives such power that it not only purifies by burning away the traces of sin but it also puts to flight the invisible powers of the evil one."

25. *Hom.* 5, 2 (148).

26. *Hom.* 2, 4 (110).

27. *Hom.* 3, 6 (128).

28. *Hom.* 2, 4 (112).

29. *Ibid.*

30. See *Hom.* 2, 2 (106): "Having stripped, you were naked and in this way too you imitated Christ who was naked on the cross."

31. *Ibid.*

32. *Hom.* 2, 5 (112–114).

33. *Hom.* 2, 6 (116).

34. The same is already true in Paul himself, as U. Vanni has very clearly shown in his article, "*Homomoioma* in Paolo," *Greg* 58 (1977): 321–345, 431–470. He correctly points out that the suffix -*ma* conveys the concreteness to be read into the word. That is, *homoiōma* is "the thing, the reality, which is like," and not simply the quality of "similarity" (which would translate the Greek *homoiōsis*).

35. *Hom.* 2, 7 (116).

36. *Hom.* 3, 2 (124).

37. On this point, see X. Léon-Dufour, "Corps du Christ et eucharistie selon Saint Paul," in the collective volume *Le corps et le corps du Christ dans la Première Epître aux Corinthiens* (Congrès de l'ACFEB, Tarbes, 1981; Paris, 1983), 225–255.

38. *Hom.* 2, 5 (114).

39. I prefer not to translate the Greek word *antitypos*, but to leave it as it is with all the nuances it carries in Cyril's conception of the sacraments. Only if this is done will it be possible to avoid forced interpretations of the text such as are clearly to be seen in, for example, the translation in the Sources chrétiennes volume.

40. *Hom.* 2, 6 (114).

41. *Hom.* 2, 7 (118).

42. *Hom.* 2, 6 (116).

43. *Hom.* 3, 1 (120).

44. *Ibid.* (122).

45. *Hom.* 5, 20 (170).

46. See, e.g., *Hom.* 4, 3 (136): "Under the figure (*en tupō*) of the bread the body is given to you and under the figure of the wine the blood is given to you, in order that, having participated (*metalabōn*) in the body and blood of Christ, you may become one body and one blood with Christ."

47. *Hom.* 1, 2 (84).

48. *Hom.* 3, 6 (128).

49. *Hom.* 4, 7 (140).

50. *Hom.* 1, 2 (84).

51. *Hom.* 1, 3 (86).

52. For example: "The former was swallowed up in the sea; the latter disappeared in the saving water" (*ibid.*).

53. *Hom.* 2, 4 (112).

54. *Hom.* 3, 1 (120).

55. *Hom.* 3, 6 (128).

56. *Hom.* 4, 7 (140–141).

57. Along the same line, see also *Hom.* 3, 7 (130).

58. *Hom.* 5, 2 (148).

CHAPTER SIX

1. *Phaedo* 100C-E; 74D; 75B.

2. I did not mention this point when analyzing the texts from Cyril, because it was not relevant; see *Hom.* 3, 2 (124).

3. G. Reale, *Per una nuova interpretazione di Platone* (Milan, 1987), 218.

4. *Ibid.*, 219.

5. *Ibid.*, 179.

6. *Ibid.*, 194.

7. *Ibid.*, 169.

8. *Ibid.*, 62.

9. *Ibid.*, 223.

10. *Ibid.*, 249.

11. On this Platonic concept, see H. Krämer, *Platone e i fondamenti della metafisica. Saggio sulla teoria del principi e sulle dottrine non scritte di Platone con una raccolta dei documenti fondamentali in edizione bilingue e bibliografia*, introduction and translation by G. Reale (Milan, 1987), 172, note 47.

12. *Ibid.*, 160.

13. *Ibid.*, 222, note 18.

14. G. Reale (n. 3), 169.

15. But the event remains external to the sacrament because it transcends it as its ontological principle.

16. G. Reale (n. 2), 169.

17. G. Reale, *Storia della filosofia antica. 3. I sistemi della'età ellenistica* (Milan, 1987), 100.

18. *Ibid.*, 107–115. "Thus the voice of Plato died out even within the walls of the Academy" (121).

19. *Ibid.*, 125; see also G. Reale, *Storia della filosofia antica 2. Platone e Aristotele* (Milan, 1987), 388–395.

20. G. Reale, *Storia della filosofia antica 3*, 127.

21. G. Reale, *Storia della filosofia antica 4. Le scuole dell'età imperiale* (Milan, 1987), 253. In addition, "the eidetic-paradigmatic aspect of the doctrine of the Ideas was maintained in its full breadth" (*ibid.*).

22. *Ibid.*, 268.

23. This is also the case when the Fathers formulate the ontological dimension only imperfectly (perhaps because of their imperfect mastery of the cultural instrument they are using, namely, Platonism).

24. And therefore as something invisible, as in Ambrose's idea of "likeness," which was explained earlier.

25. I prefer to focus on Platonism and not on Middle Platonism, since the Middle Platonists were well aware that the problem with Platonism was the excessive transcendence of the Ideas, and since they corrected this by means of elements from Aristotle. "Platonic metaphysics was

revived along with the advances made possible by elements from Aristotle" (G. Reale, *Storia della filosofia antica* 4, 336). And again: "Plato had made the world of Ideas, or the Intelligible, an absolute, and had situated it above Mind and Intelligence. . . . Aristotle, on the other hand, had made Intelligence, understood as the thought of itself (Thought of Thought), the absolute, and had made the Ideas immanent in the sensible world, thus transforming them into 'forms' that are intrinsic to things. He maintained that only thus could Plato's eidetic intuition be defended" (338).

Index

Aaron, 163

Abraham, 39, 42

Account of institution, 88
  baptism of Christ as an, 6
  epiclesis, relation with, 4

Alexandrian school, 9, 55, 166

Allegory, 9, 21, 59, 61, 62, 64, 66, 69, 70
  liturgical, 61
  mystagogy and, 55–59
  subjectivism in, 11
  typology and, 10–13

Amalarius of Metz, 13

Ambrose of Milan, x, xi, 4, 6, 14ff., 47, 53, 91, 92, 101, 104, 106, 117, 124, 132, 142, 143, 156, 161, 166, 167, 171
  baptismal rite, 31
  baptismal theology, 5
  exegetical method, 15
  mystagogical catecheses, 22–23
  mystagogical homilies, 115
  mystagogy, 4, 23–34
  tradition and, 33, 44
  typology, 30, 35, 44

Anaphora, xi, 61, 70, 78, 88, 125, 153
  Antiochene, x
  Jerusalem, 150
  Serapion, 20
  structure, 150, 151
  theology, 151

Angelic liturgy, 64, 71, 72, 81, 154
  celebrates the passion of Christ, 63

sacrament as an image of the, 62
  and the *Sanctus*, 78–81

Angels, 124–125

Anointing
  baptismal, 150, 156
  Cyril of Jerusalem, typological commentary on, 163
  oil, 168
  postbaptismal, x
  of the sick, 1, 153

Antioch, 45

Antiochene anaphora, x

Antiochene school, 9, 12, 55, 135, 166

Antitypos, 160–161

Aristotle, 171, 172

Ascension, 74

Baptism, x, 1, 6, 20, 29, 35, 37, 38, 46, 48, 49, 60, 74, 75, 86, 94, 96, 105, 109, 114, 115, 116, 117, 119, 121, 126, 127, 128, 130, 131, 132, 135, 138, 139, 142, 144, 145, 158, 159, 160, 161
  as birth, 86, 93
  blood as a witness, 31
  of Christ as seen as an act of institution, 6
  effects, 51
  as an enrollment in the books of the heavenly city, 125
  image of marriage as applied to, 126

imitation and, 154–161
Holy Spirit acting in, 26, 27, 31
of Jesus, 5–6, 35, 83
mystagogy, 6
Naaman and, 5
rite, *See* Baptismal rite
sacrament, 31
signing with the cross, 75
as a spiritual marriage, 126
three witnesses, 31
triple immersion, 156
water, 31, 35, 168
Baptismal activities, 58–59
Baptismal anointing, 150, 156
Baptismal homilies, x
of Cyril of Jerusalem, 115
of Theodore of Mopsuestia, 115
Baptismal immersion, 59
triple, 156
Baptismal instructions, Eucharist
in, 120
Baptismal rite, 27, 157
Ambrose of Milan's, 31
sacramentality, 28
Baptismal theology, 6
Ambrose of Milan's, 5
Berengarius, 92
Bethzatha, water of the pool of,
37
Biblical exegesis and mystagogy,
7–13
Biblical theology, 34, 135
Biblical typology, xi, 9, 16, 26, 43,
55, 102, 167, 174
Cyril of Jerusalem's, 164
Blood, 138
and water, 139
as a witness in baptism, 31
Bornert, R., 11
Botte, B., 23
Böuessé, H., O.P., 4
Bread
breaking of the, 71, 92
breaking of the, as a type of the
resurrection, 69

Bread and wine, 32, 60, 66, 68,
69, 87, 88, 98, 168
passion of Christ in relation to,
65–66
Byzantine period, 1

Cabasilas, Nicholas, 3, 4, 106
Catechesis, 6, 7, 115
Ambrose of Milan's
mystagogical, 22–23
Cyril of Jerusalem's, 152, 154
Cyril of Jerusalem's
prebaptismal, 150
on the Mass, 53
mystagogical, x, xi, xii, 2–6, 53
Theodore of Mopsuestia's, 150
Catechectical homilies, 141
John Chrysostom's, 106–109,
114, 115
Theodore of Mopsuestia's, 45–
46
Theodore of Mopsuestia's, purpose of, 49–55
Ceresa-Gastaldo, A., 107, 132, 134
Christ
imitation of, 121
immolation of, 90
Melchizedek as figural parallel
with, 40
resurrection of, *See* Resurrection of Christ
Christian initiation, 59, 109, 117,
119, 135, 138, 165
Eucharist as part, 118
sacraments of, 1
Christian living
John Chrysostom's theology of,
112
theology of, 120
Christian sacraments, 39–43
Church liturgy, 64, 72
Chrysostom, John, x, xi, 45, 72,
105ff., 166
catechetical homilies, 106–109,
114, 115

homilies, 116
martyrs, comment on the life of
  the, 123
mystagogical homilies, 126
mystagogy, 114, 134
mystagogy, distinguishing
  traits, 109–120
postbaptismal homilies, 117
theme of garments, 129
theology, Trinitarian evolution,
  146
theology of Christian living,
  112
typology, 134–141
Communion, eucharistic, 56–57
Communion formula, 90
Communion rites, 61
  as types of the resurrection,
    67–70
Confirmation, x
Consecration
  doctrine of, 151
  eucharistic, 4, 33
  theology of, 32
Council of Laodicea, x
Creation
  order of, unity with order of sal-
    vation, 16
Cutrone, E. J., 151, 152, 154
Cyril of Alexandria, 1, 2
Cyril of Jerusalem, x, xi, 3, 106,
  150ff., 166, 167, 169
  anointing, typological commen-
    tary of, 163
  baptismal homilies, 115
  biblical typology, 164
  catecheses, 152, 154
  imitation, concept of, 154
  Lavabo, interpretation of the,
    164
  mystagogical method, 161
  mystagogical typology, 161
  mystagogy, 152–154
  prebaptismal catecheses, 150
  typology, 161–164

Daniélou, J., 11, 12
David, 38, 42, 164
  Eucharist foreseen by, 43
Deacons, 61–64
Devreesse, Robert, 45, 49
Diodore, 105
Diodorus of Tarsus, 2, 55
Doctrine of consecration, 151
Doctrine of divine election, 126
Doctrine of imitation, 148
Doctrine of sacramentality, 168
Doctrine of the sacraments, 138

Earthly liturgy, 79, 81, 83, 125
Elijah, 32
Ephphetha, rite of, 26
Epiclesis, 66, 70, 151, 152
  account of institution, relation
    with, 4
  effects, 88
  as a manifestation of the resur-
    rection, 70
Epiphanius, 1
Eschatological gifts of resurrection, 77, 94
Eschatological transcendence, 101
Eschatology, 120, 143
  sacrament and, 93–97, 100,
    101, 121
Eschaton, 93, 98, 120, 121
Eucharist, x, xi, 1, 4, 20, 23, 42,
  49, 59, 60, 61, 66, 67, 76, 80,
  84, 86, 87, 114, 115, 117, 119,
  131, 136, 138, 151–154, 159,
  161, 164, 166, 173
  in baptismal instructions, 120
  celebration of the, 56
  Christian initiation, as part of,
    118
  as foreseen by David, 43
  as food, 86, 111
  homilies on the Mass, parts of
    in, 61
  Incarnation, parallel with, 32
  interpretation of the, 5

as memorial and narration of
the Lord's death, 100
mystagogical explanation of,
141
parallelism with the passion,
12, 101
prefigurations of the, 21
as remission of sins, 71–72
sacrament of immortality, 98
sacrament of the Lord's passion, 90
as a sacrifice, 66, 99
as a type of the passion, 61–66
as a type of the resurrection,
66–72
Eucharistic communion, 56–57
Eucharistic consecration, 4, 33
Eucharistic elements, 60
Eucharistic initiation, 1–2
Eucharistic prayer, *See* Anaphora
Eucharistic presence, 89
Eucharistic sacrifice, 4, 6, 99
Eucharistic thematic, problem of,
114–120
Eucharistic theology, 151
Theodore of Mopsuestia's, 81
Exegesis, 79
biblical, and mystagogy, 7–13
literal, 12
spiritual, 9, 12
Exegetical method, 9
Ambrose of Milan's, 15
Exemplum, 33
Explicationes Missae, 13
Exorcism, 51, 52, 58, 74, 117, 127
oil of, 155

Faith, and sacramentality, 141–
149
Fathers of the Church, xi, xii, 1,
2, 3, 7, 102, 119, 135, 141,
147, 169, 170, 171, 172, 173,
174
Federici, T., 1
Figura, 15, 16–17, 18, 21, 37, 38, 39

Figura mysterii, 17
Figura-veritas relation, 17
Firstfruits, 95, 96
Flavian, bishop, 105, 107, 108
Forma, 15, 21
Francesconi, G., xi, 14, 21, 22
Fronton du Duc, 106

Gaiser, K., 170
Gideon, 22
Gouillard, J., 3, 4
Gregory of Nazianzus, 1
Gregory of Nyssa, 1

Hager, 10
Haggadah, 8
Halakah, 8
Harkins, Paul, 107
Heavenly liturgy, 72–85
Hermeneutical method, 8
typology as a, 34
Hilary, 14
Holy Spirit, 5, 6, 30, 35, 48, 70,
71, 76, 83, 84, 87, 88, 89, 94,
95, 98, 122, 144, 145, 146,
160, 163
in baptism, 26, 27, 31
Homilies
Ambrose of Milan's
mystagogical, 115
baptismal, x
catechetical, *See* Catechetical
homilies
John Chrysostom's, 116
John Chrysostom's cat-
echetical, 106–109, 114, 115
John Chrysostom's
postbaptismal, 117
John Chrysostom's
mystagogical, 126
Cyril of Jerusalem's, 115
on the Lord's Prayer, 50–51
on the Mass, 61
mystagogical, x
on the mysteries, 51–54

Theodore of Mopsuestia's baptismal, 115
Theodore of Mopsuestia's catechetical, 45–46, 49–55
Homoiōma, 21

Identification, 35, 141
Image
   of marriage as applied to baptism, 126
   theology of the, 144, 145
Imago, 15, 18, 19–20, 21
Imitation, 6, 122, 154, 156–158
   baptism and, 154–161
   Cyril of Jerusalem's concept of, 154
   doctrine of, 148
   object of, 158
   theology of, 144, 145
   theory of, 168
   typology and, 167–168
Imitation of Christ, 121
Immanence, 168
Immersion
   baptismal, 59
   triple, in baptism, 156
Immolation of Christ, 90
Immortality, Eucharist as sacrament of, 98
Incarnation
   parallel with the Eucharist, 32
   mysteries of, 32, 43
Initiation, 3, 115
   Christian, *See* Christian initiation
   eucharistic, 1–2
   mystagogy as an, 33
   sacraments of Christian, xi, 115, 116, 132
   sacred, 144
   theology of, morality as a, 120–124
Institution
   account of, *See* Account of institution

baptism of Christ as an act of, 6
   epiclesis, relation with, 4
Invocation, Trinitarian, 59
Isaiah, 56, 78, 79, 80, 81

Jesus
   actions of, as types, 82–85
   baptism of, 5–6, 35, 83
Jerusalem anaphora, 150
Jewish sacraments, 39–43
John the Baptist, 83, 99
John of Jerusalem, 150
Jonah, 22

Krämer, H., 170

Last Supper, 71–72, 83, 84, 88, 92, 148, 153, 164
Latin Middle Ages, 13
Law of the priesthood, 152
Lavabo, Cyril of Jerusalem's interpretation of the, 164
Libanius, 105
Liber officialis, 13
Life, theology of, 51
Likeness, 158–160
   theory of, 168
Liturgical allegory, 61
Liturgical mystagogy, Origen's, 24
Liturgical theology, xii, 3, 6, 43, 135, 144, 166
Liturgical typology, 43, 55
Liturgy
   angelic, *See* Angelic liturgy
   Church, 64, 72
   earthly, 79, 81, 83, 125
   heavenly, 72–85
   of the prothesis, 63
Lord's Prayer, homily on, 50–51

Magnificat, 8
Marah, water of, 29
Marriage
   baptism as a spiritual, 126

image of, as applied to baptism, 126
Martyrs, John Chrysostom's comment on life of, 123
Mass, catechesis on the, 53
Maximus the Confessor, 1, 2, 3, 13, 25, 33, 106
  basis of his mystagogy, 24
Melchizedek, 41, 42, 162, 167
  as author of the sacraments, 39, 40
  figural parallel with Christ, 40
Melito of Sardis, 11
Meletius, bishop of Antioch, 105
Middle Ages, Latin, 13
Middle Platonism, 169, 172, 173
Midrash, 8
Mingana, A., 45
Montfaucon, 106, 107, 108, 127
Morality, as a theology of initiation, 120–124
Moses, 22, 29, 38, 139, 141, 161, 163
Mystagogical catechesis, x, xi, xii, 2–6, 53
  Ambrose of Milan's, 22–23
Mystagogical homilies, x
  Ambrose of Milan's, 115
  John Chrysostom's, 126
Mystagogical method, 3, 5
  Cyril of Jerusalem's, 161
Mystagogical theology, xx, 2–6, 44, 135
Mystagogical typology, Cyril of Jersualem's, 161
Mystagogical writings, 3
Mystagogy, ix, x, xi, xii, 12, 38, 43, 104, 124, 135, 148, 167
  allegory and, 55–59
  Ambrose of Milan's, 4, 23–34
  baptismal, 6
  biblical exegesis and, 7–13
  John Chrysostom's 114, 134
  John Chrysostom's, distinguishing traits of, 109–120

Cyril of Jerusalem's, 152–154
  definition, 1–2
  as an initiation, 33
  Maximus the Confessor's, 24
  the mystery of salvation, initiation into, 25
  Origen's liturgical, 24
  Origen's sacramental, 24
  pastoral fruitfulness, 54
  salvation and, 54
  Theodore of Mopsuestia's, 46, 54
  theology, as a way of doing, 141
  as theology, 165–167
  as theology of the mystery, xii, 53
  typology and, 9–10
Mysteries
  of the cross, 29
  homilies on the, 51–54
  of the Incarnation, 32, 43
  mystagogy as theology of the, xii, 53
  of salvation, initiation into, 25
  theology of the, xii, 53
De mysteriis, 14, 20, 22, 23, 29, 30, 31, 33, 35
Mysterium, 15, 16, 17, 21, 23, 25, 26, 27, 28, 29, 30, 31, 32, 33, 44

Naaman, 30, 31, 36, 37
  cure and baptism of, 5

Orarion, 57
Order of creation, unity with order of salvation, 16
Order of salvation, unity with order of creation, 16
Orders, sacrament, 56
Origen, 1, 2, 9, 14, 24, 25, 33
  liturgical mystagogy, 24
  sacramental mystagogy, 24

Palladius, bishop of Helenopolis, 105
Papadopoulos-Kerameus, A., 106, 107, 108, 115, 127, 143
Parable, 11
Passion of Christ, 38, 62, 63, 64, 68, 85
  bread and wine, in relation to the, 65–66
  Eucharist, parallelism with the, 12, 101
  Eucharist as a sacrament of the, 90
  Eucharist as type of the, 61–66
  prothesis as a type of the, 62, 63, 64
Passover lamb, 9
Passover texts, 136
Patristic age, 7, 47, 174
Paul, Saint, 10, 32, 49, 82, 83, 86, 99, 111, 112, 122, 124, 125, 128, 129, 131
Peripatetic School, 172
Pesher, 8
Peter, Saint, 28, 32
Phaedo, 169
Philo of Alexandria, 14, 166, 172
Piédagnel, A., 150, 152
Plato, 169, 170, 171, 172, 173
Platonism, 169, 170, 173, 174
Postbaptismal anointing, x
Postbaptismal homilies, John Chrysostom's, 117
Post sanctus, 147
Prayer
  Eucharistic, *See* Anaphora
  Lord's, homily on the, 50–51
  theology of 51
Prebaptismal catecheses, Cyril of Jerusalem's, 150
Prefiguration, 11
Priesthood, law of, 152
Priestly ordination, 1
Prothesis, 61, 66, 69, 70, 71, 92, 153, 173

liturgy of the, 63
passion of Christ, as a type of the, 62, 63, 64
Pseudo-Dionysius, 1, 24

Qumram sect, 8

Ratio sacramentorum, 23, 24
Raza, 46
Reale, G., 170, 172
Reconciliation, rites of, x
Redemption, 76, 101
  concept of, 73–74
  sacramental phase, 101
  Theodore of Mopsuestia's theology of, 73
Remission of sins, Eucharist as, 71–72
Resurrection of Christ, xii, 73, 75, 76, 83, 86, 88, 91, 96, 99, 100, 101, 173, 174
  breaking of the bread, as a type of the, 69
  communion rites as type of the, 67–70
  epiclesis as a manifestation of the, 70
  eschatological gifts of, 77, 94
  Eucharist as a type of the, 66–72
  fruits of, 93
Rites
  communion, *See* Communion rites
  of *Ephphetha*, 26
  symbolism of, 126–131
Ritual, 62, 63, 68, 70, 71, 87, 99, 151, 152, 153, 164, 166
Roman Canon, 125
Roman Church, 13
Roman Empire, 14

Sacrament of baptism, 31
Sacrament of immortality, Eucharist as, 98

Sacrament of Christian initiation,
    xi, 115, 116, 132
Sacrament of the Lord's passion,
    Eucharist as, 90
Sacrament of orders, 56
Sacramental mystagogy,
    Origen's, 24
Sacramental realism, xi, xii, 62,
    64, 85–93, 97–101, 103, 144,
    145, 153, 159, 162, 168, 172,
    174
  of salvation, 99
Sacramental salvation, 96, 98, 99
Sacramental sign, 53
Sacramental theology, ix, 31, 43,
    44, 48, 60, 96, 97, 98, 102,
    144, 146, 148, 167
Sacramental typology, 60
Sacramental vocabulary, ix, 34,
    46, 47, 85
Sacramentality, 15, 34–44, 47, 53,
    64, 69, 92, 144
  of baptismal rite, 28
  doctrine of, 168
  faith and, 141–149
De sacramentis, 14, 20, 29, 30, 33,
    35
Sacraments
  angelic liturgy, image of the, 62
  Christian, 39–43
  and content, 93–104
  definition, 91
  doctrine of the, 138
  eschatology and the, 93–97,
    100, 101, 121
  function, 98
  Jewish, 39–43
  Melchizedek as author of, 39,
    40
  natural realities, relation be-
    tween, 59–60
  ontological content, 3
  redemptive contents, 102
  salvation and, 74–77
  theology of the, 167

value of the, 51
Sacramentum, 15, 21–23, 25, 27,
    29, 30, 32, 33
Sacred initiation, 144
Sacrifice, Eucharist as, 45, 66, 99
Salvation, 96
  effect implementation of, 99
  history of, 14–23
  mystagogy and, 54
  mystagogy as initiation into the
    mystery of, 25
  order of, unity with order of
    creation, 16
  sacrament and, 74–77
  sacramental, 96, 98, 99
Sanchez Caro, J. M., 151
Sanctus, 70, 92, 147, 151, 154
  angelic liturgy and the, 78–81
  Trinitarian interpretation, 81
Sarah, 10
Sartore, D., 107
Satan, 73, 118, 120, 148
  renunciation of, 117, 125, 132,
    134, 155, 161
Serapion, anaphora of, 20
Sick, anointing the, 1, 53
Sign, sacramental, 53
Similitudo, 15, 18, 20–21, 23, 35,
    53
Sins, Eucharist as remission of,
    71–72
Sophist, 105
Species, 15, 18–19, 24
Speusippus, 172
Spiritual exegesis, 9, 12
Spiritual theology, 6
Stavronikita, monastery of, 107
Stavronikita manuscripts series,
    107, 108, 109, 115, 129, 134,
    143
Subjectivism in allegory, 11
Superimpositions, 35, 139, 141

de la Taille, M., S.J., 4
Targum, 8

Tarsus, 45
Theme of garments, John
    Chrysostom's, 129
Theodore of Mopsuestia, x, xi,
    xii, 12, 45ff., 106, 120, 126,
    129, 141, 142, 143, 151, 153,
    164, 166, 167, 173
  baptismal homilies, 115
  catechesis, 150
  catechetical homilies, 45–46
  catechetical homilies, purpose
    of, 49–55
  eucharistic theology, 81
  mystagogy, 46, 54
  redemption, theology of, 73
Theodore of Studios, 1
Theology
  Ambrose of Milan's baptismal, 5
  Ambrose of Milan's typologi-
    cal, 30, 35, 44
  of the anaphora, 151
  baptismal, 6
  biblical, 34, 135
  of Christian living, 120
  of Christian living, John
    Chrysostom's, 112
  John Chrysostom's, Trinitarian
    evolution of, 146
  of consecration, 32
  eucharistic, See Eucharistic the-
    ology
  of the image, 144, 145
  of imitation, 144, 145
  of initiation, morality as a, 120–
    124
  of life, 51
  liturgical, xii, 3, 6, 43, 135, 144,
    166
  mystagogical, xii, 2–6, 44, 135
  mystagogy as, 141, 165–167
  of the mysteries, xii, 53
  of prayer, 51
  sacramental, ix, 31, 43, 44, 48,
    60, 96, 97, 98, 102, 144, 146,
    148, 167

spiritual, 6
  of redemption, Theodore of
    Mopsuestia's, 73
  Trinitarian, 71
Tonneau, Raymond M., 45
Tradition, 96
  Ambrose of Milan and, 33, 44
Transcendence, 168
  eschatological, 101
Transfiguration, sacramental con-
    cept of, 171
Transsubstantiation, 171
Trinitarian invocation, 59
Trinitarian presence, 6
Trinitarian theology, 71
Trinity, 130, 148
  doctrine of, 79
Triple immersion in baptism, 156
Typological application, 34–41
Typological method, 33
Typological theology, Ambrose of
    Milan's, 30
Typology, 7, 28, 29, 35, 37, 38,
    41, 43, 55, 62, 70, 80, 101,
    103, 106, 131, 135, 139, 140,
    141, 144, 147, 154, 156, 162,
    166, 168, 171, 173, 174
  allegory and, 10–13
  Ambrose of Milan's, 35, 44
  biblical, xi, 9, 16, 26, 43, 55,
    102, 167, 174
  John Chrysostom's, 134–141
  Cyril of Jerusalem's, 161–164
  Cyril of Jerusalem's biblical,
    164
  Cyril of Jerusalem's
    mystagogical, 161
  as a hermeneutical method, 34
  imitation and, 167–168
  liturgical, 43, 55
  mystagogy and, 9–10
  sacramental, 60
Typos, 8, 10, 15, 21, 46, 47, 48, 154

Umbra, 15, 18

Vaccari, A., 55
Veritas, 18, 37, 38
Vestments, 57–58
Vocabulary, sacramental, ix, 34,
  46, 47, 85

Washing of the feet, rite of, 27, 28
Water of baptism, 31, 35, 168

Water and blood, 139
Water of Marah, 29
Water of the pool of Bethzatha,
  37
Witnesses of baptism, three, 31
Wenger, Antoine, 107, 108, 109,
  129, 132, 138